D0908355

WHITE TEACHER, BLACK SCHOOL

WHITE TEACHER, BLACK SCHOOL

The Professional Growth of a Ghetto Teacher

by Forrest W. Parkay

Associate Professor of Education,
The University of Florida, Gainesville

PRAEGER

PRAEGER SPECIAL STUDIES • PRAEGER SCIENTIFIC

Library of Congress Cataloging in Publication Data

Parkay, Forrest W.
  White teacher, black school.

  Includes index.
  1. Parkay, Forrest W. 2. High school teachers—
Illinois—Biography. 3. DuSable High School—Students.
4. Teacher-student relationships. 5. English language
—Study and teaching—Afro-American students. I. Title.
LC2852.C483P37   1983   373.11'0092'4   83-6227
ISBN 0-03-062950-0

Published in 1983 by Praeger Publishers
CBS Educational and Professional Publishing
a Division of CBS Inc.
521 Fifth Avenue, New York, NY 10175 USA
© 1983 by Praeger Publishers

3456789 052 987654321

Printed in the United States of America
on acid-free paper

To the memory of

MARVIN L. SIEGEL

who first encouraged me to write this book.

FOREWORD

THE schools of the United States differ among themselves in many
ways: academic vs. vocational goals; parochial vs. public gover-
nance; middle-class vs. lower-class students; employed vs. welfare parents; and so on. Some schools seem to collect all the
"good" attributes: bright, middle-class ambitious students, well-
prepared teachers, humane but firm management. Other schools
have the opposite reputation—they are at the bottom of everyone's
list. These are large high schools located near black welfare housing in deteriorated quarters of big cities. Such a school is the subject of Forrest W. Parkay's telling and compassionate book.

There has been plenty of discussion and writing about the
"inner-city black" school. Much of the discourse is either highly
abstract or luridly melodramatic. On the one hand, the school is
represented as a place where middle-class curricular and role expectations are laid on lower-class students who can't deliver. From
this "fact" conclusions are often drawn: that the school seems to
afford "equal educational opportunity for an education" but under
conditions that virtually guarantee failure—for a number of reasons
among which various forms of racial prejudice are well represented.
On the other hand, the melodramatists document how sadistic
teachers, egged on by the administration, destroy the souls of
children, turning them into either vegetables or monsters; and how
any teacher who dares to treat children humanely will be hounded
out of the school.

Then there are the "scientists," using IQ and other test
scores to prove that black children are—or are not—genetically
inferior to whites. The arguments depend on the persuasiveness
of statistical treatments of data, and the critics have a field day
assessing the "scientificness" of the procedures. As for the relevance (if any) of IQ and other scores to the child's prospects of
effective living, nothing is said.

In the midst of these overheated and pretentious abstract,
melodramatic, and statistical arguments, Parkay has come up with
a careful, lucid, straightforward account of the persons and classes
in an inner-city school. To Parkay, the school is not just a symbolic counter in a large thesis about society; it is not merely the
locus for occasional instances of lurid bestiality; it is not a test situation in which to rationalize prejudices. It is a particular sort of
community in which human beings cope with tensions and conflicts.
Parkay shows that there are several ways of coping, ranging from

vii

destructive to maturely constructive; and he describes the "types" of students and teachers likely to employ these coping methods. He shows, at least by implication, that different classroom combinations of types of students and teachers produce different outcomes, ranging from college success down to jail and welfare.

Parkay's common sense is refreshing. From now on the proper response to the big, glib, sweeping generalizations about inner-city schools is "which teachers and which students are you talking about?" If you are selective enough in your choice of students and teachers, you can "prove" anything.

But all of this is far from the author's real concerns that center in the classrooms and come to a focus in the question: How can we arrive at methods of teaching that will make the school more educative for more of its students? What is there about the successful teacher-student combinations that can be extended to a wider range of pupils and teachers? And, in his final chapter, Parkay suggests answers.

This book has two aspects. It presents the "findings" about teachers, students, and classes. And it narrates the personal and professional inquiry of the teacher who produced the findings. This is important, for the findings (about student types, for example) may well differ from school to school and among observation instruments; but the inquiry itself, imbedded in Parkay's continual quest for teacher effectiveness, is at the very center of teaching as a profession. Here, then, is a model that experienced teachers will find making sense out of their own explorations over the years and from which novice teachers can muster their own resources for coping with the at first overwhelming difficulties of the inner-city school.

Herbert A. Thelen
Professor Emeritus
The Department of Education
University of Chicago

PREFACE

THIS book is my account of how I learned to teach—and learned to go beyond burnout—at an all-black high school on Chicago's crime-scarred South Side. I spent eight years at Du Sable High School and, during those years, I learned a lot—a lot about what teaching really is and a lot about myself.

I hope the book presents a balanced view of what it feels like to teach in a ghetto school; neither dwelling exclusively on explosive teacher-student confrontations as so many books by inner-city teachers have done, nor failing to point out the authentic caring and respect that mutually exist between most ghetto teachers and students. While at Du Sable I was cursed, spat upon, assaulted, and threatened; but I was also, I feel, loved and respected by countless more young people who showed me daily their sincere, unconditional appreciation for helping them learn.

This book is also about other ghetto teachers and the styles of teaching they develop to cope with the stress of inner-city teaching. Once I had learned to see beyond the occasional outbursts of street-corner violence in the school and had learned how to be as effective as any conscientious, caring teacher could be at a place like Du Sable, I became interested in other teachers and their responses to environmental stress. Chapters 6 through 9, then, describe three teacher "types" I developed based on observations of and interviews with 21 other teachers at Du Sable.

Many people contributed significantly to the writing of this book and to my personal and professional growth while I taught in Chicago. I am deeply indebted to the late Marvin L. Siegel, who always unswervingly believed in me. This book is, in a fundamental and inexpressible way, attributable to the love, guidance, and encouragement he gave me during those eight years at Du Sable.

While at Du Sable, I also worked on a Ph.D. in Teacher Education at the University of Chicago for six years, and several professors under whom I studied greatly influenced my conceptions of what education is all about. My greatest debt is to Professor Herbert A. Thelen. The elegance and profundity of his writing and our long-standing dialogue about the educative process stimulated me immeasurably. Other faculty whose rich ideas have no doubt found their way into this book in one form or another are professors Philip Jackson, Jacob Getzels, Benjamin Wright, Roger Pillet, Benjamin Bloom, Jack Glidewell, Edgar Epps, and Sharon Feiman-Nemser.

To my colleagues and friends at Du Sable High School I also owe a special thanks; the observations they shared with me about inner-city teaching were always helpful and thought-provoking. Larry Barkan, one of the most caring and sensitive teachers I have known, provided a model of a style of teaching that let me know it was all right to make friends with the kids I taught. Moreover, he always had a fresh and perceptive interpretation to the often puzzling events we witnessed at Du Sable. For their friendship both on and off the job, I would like to thank Virginia Evard, Charles Pugh, Marta Stingley, and Charles Abele. In addition, Professor Katherine K. Newman of Sacramento State University's Department of Education, and formerly a fellow teacher at Du Sable, graciously and sensitively responded to earlier portions of this book.

I am deeply obligated to Du Sable's students. Teachers often casually report that they learn more from their students than their students learn from them—this was certainly true regarding my work at Du Sable. Through their example I learned never to underestimate the human being's capacity for change and growth.

To my daughters Anna and Catherine I apologize for the times that my involvement with this book prevented us from being together. And most of all I thank my wife, Arlene, whose constant encouragement and perceptive suggestions made this book possible.

F.W.P.
San Marcos, Texas

Note: Pronouns in the masculine gender are used throughout this book to refer to any person whose sex is not specified. This usage is to promote clarity and tightness of writing and in no way reflects negatively on female persons.

CONTENTS

ERRATA

The texts of Figure 5 (p. 202) and
Figure 6 (p. 207) are transposed.

INTRODUCTION:
THE STRESS
OF GHETTO TEACHING

The reality of Du Sable has nothing to do with the reality of the
rest of society. It bears no relation to it . . . it's a world of its
own. The hopelessness of the
situation is what bothers me most.
I'm in a situation with all these
crazy things going on and I can't
do anything about it.

A Du Sable High School Teacher

IN July of 1970, armed with bachelor's and master's degrees in
English from the University of Illinois at Urbana and a piece of
paper certifying my fitness to teach high school English, I threw
all of my belongings into my 1955 Buick convertible and drove to
Chicago in search of my first teaching job.

From my present vantage point as an assistant professor of
secondary education, I would judge the teacher education program
I completed at the University of Illinois as quite adequate and perhaps better than most other teacher education programs around the
country. What my education had not prepared me for in the least,
however, was the shock of beginning a teaching career at a Chicago
inner-city high school. My expectations of what teaching would be
like, for example, had been fueled by a university field trip my
senior year to Ernest Hemingway's rather prestigious alma mater,
Oak Park-River Forest High School. How much more educative,

I realize now, would it have been for us to have visited Du Sable, only a ten or fifteen-minute drive from Oak Park-River Forest.

Several of my friends had forewarned me about the difficulty of finding a teaching position in any of the suburban schools. They also told me, however, that if I had the stamina to wade through the Chicago Board of Education's endless forms and procedures for new employees and if I didn't mind teaching under conditions they described as "difficult," I could land a teaching job that, if I chose, would last the rest of my life.

After being informed by four suburban school districts that I was searching for employment at a time when teachers glutted the marketplace, I quickly found myself at the Chicago Board of Education's vast complex of administrative offices at 228 North La Salle Street in the Loop, a command and policy-making center teachers know as "Downtown."

A receptionist in personnel informed me of the hurdles I would have to clear if I wished to teach in the city's schools. The next five days I spent tending to these requirements, not the least of which were written, oral, and physical examinations (which, incidentally, struck me as not at all unlike the Army exams I had taken three years earlier). Two weeks later, after an apparently satisfactory showing on the board's exams, I received a written notice to report to the Office of Teacher Placement for my "assignment." I was assigned as an English teacher, Position No. 52121, at Du Sable High School. Because the position was newly created and had not yet been formally approved, I was told not to report until the start of the second week of school.

When I first began teaching at the school, I found myself plunged into an environment that I found chaotic, threatening, and beyond my understanding. Continuing the habit I had developed as a university student, I began to read about those things I didn't understand. I eagerly consumed anything written by anyone who had survived his own rights-of-passage as a ghetto teacher.

I soon found that front-line reports on the vicissitudes of inner-city school teaching were commonplace in popularized educational literature (Herndon, 1969; Kohl 1967; Kozol 1970). With evident frustration and, frequently despair, these reporters told of trying to motivate classes whose behavior alternated between chaos, sluggish compliance, and blank inattention, and of dealing with administrators and boards of education that neither understood the stresses experienced by teachers nor supported them in the search for more appropriate, realistic teaching methods.

It was to these and other books written predominantly by young, white, and humanistic teachers that I turned when I began my eight-year stint as a white teacher at Du Sable. What I found in these autobiographical, largely anecdotal reports, however, was that little inquiry had been conducted into the psychological effects on teachers of working day after day in difficult ghetto schools. The aim of this book, then, is not only to describe the kinds of stress that I and my Du Sable colleagues had to cope with, but to tell what it <u>feels</u> like to teach in a ghetto school for several years. (Several other ghetto teacher-authors have told their stories, but most have done so after teaching at their schools for only one or two years.)

To set the stage for what follows, though, it is necessary first to chronicle briefly the United States' slowly dawning awareness that it is confronted with a "crisis" in urban education and that, in the words of a recent news article headline, its ghetto teachers are "taking a beating."

CRISIS IN U.S. GHETTO SCHOOLS

During the years following the Civil Rights Act of 1964, educational policy makers and the general public became increasingly aware that urban schools, in alarming numbers, were failing to educate their students for meaningful participation in our complex society. The gravity of this failure was evidenced by the frequency with which educators came to refer matter-of-factly to the "crisis" situation in many inner-city schools. (The professionally prestigious <u>Second Handbook of Research on Teaching</u>, Travers, 1973, even devoted a chapter to investigating this "national dilemma.")

Spurred to self-examination by increasingly militant minorities in the late 1960s, educators began to realize that ghetto schools, reflecting the subtle, yet powerful, biases of the larger society, had in effect "institutionalized" failure. In 1968, for example, the National Advisory Commission on Civil Disorders (Kerner 1968) concluded that for many minorities urban schools had failed to provide educational experiences necessary to overcome the effects of prejudice and deprivation. Silberman (1970, p. 53) similarly described the "crisis" situation in many urban classrooms:

the public schools are failing dismally in what has
always been regarded as one of their primary tasks—
. . . to be "the great equalizer of the conditions of
men," facilitating the movement of the poor and disadvantaged into the mainstream of American economic
and social life. Far from being "the great equalizer,"
the schools help perpetuate the differences in condition, or at the very least, do little to reduce them.

To meet the challenge posed by urban education, many training programs for teachers of disadvantaged youth were started throughout the country. Many of these training programs were in response to the demands of minority group parents, school officials, and frustrated teachers—all of whom realized that traditional teacher education programs were not adequately preparing teachers to practice in the inner city. It was felt, therefore, that the way to improve instruction for the disadvantaged was to improve the preparation of their teachers and to insure that these prospective teachers possessed certain personal characteristics. Thereupon, numerous educators began to make broad recommendations for the training of inner-city teachers (Haubrich 1963; Bloom, Davis, and Hess 1965; Clark 1965; Coleman 1966; Fantini and Weinstein 1968; Getzels 1967; Wisniewski 1969; Silberman 1970).

In spite of successes reported (but seldom empirically verified) by individual preservice and inservice training programs (Haubrich 1963; Gordon and Wilkerson 1966; Fairfield 1967; Olsen 1967; Teachers Corps 1968; Stone 1969), the problems of inner-city education have continued to remain frustratingly obdurate into the 1980s. Patterns of low academic achievement among many inner-city youth continue; teachers are frequently reluctant to accept teaching assignments in urban schools; and many teachers, because of workload pressures, personal limitations, or inadequate training, are unable to bridge the gap between their middle-class culture and the lower-class culture of the students they teach. As a result, Clark's (1965, p. 603) contention of a decade and a half ago remains as apt today as it was then: "The schools in the ghetto have lost faith in the ability of the students to learn and the ghetto has lost faith in the ability of the schools to lead." In short, the malaise affecting urban education seems beyond the influence of all but the most radical ameliorative proposals.

TEACHER STRESS

The incidence of job-related stress among teachers has been found to be quite common and has received considerable attention since early in this century (Coates and Thoresen 1976). In a 1967 survey of 2,290 teachers (National Education Association 1967), 16.2 percent responded that they were working under "considerable strain," and another 61.7 percent of the sample reported they were working under "moderate strain." Coates and Thoresen (1976, p. 165) summarize the chief sources of anxiety reported by experienced teachers as related to: time demands, difficulties with pupils, large class enrollments, financial constraints, and lack of educational resources.

While the literature ostensibly dealing with teacher stress or strain is familiar, such research appears to be limited mainly to cataloging specific teacher responsibilities that account for stress or strain—researchers have seldom probed the "deeper" conflicts teachers may experience in adjusting to threatening aspects of their work. Waller's (1932) contention that "shock" and "traumatic learning" are endemic to teaching—a finding perhaps more appropriate today than it was two generations ago—has apparently received little in-depth analysis. In a study of beginning elementary school teachers in Chicago, Wagenschein (1950) found that these teachers commonly experienced "reality shock." The teachers were "shocked," she found, because the real world of the schools violated so many teacher expectations. Likewise, Gabriel's (1957) survey of the emotional problems of teachers revealed that, depending upon their character and personality, teachers experienced varying degrees of "psychological buffeting"—attempts by students to weaken the teacher's self-esteem. In her study of beginning teachers in urban schools, Fuchs (1969) found many teachers who reported symptoms similar to the phenomenon described by anthropologists as "culture shock."

While today one seldom hears of teachers who must cope with the stress of student activism so characteristic of the late 1960s and early 1970s, the mass media is, nevertheless, giving increasing coverage to what it frequently terms an "epidemic" of violence, vandalism, and disrespect for authority that is sweeping our nation's secondary schools and "threatening" the very structure of public education.

A pioneering study of the effect this trend can have on teachers was made in the late 1970s by Alfred M. Bloch, M.D., Department of Psychiatry, University of California at Los Angeles. Bloch interviewed, over a five-year period, 250 classroom teachers who had symptoms of prolonged psychic stress. All of his interviewees— some of whom had been physically assaulted in addition to being mentally harassed and intimidated—showed signs of severe anxiety and depression, or what he termed "combat fatigue."

Similarly, the Chicago Teachers Union (Kotaskis 1977) has revealed that increasing numbers of teachers report that their personal and professional lives are severely disrupted by job-related stress and their inability to cope effectively:

In an atmosphere in which there seems to be little one can do to change things a sense of despair grows. For example, what can an individual teacher do about: an inadequate budget, students who come to school from disorganized families and communities, students barely literate in English, outsiders entering the school, often gang members who bring their fights into the school, etc. ? Increasingly, teachers are becoming aware of the severe limits of their ability to control student behavior. The stress created by these factors, combined with the lack of academic progress many students display (thus depriving many teachers of the "rewards" they may get from doing their job well) leads to something styled the "burn-out" syndrome.

To determine the amount of stress teachers perceive in their work, the union conducted a stress survey of its 22,488 members in 1977. Of the 4,934 who responded, more than 50 percent reported experiencing physical illness they believed to be related to their work stress, and more than 25 percent reported mental illness associated with their work (Chicago Union Teacher, March 1978). The survey also identified four general themes that concern teachers about equally regardless of their sex, age, race, or the type of school to which assigned. These four clusters of concerns, in order of their importance to teachers, are summarized below:

1. The first cluster involves issues that appear to be "priority concerns": managing "disruptive" children, being threatened with personal injury, hearing of a colleague assaulted in school, and being the target of verbal abuse by students.
2. The second cluster could be called "management tensions": involuntary transfers, overcrowded classrooms, notice of unsatisfactory performance, lack of books and supplies, reorganization of programs and classes, implementation of Board of Education goals, denial of promotion or advancement, and disagreement with supervisors. These stressors are "imposed" upon the teacher in the form of action constraints.
3. The third cluster concerns the theme of "doing a good job": maintaining self-control when angry and teaching students who are below average in achievement level.
4. The lowest ranked cluster of events concerns "pedagogical functions": attending teacher-parent conferences, dealing with bilingual students, discussing children's problems with parents, taking additional coursework for promotion, attending

inservice meetings, evaluating students, having
conferences with the principal, and doing lesson
plans.

In an attempt to ameliorate the foregoing stressful events, the
Chicago Teachers Union, with the University of Illinois School of
Public Health, has proposed the nation's first self-help program
for "stressed" teachers in the public schools.

Others have also suggested that school districts could offer
professional support services to educators who are experiencing
stress, before the symptoms of burnout become irreversible.
Dixon et al. (1980) have suggested a fringe benefit package for
teachers that would include confidential counseling for job-related
stress. Leffingwell (1979) has suggested strategies for the school
counselor to follow in reducing teacher stress. His approach suggests the importance of identifying and accurately labeling the type
of stress and its effect on the individual.

Many teachers report stressors that are quite apart from
teacher-student relationships. Jameson (1980) and Styles and
Cavanagh (1977), for example, report a number of stress factors
that restrict the professionalism of educators (lack of power, lack
of decision-making opportunities, and professional constraints).
Needle et al. (1980) and Walsh (1979) both report adminstrative
harassment and incompetence as stressors. Finally, lack of recog-
nition and lack of appreciation have also been identified as stressful. Jameson cites the lack of appreciation as a major cause of
job dissatisfaction and reports the lack of personal fulfillment as a
factor that motivates teachers to change jobs.

THE EFFECTS OF STRESS ON TEACHERS'
BEHAVIOR AND ATTITUDES

Clearly, it is impossible to say what effect stress will have
on any given teacher's behavior and attitudes. The experiential
impact of teaching upon the teacher is determined not only by the
teacher's idiosyncratic perceptions of his school as a psychosocial
system but also by his transactions with the cultural community
in which the school is embedded. In most cases, the culture of
the school and the larger culture of the community are more or
less compatible with each other and with the teacher's values—
thus the teacher can function without undue conflict so that he
simultaneously satisfies his own professional needs and the needs
of students, school, and community.

In inner-city schools such as Du Sable, however, the disparity between the school's espoused policies and the culture of the community can be overwhelming—and this difference may have a profound, if not aberrant, effect on teacher attitudes and behavior. In particular, middle-class teachers are apt to experience a high level of anxiety and stress when confronted with cultural and behavioral patterns that differ radically from their own. During the course of their ghetto teaching assignment, some of these teachers may become acclimated (perhaps, though, at an unrevealed psychic cost) to their teaching situation, while others may continue to feel threatened by their teaching environment and maintain a high level of anxiety.

Because inner-city teachers frequently have to teach day after day in situations characterized by pervasive student apathy, the periodic acting out of destructive, antisocial impulses, or occasional disorder and confusion, they may be compelled to minimize their resultant anxiety through defensive, perhaps regressive, coping measures that facilitate neither their own professional growth nor the growth of their students. Furthermore, as they respond to impulsive student behavior that may reflect unresolved conflicts from the student's past, it is possible that the residues of a teacher's own unconscious infantile fears and latent conflicts may be "set in motion." Once these conflicts are "reawakened" for the teacher, then they must, in some way, be "resolved."

In the chapters that follow, I recount chronologically my attempts to deal with the painful, many-faceted conflict I experienced when I first began to teach at Du Sable. What began as a personal and immediate need to cope with a threatening environment, however, gradually evolved into a professional quest for a deeper understanding of the educative process.

As I find it impossible to separate my development as a person, a teacher, and an educational researcher, this book includes not only the firsthand reports of the particpant-observer but also more "objective" research-based studies of the Du Sable environment. For me, the personal need to understand informed my professional quest for understanding and vice versa. There are, of course, limitations to this approach to research; however, as Cusick (1973) suggests, the approach has a validity unobtainable through other means of study:

> Becoming a member of the social unit under study is
> basic, but it is also a source of validity problems.
> As the researcher identifies more closely with his
> subjects, he may lose his objectivity, may become
> the subject of his own research and thus invalidate

his findings. However, "the study of action has to be made from the position of the actor: such action is forged by the actor out of what he perceives, interprets, and judges; one has to see the situation as he sees it." Proximity to the subject, therefore, becomes a condition necessary for validity.

Moreover, if one conducts his research "as a full-fledged member of the group, he will be privy to knowledge that would normally be shared by such a member and might be hidden from an outsider" (Becker 1958). A position of intimacy within a psychosocial system such as Du Sable coupled with an awareness of the dangers of sharing group "myths" is essential, I feel, for a full, rich understanding of that system and the pressures it exerts on members.

REFERENCES

Becker, H. S. "Problems of Inference and Proof in Participant Observation." American Sociological Review 23 (1958):655.

Bloom, B. A.; Davis, A.; and Hess, R. Compensatory Education for Cultural Deprivation. New York: Holt, Rinehart and Winston, 1965.

Chicago Union Teacher, March 1978.

Clark, K. B. Dark Ghetto. New York: Harper and Row, 1965.

Coates, T. J., and Thoresen, C. E. "Teacher Anxiety: A Review with Recommendations." Review of Educational Research 46 (1976):59-184.

Coleman, J. S., et al. Equality of Educational Opportunity. Washington, D.C.: U.S. Government Printing Office, 1966.

Cusick, P. "Adolescent Groups and the School Organization." School Review 82 (1973):116-17.

Dixon, B.; Shaw, S.; and Bensky, J. "Administrators' Role in Fostering the Mental Health of Special Services Personnel," Exceptional Children 47 (1980);30-36.

Fairfield, R. P. "Teacher Education: What Design?" The Antioch-Putney Graduate School Report no. 1 (Fall 1967): Updating.

Fantini, M. D., and Weinstein, G. "Toward a Contact Curriculum." In The Disadvantaged: Challenge to Education. New York: Harper & Row, 1968.

Fuchs, E. Teachers Talk: Views from Inside City Schools. Garden City, N.Y.: Anchor, Doubleday, 1969.

Gabriel, J. An Analysis of the Emotional Problems of Teachers in the Classroom. London: Angus and Robertson, 1957.

Getzels, J. W. "Education for the Inner City: A Practical Proposal by an Impractical Theorist." School Review 75 (1967):283-99.

Gordon, E., and Wilkerson, D. A. Compensatory Education for the Disadvantaged. Princeton, N.J.: College Entrance Examination Board, 1966.

Haubrich, V. F. "Teachers for Big City Schools." In Education in Depressed Areas, edited by A. H. Passow. New York: Columbia University Press, 1963.

Herndon, J. The Way It Spozed to be. New York: Bantam Books, 1969.

Jameson, S. A. "Distress Signals." School and Community 66 (1980):17-19.

Kerner, O. et al. Report of the National Advisory Commission on Civil Disorders. New York: E. P. Dutton, 1968.

Kohl, H. 36 Children. New York: Signet Books, 1967.

Kotaskis, J. Mimeographed. Chicago Teacher's Union, 1977.

Kozol, J. Death at an Early Age. New York: Bantam, 1970.

Leffingwell, R. J. "The Role of the Middle School Counselor in the Reduction of Stress in Teachers." Elementary School Guidance and Counseling 13 (1979):286-90.

National Education Association. "Teachers' Problems." Research Bulletin 45 (1967):116-17.

Needle, R. H.; Griffin, T.; Svendsen, R.; and Berney, C.
"Teacher Stress: Sources and Consequences." The Journal of
School Health 50 (1980):37-39.

Olsen, E. G. "Teacher Education for the Deprived: A New Pattern." School and Society 95 (1967):232-34.

Silberman, C. E. Crisis in the Classroom: The Remaking of
American Education. New York: Random House, 1970.

Stone, S. H. "Chicago's Center for Inner City Studies: An Experiment in Relevancy." Social Education 33 (1969):528-32.

Styles, K., and Cavanagh, C. "Stress in Teaching and How to
Handle It." English Journal 66 (1977):76-79.

Teachers Corps. Two Full Years of Progress and Plans for the
Future Teachers Corps. Washington, D.C.: Washington School
of Psychiatry, October, 1968.

Travers, R. M. W., ed. Second Handbook of Research on Teaching. Chicago: Rand McNally, 1973.

Wagenschein, M. "Reality Shock: A Study of Beginning Elementary
School Teachers." Master's thesis, University of Chicago, 1950.

Waller, W. The Sociology of Teaching. New York: John Wiley
and Sons, 1932.

Walsh, D. "Classroom Stress and Teacher Burnout." Phi Delta
Kappan 61, no. 4 (1979):253-64.

Wisniewski, R. "Urban Teacher Preparation Programs." Social
Education 33 (1969):77-82.

FIRST IMPRESSIONS

"Class"

Every day is when the South Side shows its class.
Sisters play it cool; brothers act an ass—
Like throw'n barbecue bones at each other,
Or call'n nobody in general a motherfucker,
Or maybe stand'n on the corner say'n
"Hey, Slick, you gotta dime?"
Or call'n out to the fine young ladies
"You can walk with me any time, Baby."
Some hang around a dark alley and wait
To snatch an old lady's purse who's com'n home late.
Yes, every day is when the South Side shows its class.
Sisters play it cool; brothers act an ass.

From Write On, a Magazine of Student Writing at
Du Sable High School

ON a Wednesday, five days before the Monday I was to begin at Du
Sable, I decided to visit the school and meet the principal and perhaps chat with a few teachers and students. With a better "feel"
for the school, I thought, my final planning that weekend before I
started teaching would be more appropriate.

Seventy-five blocks south of my Near North Side apartment
was Du Sable—a distance, I was told, most efficiently traveled on
public transportation. Rush hour congestion on the north-south

Dan Ryan Expressway that ran right by Du Sable occurred, Monday through Friday, between 6:30 A. M. and 7:30 P. M.

As I had no desire to prove myself in a daily traffic battle to and from school, and I doubted that my Buick's ailing Dynaflow transmission could withstand all that stop-and-go driving, I decided to take the elevated every day to school.

That Wednesday, then, I caught a southbound B train at Fullerton Avenue for the ride to Fifty-first Street. At Fifty-first, I would walk the remaining five blocks to the school.

From Fullerton to the underground Loop stops the ride was deafening, hot, and crowded. I wondered if it could be any more unpleasant on the Dan Ryan.

Washington . . . .

Madison . . . .

Adams . . . .

Jackson . . . .

Gradually the cars emptied their cargo of Loop-bound workers and the ride became less crowded, though no less noisy or hot.

After the Twelfth Street/Roosevelt Road stop, I was the only passenger in my car—that is until the train emerged from darkness and rose above the street to make its Thirty-first Street/Illinois Institute of Technology stop. The nine people who entered my car, I noticed, were black.

As the iron-wheeled cars lurched and screeched hideously southward, the dreariness of life in Chicago's South Side slums began to press heavily upon me. We inched around an S-turn and I could see what life was like in the many flats whose rear entrances now jutted up against the elevated tracks.

Sagging wooden porches revealed the junk and clutter of current and past tenants—broken and twisted bicycles; antique wringer-type washing machines frozen forever by years of neglect and weathering; faded shirts, trousers, and underwear hanging on a line to dry. On an occasional porch hung a potted plant, testament to the fact that life in the ghetto can go on with even the smallest snatch of air and sunlight.

It was sweltering, and through the open window at my seat I caught a rank odor that made me move back and opt for the heated, graffiti-scarred interior of the car.

As I rode further southward, I had the impression of traveling into a foreign land, a land that communicated to the traveler the need to beware. I contemplated the messages left on the clapboard siding at each train stop by urban warriors whom I hoped never to meet.

"Willie Williams—43rd Street Gangster."

"Stone Thang."

"Death to White Motherfuckers."

To get off of the el at Fifty-first Street took some nerve, for I had to give up what little security I had felt while inside the train. Alone and on foot for the first time in the ghetto, I had to admit to myself that I was afraid.

I whirled through the heavy iron turnstyle, knocking aside an empty Swiss Colony port wine bottle, evidence of the previous night's seamy activity on the platform. I descended the stairs to street level, trying all the while to ignore the sharp intrusive smell of urine.

Down on Fifty-first Street, I was aware of trying to act as though I was not a displaced white person and knew exactly where I was going. However, my need to appear externally "at home" was belied by a knot of anxiety within as I faced the five-block walk alone to Du Sable.

Fifty-first Street, even at 8:00 in the morning, was surprisingly alive. A Seagram's liquor truck, making an early morning delivery to Golden Black Food and Liquor, had double-parked and now blocked in an angry driver of a battered 1961 Chevrolet.

The Chevy owner hung out of the driver's window and yelled, "Hey, man, I gots to go. Can't ya see? Like I got places to go, things to do and your motherfuckin' truck is getting me down."

The uniformed driver, a lanky black with a reddish Afro and no doubt used to such harassment, waved good-naturedly to his antagonist. He then swung up into his truck and pulled ahead a car length and a half.

The impatient motorist continued his barrage of complaints against the world as he maneuvered his car out of the tight parking spot. Once free, he roared off westward, leaving behind a trail of heavy blue gray smoke.

In front of United Loan Bank, the neighborhood pawn shop, I walked near the curb to avoid the broken glass from last night's assault on the shop's window display. The heavy steel lattice work behind the window apparently thwarted the would-be thief as the display still looked complete—three television sets, a trombone, several table radios, and some electric hand tools.

At Fifty-first and Michigan Avenue, in front of Family Cut-Rate Liquor, I saw an old man suffocatingly overdressed in a tattered brown overcoat and rumpled black hat weaving and lurching toward me as he talked very loudly. An appropriately hip refusal to this panhandler flashed through my mind—"Sorry, brother, I'm kinda short myself."

When the two of us passed in the middle of Michigan, however, I wondered if I had even been seen, so intent was the old man on his wild-eyed religious ramblings.

"Do you understand? Or is it too late? Has hate spread this land like a wide gate? Praise Jesus before it's too late. He knows—he knows. He knows, brother. Amen."

At last Wabash Avenue. I turned off of Fifty-first Street at Erie Vehicle Company. Now I could see Du Sable High School, one block ahead on the west side of Wabash. It was a monolithic three-story yellow brick building that appeared to cover almost a city block. On the opposite side of the school, facing State Street, loomed several red brick high rise buildings—part of the Robert Taylor Housing Project that lined a mile or two of the Dan Ryan Expressway. Touted as the largest housing project in the world, the buildings overshadowed Du Sable High School both physically and spiritually. On each city block of the project stood three 16-story buildings with ten apartments per floor. With an average of over 10 people per apartment, about 5,000 people lived in any given one block area.

In many buildings of the project, children outnumbered adults three to one. Gang violence was a way of life, and police and firemen had refused on occasion to enter certain buildings such as the building at 4848 State Street right across the street from Du Sable. Vandalism in the projects was reported to run well over $30,000 a month—not including the $500,000 needed annually to repair the damaged elevators in the project's buildings. According to a former manager of the project, 15 percent of the project's residents were involved in crime.

As I neared the school, students began to appear from various directions. They crossed littered, windblown Wabash Avenue and clustered by a battered green door of the building, waiting for the first period bell to ring. They milled restlessly, but quietly. A little pushing, a little razzing, was all that broke through of the bottled-up energy of kids kept too long in crowded places.

Outside the school, hundreds of broken, boarded-up windows on all three floors were in evidence. Heavy chain-link meshing over the first floor windows appeared to have minimized the street level damage.

On the walls were countless spray-painted messages. Each message, I thought, perhaps a cry against a school system that seemed to teach only frustration and failure and a society that recognized ghetto students only as statistical entries in the categories of race, poverty, and crime. Most of the graffiti seemed done not only out of boredom and spite but also for identification, distinction. Here I am, and here is my mark. This now has my character and is part of my personality, my property.

"Cher-o-Kee Stone."

"B P Stone."

"Ne Bone Fuzzy."

"L. L. Junior."

"Skull."

I climbed the three steps to the entrance and the nine students clumped around the door moved aside languorously—uncannily using their body language to communicate their hatred of me, a white person, an outsider on their turf.

"Hey, man, wha's happinin?" growled one kid at least six feet tall. "You gonna sub? Huh? I is gonna be in your class, and, you know, I be baaaaad."

"Say, Jack, the dude's right. You better go in there and get ready real good. We all be in your third period class."

A short muscular kid chimed in, "What's a matter with you guys, can't you see the chump wants to get through. Let the pecker through."

Even though I knew he hated my guts, I appreciated the short boy's efforts to allow me to enter the building.

After squeezing through the narrowly opened door, I found myself in a smoke-filled eight-by-ten-foot entrance foyer filled with students pressing toward a set of double doors through which they would surge the instant the bell rang.

In a flash, I thought of going back out the door, but the prospect of facing again my so-called "third period students" didn't seem wise. So, again, I pressed ahead in my quest to enter the building. Someone from behind touched the hair on the back of my head—a move I decided to ignore.

Finally, I reached a door and began to inch it open wide enough so I could slip through. As the door began to move, a woman's voice thundered out from the other side.

"Don't come through that door!"

Hoping that my white skin would allow me to enter before the bell—and not knowing where else to go—I slid through the opening and out into the first floor hallway.

A huge-chested black lady, seated behind a teacher's desk that had been dragged out into the hall, was the owner of the magnificent voice. Sheepishly, I informed her of my wish to visit the school. She motioned down the hall toward the main office and ordered me to "sign in there."

About five paces down the wide, barren hall I jumped when a bell above my head rang for five irritating, nerve-jangling seconds. First period had begun! A steady crescendo of noise built as students poured past and zigzagged up a set of nearby stairs. Down at the other end of the hall, two doors slammed open and dozens of additional students filtered out from the cafeteria.

I gladly entered the main office to escape the hallway chaos. While seated on an uncomfortable wooden bench waiting my turn to see the principal, I struck up a conversation with two teachers—both of whom I suddenly felt close to because they too were white. One, a male English teacher whose skeleton key wouldn't open his classroom door that morning, was waiting to see an assistant principal in charge of keys. The other, a female and also an English teacher, had an 8:30 A.M. meeting with another assistant principal regarding three unruly girls in her ninth period class.

The male teacher willingly commented on the stressfulness of working at Du Sable. "When I came here there was complete chaos. The behavior of the kids is very disturbing. The noise is very disturbing. Sometimes it's so noisy I have to shut my eyes in order to think clearly."

Pausing a moment, searching thoughtfully for the proper words, he continued, "The students are like children. You have to play with them, and yet they easily get out of hand, just like little kids. The abuse teachers take is tremendous. It takes a million forms."

The other English teacher was also anxious to share her perceptions of Du Sable. With a rapid-fire torrent of words, she began to describe her first year at the school.

"You want me to be polite or you want me to swear? Well, it sucked. When I came here I was terrified. Black school, not the best of neighborhoods. Shaking like a leaf, not knowing anybody. Never having been around black people."

She raced on to tell about her first year of classes," They stuck me with two double-period basic classes my first year. No materials, nothing. No paper, never. Once in a while you could scrounge up five or six books and share them."

Though she'd been at Du Sable for five years now, the strident tone of her voice indicated that she still continued to carry within the anger and frustration from that first year. This teacher, I suspected, was burned out.

"For twenty weeks we'd work on the alphabet. This is the sound of long 'A.' Uh—uh—uh. They had zero reading levels. Imagine teaching fifteen of these in class. The kids here are dumber than hell. These kids are so slow. So slow. And they are lazy. They don't want to learn anything."

Referring to her meeting that morning with the assistant principal, she told me that she wanted to have three disruptive students removed permanently from her last period class. Willingly, she shared with me a typed, two-page statement that outlined in detail how three girls had harassed her for over four months and how they had whittled away at her professional self-esteem.

By "interfering with the learning of others" I refer to
the behavior described in the remainder of this paragraph. The behavior comprises dancing, singing,
yelling during class, walking around the room, writing on the blackboard, opening and closing the doors.
It is hard for the other students to study with this
constant motion and noise going on around them.
The behavior also comprises interrupting my explanations to the class by such remarks as: "This
ain't nothing." "I ain't doin' this work!" "Ms.
Liston, when are we going to do something else?"
"You give too much work, Ms. Liston." "Ms. Liston,
what time is it?" "Ms. Liston, when are we going to
do something interesting?" "Ms. Liston, how many
days I been absent?" It is impossible for me to deliver one complete sentence of speech without such
rude and irrelevant interruptions.
By "inappropriate behavior" I refer to the behavior described in the remainder of this paragraph. The behavior comprises the before-mentioned dancing,
yelling, singing, etc. The behavior also comprises
incidents which were abusive to me and to which the
physical proximity of the students to me—along with
the remarks made and the emotional tension of the
remarks—was threatening. At various times they
have surrounded my desk as a group and have begun
remarks which usually follow a path similar to the
following one: "Why'd you call my home? I want to
talk to you. No, now! I want to talk to you out in
the hall then. Why not? You're supposed to teach us
something. You're supposed to learn how to talk to
us. We are different from you. You don't know how
to talk so we can understand. You have to understand
that we can't do this grammar because we don't talk
the same as you do. You aren't supposed to fail us if
we try. You just don't like us." And then glancing
down at the open record book, they perhaps say,
"What's that? I ain't never been absent from this
class. Why you got me absent? You know that's not
right! Why'd you tell my counselor I was going to
fail? You aren't supposed to fail me." This behavior is not something which has happened just
once, but repeatedly. This behavior also occurs in
front of all members of the class present, not only
causing embarrassment to me as a teacher, but also

causing a general atmosphere which seems to say
that at Du Sable teachers are less than nothing, not
even people, but just instruments to be used or abused
as the student sees fit and without recourse. Not only
does the behavior create a bad image for me and for
the school, but it also fails to create anything of
value for anyone involved. The only energy I have
seen these students expend in my class has been expended in this type of behavior.
At the times when I have reminded these students
they were not doing their class work during class,
they have replied to me with such remarks as: "I
do my work at home." "I already did it." "I can't
understand this stuff and you don't want to help me."
"I already know all this stuff; we had this last year."
"I don't need to learn this stuff." "Aw, go on!"
Class time spent by them on assignments is nil,
if any.

Both teachers also commented bitterly on what they perceived
as their inadequate preparation for teaching at Du Sable. Especially poignant were their almost identical accounts of how their
idealized professional aspirations were uncompromisingly shat-
tered by the brutality of ghetto life. Daily psychological (and, at
times, physical) survival was now their priority—teaching kids
seemed tragically, but understandably, second. I wondered what
price these and countless other teachers at urban schools were
paying to teach day after day in an environment that, after one-
half day, I found depressing, oppressive, and threatening.

At last, I had the opportunity to meet with Du Sable's principal. I was anxious to see if his perceptions of the school paral-
leled those of his teachers. Moreover, I hoped to encounter a
wise and supportive leader—one whose goal it would be to develop
an educational program that emphasized the humaneness of teachers and students and made it possible for teachers to be professionally satisfied. It was with a great deal of interest, then, that
I entered the principal's office before taking my own tour of the
building.

At once, I realized that the principal's view of Du Sable bore
no resemblance to the "front line" reports of the two English
teachers—nor to my own initial impressions of the place.

I described to him my experiences while trying to enter the
building and I recounted briefly the English teachers' reports of
psychological abuse at the hands of students who didn't give a damn
about learning. The principal, a white, beefy ex-coach in his
early fifties, dismissed it all with a wave of his hand.

"We have a very sound educational program," he began in noticeably tentative, measured tones. I sensed his defensiveness and how his proficiency for cover-up in the face of incontrovertible evidence had made him a successful Board of Education administrator.

"We could be a fantastic school if we could just get the right elements together," he continued. "It's just like a chemical reaction. We have the right ingredients, but we don't have the catalyst.

"There are those teachers in this school who suggest that there is violence and pot smoking, and yet when you ask them where and when, they can't say. This is one of the best high schools in the city. There are many positive aspects to Du Sable." With this, he pointed to a crudely hand-lettered sign leaning up against a file cabinet—it read, "We are No. 1."

"Du Sable has always been a prime target to be maligned by anyone. News items sometimes imply that Du Sable is a den of dope peddlers and users. But the real truth is that our students are well behaved and well groomed. Participation by our students in events in and outside the school always elicits positive comments from viewers. We are good!"

I went along with the principal's comments about his school— almost lulled by his high sounding praises into believing that maybe my initial impressions were wrong. Maybe the English teachers I had spoken to earlier didn't really care about kids and had "brought on" a lot of their own suffering.

Believing that I had seen the rightness of his views, the principal agreed to let me spend second and third periods visiting with teachers throughout the building.

While on my way to visit the English and physical education teachers in their departmental offices near the State Street side of the building, I had the opportunity to peer into several classrooms and to linger beside open doorways to catch the teacher-student interactions within.

In one room, a history teacher lectured on the Bill of Rights. The 15 students in the room seemed attentive—some squirming, an occasional snap of gum, and one student with his head on the desk were the only signs that learning might not be taking place. A discussion of the rights of individuals arrested on the street brought forth eager student participation. Even the catnapping student raised his head in a show of interest at this topic.

Further down the hall were two remedial English classes in adjacent rooms. Students in both rooms were quiet as they concentrated on dittoed assignment sheets. One teacher, a thin black male in his late fifties, sat ramrod straight at his desk while he alternately graded papers and monitored his students' activity. Four students in his class of 16 had fallen asleep at their desks—

a fact that evidently caused this teacher no alarm as he made no attempt to rouse them from their slumbers. The relative absence of noise and activity suggested a hushed library reading room rather than a high school classroom.

The other teacher, a white woman in her late twenties, sat behind her big wooden teacher's desk, staring out vacantly at her class also at work on a dittoed assignment sheet. Like her next door neighbor, she did not talk with (or even <u>at</u>) her 17 students, five of whom were asleep.

Her second floor classroom in a newer section of the building bespoke a sturdy, functional practicality—new blackboards lined the front and rear walls; four banks of fluorescent lights hung from the ceiling; and 20 movable desks were scattered about the room. Several students, though, had lined themselves up along the open windows through which came street sounds and the occasional blare of a transistor radio toted by a student arriving late for school.

The walls of the room were a bland, institutional pink. The back wall was dotted with shreds of masking tape and paper—remnants of previous years' posters and charts. The color of the walls was repeated in the pink and brown speckled tile floor. The greatest contrast in color was the lower four feet of each cinder block wall. Here were dirty black smudges and cryptic felttip scrawls: "Chunky & S.O.S." "Wank & Smitty." "CCAS ain't Shit."

On one bare expanse of wall was taped a small, color map of Disneyland. An educational poster entitled "The Play's the Thing" hung on another wall; here, too, cartoon scenes illustrated four terms used in drama. Beneath this was a commercial poster for a paperback book publisher—several books were pictured on a sloping green lawn with a bold headline that asserted, "It's Your World."

Above the door—near the clock and intercom, both broken for years—was taped a large color photo of an exotic, probably foreign, marketplace taken through a fish-eye lens. To the right of the door was a bulletin board with various newspaper and magazine articles—one about Cicely Tyson, another about a black high school quarterback who couldn't read, and another about a new home for the Du Sable Museum of African Art. Above the front blackboard, in a long thin collage, were 50 paper covers from different hard-cover books.

The slight efforts to enliven the room and to make it more interesting seemed instead to accentuate the room's elemental drabness. For the student, the psychological message such an environment conveyed was clear—here was another sterile classroom (no different from those down the hall) designed for years of efficient, practical service at the expense of individual feelings

and preferences. The room subtly, but powerfully, mitigated
against any strongly felt feelings or individual actions. Instead, it
blended all (teacher as well as student) into an institutionally "safe"
unit within the total impersonal milieu of the school.

Inner-city schools, I knew, were frequently housed in rundown
buildings. Du Sable was no exception I realized as I reentered the
older section of the building. The halls here were gloomy, dank,
and depressing. Windows were smashed at a rate that evidently
surpassed the building engineer's ability to replace them or to
board them up. Heavy door frames had been loosened by countless
students who would viciously kick and slam doors not immediately
open to them.

I peered into empty room 114 and saw that several bolted
down desks had been yanked off the floor and broken. Large chunks
of the slate blackboard had been ripped out, revealing the brickwork
of an interior wall.

In a dark entrance foyer on the State Street side of the building, four male students furtively passed around an early morning
marijuana cigarette. The pungent odor that assailed my nostrils
was unmistakable.

One of them stopped his loud, rapid-fire challenging of another boy for a moment and called out to me, the menacing mockery
in his voice very, very clear, "Hey, man, is you a narc?" His
pals laughed hysterically, slapped each others' open palms, and
resumed their banter, not at all concerned about who I really was
or what steps I might take to remove them from the building.

The boy that yelled out to me gave another boy a sharp jab
on the collar bone and said, "Check this out, chump":

I was walk'n through the jungle
With my dick in my hand.
I was the baddest mother fucker
In the jungle land.
I look up in a tree,
And what did I see?
Your big black mama
Try'n to piss on me.

At this surprising turn to the limerick, the others, even the boy who
was being insulted, emitted hoots and howls of approval. Spurred
on by his comrades, the boy continued his frenzied rhyme:

I picked up a rock
And hit her in the cock
And knocked that ole bitch
About a half a block.

> I hate to talk about your mama;
> She's a sweet ole soul.
> She's got a rap-pa-tap-pa dick
> And a pussy hole.
> Listen mother fucker,
> You a two-timing bitch.
> You got a ring around your pussy
> Make a old man itch.

By this time, the boy who had been ridiculed had prepared his rejoinder. He strode up, nose-to-nose with his contender, and, with bulging eyes and ostentatious hand movements, began his counterattack:

> Your mama don't wear no drawers.
> She wash 'em in alcohol.
> She put 'em on a clothesline;
> The sun refused to shine.
> She put 'em in a garbage can;
> They scared old garbage man.
> She put 'em on the railroad track;
> The train went back and back.
> She put 'em in the midnight train;
> They scared old Jesse James.

I heard their shrieks of laughter as I climbed the stairs to room 260, the English office. I admitted to myself that those hoodlums in the doorway were frightening; I was aware, too, of some anger toward a system that would allow me to confront, alone, such a threatening situation.

During my brief stay in the English office, I learned that conflict (with students, administrators, other teachers, and the surrounding ghetto environment) characterized nearly every facet of the English teacher's professional life at Du Sable. The major task of the English teacher, it seemed, was to cope with the situation in a way that reduced, or at least managed, the tension that arose from this multidimensional conflict. Therefore, the discharging of accumulated tension was often the order of the day for those teachers who spent a conference and preparation, or a self-directed, period in the English office.

Of the four teachers now in the office, I first chatted with a black male who entered the office just after me, exclaiming in mock hysteria, "It's a mockery—it's a mockery. I just skipped to class. I told my kids, "Let's skip education!"

Humor, he explained, helped him and others similarly inclined to cope with the demands of ghetto teaching.

"In the English department we have a sort of humor that comes from experiences in the classroom and with the administration. It's really a downer when you come in here. If you don't see it this way, it's hard. You have to see it as a joke—a joke. It's like a Catch 22 or Mash situation."

Through his humor, this teacher made it clear that the demands of ghetto teaching were really beneath his capabilities. The job was not worth taking seriously nor becoming involved with.

Du Sable teachers, I was beginning to realize, must counteract several stressors—stressors that could originate with the administrators, with the students, with the ghetto environment, or with the teacher himself. Another teacher in the English office, a young Jewish male who commuted daily from the North Side, insightfully characterized these stressors as free-floating "fears" related to professional competence, job security, the students he taught, and the intentions of the administration.

"I'm scared," he began, "scared I'll be told I'm doing a horrible job—by other faculty and by the administration. I'd rather the administration, and some other teachers, don't know what's going on in my classes. Also, I think I have some fear of the kids' irrationality."

This teacher went on to tell me how he believed that most teachers in the English department, and perhaps most teachers in the entire school, "offset" their job-related stress by cultivating social relationships within the English office instead of pursuing unrewarding relationships with either the administration or the students. In effect, such teachers formed coalitions to combat or to "balance off" particular conditions within the school that they found intolerable.

I was about to chat with another teacher, when the office door swung open and a teacher, obviously distressed, entered, threw her green record book on the long oak conference table, and plopped in a chair.

"Goddamn place," she moaned. All eyes were on her—fellow teachers waiting for the familiar, ritualistic ventilation of anger and frustration.

"What happened?" one teacher asked with just enough nonchalance to suggest that it was a frequently asked question around Du Sable.

The teacher, a heavy-set white woman in her late thirties and wearing a sweater, corduroy pants, and earth shoes, began her story.

"Yesterday, during ninth period, I was teaching in room 208 when two boys outside the door began yelling, 'Fuck! Fuck! Fuck!'

"Finally, I had enough and went to the door and asked them politely to leave. Then one of them asked me if I wanted to fuck. And I said, 'I'm going to ask you once more politely to leave, and then I'm going to get mad.'"

"Right on, that's the way, Miss Wacker," said the humorous-minded black teacher. "We gots to communicate with our student body."

She paused for a moment here and, letting the drama of the story escalate a bit, dug through her purse for a package of Salem and a lighter. She lit up and took a long slow puff before exhaling and continuing.

"Well, they finally left. But five minutes later they came back and crashed the door open. They walked in and one of them yelled to me, 'Do you want to fuck?' I told him no, and then he said, 'Well, does anyone else want to fuck?' My class went absolutely berserk!

"Then I really got mad and threw a fit. I told them, 'If you goddamn son-of-a-bitches don't get out of my room right now, I'm going to beat the hell out of you. Now get your asses out of here!'

"Then one of the bastards, the one that was yelling, spit in my face and slammed the door when I went to run after him."

"Did you tell the principal about it?" one of her colleagues asked. "What did he say?"

"I just came from his office. He said I shouldn't let them talk to me like that. I said, 'What do you want me to do—cut their tongues out?'

"Then he had the gall to say, 'You must have done something to provoke them.' I told him, 'It takes a lot of nerve to say that,' and then I walked out. That man's such a turd. He's more frustrating to deal with than the kids."

My final stop before leaving Du Sable was the departmental office for the school's five male gym teachers. This office, also on the second floor, was in an isolated corner of the building.

I headed down a dimly lit corridor of bashed in lockers. As I turned left, I noticed several kids dart up a set of stairs in front of me. Evidently, they thought I was on hall patrol. Moments later, they miraculously reappeared behind me, only to flee again when I stopped and looked their way.

The gym office was a small narrow room, just barely large enough to accommodate the three teachers' desks that had been crammed in—two on the west wall, the other on the opposite wall next to a gray, dusty radiator. The glass window on the heavy office door was covered with a black steel mesh. Two extra-heavy hasps gave additional security for the office's cache of baseball mitts, bats, basketballs, and so on. And lest anyone overlook these security measures, a plastic sign on the door warned, "Students—Keep Out! "

At each desk was seated a coach. One of them, white and in his late twenties, was absorbed in the morning edition of the Chicago Sun Times. Appropriately, perhaps, he was reading about the Muhammed Ali-Joe Frazier heavyweight fight the night before. Another coach, a tall muscular black in his late forties, was reading a copy of Chicago's black-owned newspaper, the Daily Defender. The third coach, also black, was asleep—his spring-loaded swivel chair tilted at an alarming angle.

The coach with the Defender identified himself as Coach Tanner, chairman of the physical education department. His voice, a booming baritone capable of incredible projection, conveyed impressive self-assurance. If I had to go into battle, I thought, this was the kind of man I would want on my side.

Coach Tanner told me that he had been at Du Sable for 12 years now. With a manner that was confident and nonchalant, he shared with me his perceptions of Du Sable's students.

"We got all kinds here, but nothing we can't handle. Some of these kids have never had discipline of any kind, and that's what we give them in here—a good shot of discipline.

"Some of the teachers in other departments complain about not being able to control the kids, but, hell, they let the kids walk all over them. You can't do that with these kids. Stand fast and let 'em know you won't take no guff—that's what you got to do. "

By this time, the other black coach had been roused from his slumbers. Coach Washington, a gravel-voiced ex-professional football player and one of the school's two representatives for the Chicago Teachers' Union, was a man, I immediately sensed, who did not mince words.

"Teaching here, you realize it's you against them bastards," he said contemptuously, waving his big right hand in the general direction of the Robert Taylor Housing Projects.

"When I see a kid in the hall, I tell 'em they better get their black ass outa here. I'll jam the fuckers up against the lockers and break their goddamn necks.

"The other day during fourth period I caught a kid right outside this door. " He motioned toward the hallway that was now beginning to fill with students who had showered and dressed and were now awaiting the bell. "I said, 'You're a funny-looking nigger—get on to class. ' The little shit told me to go to hell.

"I grabbed him by the collar, pulled him in here, and made him grab hold of this desk and bend over. "

He pointed to a large wooden paddle with several half-inch holes in it. "See that? I damn near split that on that black fool's ass. Yes I did. That's just how you survive and get respect here at Du Sable."

Just as I left the gym office, the bell signaling the end of the period rang. Quickly the halls filled with yelling, pushing, running kids. I was jostled and bumped along as I headed for an exit door on Wabash Street.

During the long ride back to Chicago's North Side, I tried to sort out my first impressions of Du Sable and those who had to spend the best parts of their lives there. I had felt, alternately, fear, anger, powerlessness, and humor.

I was aware, though, of another emotion—not the sense of relief that I expected when I left behind Chicago's expansive South Side ghetto, but a feeling that can best be described as sadness. Sad that my society allowed human tragedies like Du Sable to continue in its midst. And sad because I was in touch with the humanity that I knew I shared with all of those—black and white, teacher and student—whose fate it was to work out their lives in a place like Du Sable.

The fact that I would soon be taking my place by their side, however, cut short my humanitarian reverie. I knew I had a lot of preparing to do before that Monday.

2
CULTURE SHOCK

Over the years, it has become increasingly important that students
identify themselves as they enter
the building, lunchrooms, athletic
events, and other special activities. This is because outsiders
have taken advantage of the opportunity to remain anonymous and
create problems in the halls,
lunchrooms, classrooms, and
during activities. Students, teachers, teacher-aides, and others
have been attacked, abused,
robbed, and learning has been
disrupted.

Special Bulletin No. 15, Du Sable
High School

"HEY, white man, you gonna teach here?"

I looked up from my desk that Monday morning and saw three
boys crowded into the open doorway of room 207, my new classroom
for the year.

"Yeah, I be talkin' to you, man! Is you a teacher or something?"

"Yes. I'm a new English teacher here," I said, getting up from my desk and my preparations for my new students who were to arrive in 30 minutes. The three tall, slender youths eyed me with bemusement as though I not only was of a different skin color but wore antlers as well.

The boy that spoke to me began to laugh and the others quickly joined in.

"What you teach? Sewing?"

They laughed again and then turned to leave.

"You'll be sorry you came here, white motherfucker," one of them called out just before he slammed the door.

When I stepped out into the hall they were gone—their loud footsteps as they raced down a set of nearby stairs the only sign that they had, a moment ago, been in my room.

That was my formal introduction to Du Sable High School's student body—an introduction that made me feel that my students might be more prepared for me than I was for them.

I was, on that first day, frightened. If I had been told that I would spend the next eight years of my life at Du Sable, I would have quit—right then. As it was, though, I had no crystal ball with which to foretell my future—and so I began my slow, often painful, professional growth as an inner-city teacher at a school most Chicagoans knew as a "dumping ground" for underachievers and delinquents.

The exact nature of the anxiety I felt as a ghetto teacher was not readily apparent at the beginning of my assignment. During my first year at Du Sable I was frequently very anxious and frightened. On occasion, I even had nightmares about the place. I despaired of ever understanding or accepting the students' behavior and attitudes that were so strange and threatening to me. I experienced what anthropologists and sociologists have termed "culture shock," a kind of free-floating anxiety that afflicts the sojourner in a "foreign" culture.

Initially, I tried to locate the source of my discomfort primarily in the disturbing behavior of my students, much as Wright (1957, pp. 13-14) did during his early work at the University of Chicago's Orthogenic School for autistic children:

> At the time, I explained my unhappy situation to myself as the result of the children being basically different from me, in a different world. I was sane, an adult, a counselor. The gist of these efforts was to protect myself by maintaining a gap between me and them, a gap which could account for my lack of success.

In an effort to understand my situation (and my response to it), I read extensively from the literature on teaching the "disadvantaged" and on the psychology of black ghetto life. I also at that time, for reasons quite apart from my need to cope with the stress of teaching at Du Sable, entered analytically oriented psychotherapy. The increased awareness I achieved about my teaching directly reflects, and is inseparable from, discoveries made during my nine years of personal therapy. I do not intend to suggest, however, that therapy is necessary for a teacher to adjust effectively to the demands of ghetto teaching; I merely wish to make known what was for me an invaluable aid in clarifying the anxiety I felt about teaching at Du Sable.

Prompted by my therapy, then, I began to monitor more precisely what was really going on within me while I was at Du Sable. Gradually, I realized that some of my anxiety about the school had its origins within myself, often springing from my own dimly perceived fears—fears that had nothing to do with Du Sable.

In the remainder of this chapter, I will recount several episodes that increased the intensity of the culture shock I had to work through. Though there is much in the following that is legitimately upsetting, the almost uncanny way these experiences seemed to parallel some of my earlier fears may have allowed them to be distorted and transformed into unconscious anxieties that limited the formation of educative relationships between my students and me. And all of these examples highlight what was for me a fundamental "crisis"—my inner struggle between trust and mistrust at the Du Sable environment.

FEAR OF SUDDENNESS OR SURPRISE

The most pervasive, free-floating anxiety I experienced while teaching at Du Sable was my fear of suddenness or surprise. On a deeper level, I interpreted fearful events at Du Sable as attacks on my integrity as a human being. And, to heighten my anxiety, these forays against my personhood were initiated from sources that I seldom could identify. Furthermore, the very randomness of such events increased my resultant anxiety—if I could have predicted such noxious, threatening episodes in my environment, then my anxiety would certainly have lessened.

Example 1. I had just begun a review of paragraph writing with a morning English class. The 15 students and I were seated in a circle. My back was to the door, which I had left open (poor practice, as any seasoned ghetto teacher will tell you) in an attempt to cool off the room.

"Remember, each paragraph should deal with one main idea. And if you have another idea you want to write about, what should you do?"

Before any of my students could provide me with the rather obvious answer to my question, I was startled by a gasp of hoarse laughter from someone literally breathing down my neck. With the racing heart of a person who has just been startled in a carnival fun house, I turned in time to see an unidentified student dart through the doorway.

I tried to appear calm and not upset in front of my students. I got up, walked to the door, and, before closing it, set the lock with my key.

Example 2. During one of the three years that Du Sable was on an experimental year-round schedule, I taught a small make-up class in freshman English. Our room was just across the hall from a second floor lunchroom exit door and cater-corner from a set of stairs leading to the faculty parking lot.

Yesterday and the day before, plate-flinging, chair-throwing riots had exploded in both the first and second floor lunchrooms. When these eruptions occurred, scores of screaming students surged out into the halls—the noise and chaos creating havoc with my remedial kids who always looked for the slightest excuse to act out and go wild. And the irritating staccato ringing of bells to signal security guards elsewhere in the building only further disrupted my efforts to restore order.

Since the heavy glass was missing from our classroom door, it was also not unusual for second floor lunchroom students driven out into the hall during a riot to stick their heads through the opening and hurl wisecracks at my students or at me.

Today, then, I was hoping desperately for one day of relative calm with my fourth period class. 11:05 A.M. We had about made it through the period. My students were reading aloud from a book in the Checkered Flag Series, simple stories about teenage race car drivers. I moved about the room as students read, most stumbling terribly on the simplest of words: "because," "miles per hour," "track," and "second."

Suddenly, I jumped as I was hit in the chest by a snowball thrown through the opening in my classroom door. The smashed snow splattered the pages of my book. I looked up in time to see two boys running down the stairs. By the time I stepped out into the hall, they had reached the parking lot and were rearming themselves with the snow they would need for another commando-style raid within the building. I returned to the room, determined never again to make myself an easy target by standing directly across from my classroom doorway.

FEAR OF BEING ATTACKED FROM THE REAR

Similar to my fear of suddenness or surprise was my fear of being attacked from the rear. While at Du Sable, I found that those few students who would dare to assault a teacher would often do so through means of a "surprise attack" from the rear—whether throwing an object at the teacher's unguarded back or actually touching the teacher from behind. Thus, I was frequently aware of being "instinctively" poised to react suddenly if threatened from the rear.

Example. While on ninth period hall duty during my first year at Du Sable, I approached two young men to ask if they had a hall pass. (Later, I learned that they were not students but "gang-bangers," a neighborhood term for hoodlum.)

"Hey, the man wants to know if we gots a hall pass," the tall, athletic boy said to his pal.

The other, one or two inches taller than my own six-foot-one frame, strode up to me and, nose-to-nose, leered, "Motherfucker, don't you know who that is? That's Muhammed Ali, and he don't need no pass."

"Yeah, chump, I'm Muhammad Ali."

The lean, muscular boy started shadow boxing, fists knifing through the air with impressive speed.

"I'm Ali," he shrieked. "And you—you Jerry Quarry. We gonna get it on!"

I saw that the long hallway was deserted. Uncertain as to what my best response would be, I tried faintly to reestablish any authority I might have had. "You're supposed to have a hall pass," I said.

Then I turned to continue down the hall, hoping to make, without further incident, the main corridor near the front of the building. About five steps away, I caught the movement of a large object near my head. I whirled in time to deflect a wooden chair thrown at my back.

The pair of desperados then raced down a nearby set of stairs and effortlessly disappeared somewhere within the school's vast network of dimly lit, dank corridors.

INTOLERANCE FOR BEING INTERRUPTED

While teaching at Du Sable, I was interrupted countless times by students whose behavior, regardless of its underlying causes, I saw as purposefully rude and thoughtless. Interrupting, then, was just one more way Du Sable students had of psychologically wearing down their teachers. While some students, of course, would try not to interrupt me, they were usually unable to subvert their individual desires and needs of the moment for the benefit of the group; they were arrested at the level of childish egocentrism that Piaget (1965) has described in much younger children. In short, these kids had no respect for the "rules" required in the "game" of classroom give-and-take.

FEAR OF BEING MANIPULATED AND FEAR OF AGGRESSIVE, INTRUSIVE BEHAVIOR

A necessary attribute for kids to survive at Du Sable, particularly for males, was the ability to overwhelm and manipulate an "opponent" (other student, teacher, or staff person) toward a desired end. The behavior of girls as well as boys was often provocative, intrusive, and manipulative. Such young people, as Redl and Wineman (1952, p. 20) note, have an uncanny ability to keep an adult anxiously off balance: "How fascinating to observe here the ego, which seems to be so stupid in its perception of social reality, so 'socially blind,' operate with such diagnostic acuity about the feelings and attitudes of the adult."

Example 1. While stationed on eighth period hall duty near room 260, an older student whom I didn't know came up to me and put his foot on the chair next to mine.

"Tie my shoe!" he commanded menacingly.

"Man, I ain't gonna tie your shoe," I said. I could feel the blood rush to my face—partly from anger and partly from fear. Is he going to kick me in the face and then run down the hall, I wondered.

"Tie my shoe," he ordered again.

I stood up now, determined that if we got into a fight my opponent was not going to have the advantage of jumping me while I was seated.

"You better move on down this hall—now!" I yelled, clenching my fists in preparation for the struggle that I was certain would follow. Dimly, I was aware of how unprofessional my behavior was, yet I almost had to chuckle at how sweet it felt to be responding naturally—free, for the moment, of the constraining role of the teacher.

To my surprise, however, the kid left, peering into different classroom doors as he weaved his way down the hall in search of another victim whom he could bait just to the brink of aggressively acting out.

Example 2. As I left school one day, I decided to go through one of the entrance foyers on the Wabash Street side of the building.

Ordinarily I would leave school by walking through the boiler room and out into the faculty parking lot. But today the head engineer, displaying his ultimate control over his building, had decided to lock the door to the boiler room, thus putting an end to teachers strolling through his domain.

I slowly eased open the door to the foyer and saw that it was filled with students tightly huddled together, escaping the frigid, swirling Chicago wind outside. The familiar sweet odor of marijuana was unmistakable in that cold dry air. I was not surprised when the kids made no move to step aside and let me get to the door. So I zipped up my parka and started to press through the crowd.

Just before I reached the door, one kid, whom I suspected might not be a student because of his extremely surly, jail-hardened look and the earring he wore in his left ear, leered at me with bloodshot eyes and growled, "I'll kill you!"

I brushed past him and pushed the door open. As I crossed the snow-covered street to my car, I reminded myself that one day I would be able to leave Du Sable for the last time.

Example 3. The bell rang signaling the start of my ninth period freshman remedial reading class. No more than half of my 15 students were in their seats, however. The hall was still crowded with noisy, boisterous kids, a few of whom would enter my room by the back door only to wander out again. A handful of my students continued to mill about the room under the pretext of borrowing paper or pencil from a classmate.

"Sherman, sit down right now. Let's get started."

"But, Mr. Parkay, he stole my pencil."

"He a story. I did not."

"Bobby, get back from that window," I yelled, momentarily directing my attention to yet another trouble spot in the room.

"What page, Mr. Parkay? What page?"

"Page 41," I said to the girl who sat directly in front of my desk. Thank God at least one student is ready to begin, I thought.

I went over to separate Melvin and Nancy who were skirmishing over a pick (a special comb for Afro hairstyles). I pulled them apart and tried to steer them toward their seats.

"She stole my pick," Melvin continued to whine.

"I did not. You a lie!" Nancy screamed and tried to push me away to get at Melvin.

"All right, all right. I want everyone in their seats right now!" I yelled. Inwardly, I marveled at the uncanny ability of my students to seize on the slightest excuse to resist me—thereby prolonging the present chaos and adding to my frustration and anger.

"Page 41," I said again before turning to my next objective— clearing the room of those kids who didn't belong in my class and then securing the front and back doors and trying to keep my kids from opening them to readmit troublemakers from the hall.

I had just shooed two kids back out into the hall and was closing the door when a fat older kid forced his way past me and into my room. For the last three days now this kid had followed the same pattern. He would enter my room at the start of the period to horse around with a few of my students and then attack me with obscene verbal abuse when I asked him to leave—as though I was being unfair with him.

Before today's class I had made arrangements with Sergeant Smith, one of the school's three uniformed policemen, to point out this kid at the start of class. Now I looked up and down the halls and saw no sign of Smith. Again, I would have to handle this alone.

"Come on, let's get to class," I said, stepping back into the room. "My class has got a lot of work to do today."

"Get fucked, white man," he said. "I'll leave when I'm goddamn ready." He went back to trying to kiss the neck of one of my girls. Unsuccessful, he loped over to another girl in the next row.

"Get away from me," she howled and pushed him back. He stumbled backward in mock astonishment as though overpowered by the slim girl. "Stay away, you pig," she said laughingly. It was clear she was enticing him to return.

"Right now, I want you out of here!" I said as I moved toward the back of the room where he stood.

"Suck my dick, honky, and then I'll leave," he howled hysterically.

I knew this kid would continue his intimidation of me until he realized that I simply would take no more. At that moment, I had reached that limit.

Fists clenched so that my knuckles must have been snow white, I quickly closed up the remaining 15-foot distance between us. I could feel the adrenalin coursing throughout my body. My kids gawked at me as though I had gone mad. At least they were all quiet—15 pairs of eyes staring at us, waiting to see what their teacher would do.

"You goddamn son of a bitch, I'll beat the shit out of you if you don't get your big butt out of here—right now! And if I ever see your fat fucking face in my room again, it'll be the last time you'll be able to walk through that doorway."

He knew I meant business and would have fought him right on the spot.

"Yeah, man, I'll go. Be cool," he said. He then turned and shuffled toward the door.

For the rest of that period I vented my smoldering anger on my class. I was furious and blamed Du Sable kids, my principal, and the entire Chicago school system that I had to contend, unaided, with such abuse in the practice of my profession. For several days thereafter I felt that all Du Sable kids were "unteachable" and education at the school a complete travesty.

FEAR OF ENCIRCLEMENT AND LOSS OF AUTONOMY

During my years at Du Sable, I was frequently aware of strong anxiety when I found myself the only adult in a crowd of excited kids. And even if they were not acting out antisocially, I still seemed to fear what they might do. Only gradually did I come to realize that I was projecting some of my own inner anxieties onto students whom I perceived as radically different from myself.

Example. To reach the second floor teachers' lunchroom, it was necessary either to walk across the students' lunchroom or to cut through the kitchen, a route that the spatula-wielding cooks let any and all trespassers know was against Board of Education regulations.

Today, I was running late for lunch and didn't feel like experiencing the cooks' contemptuous looks if I passed through their kingdom, so I decided to cut across the students' lunchroom.

I showed my white face at one of the lunchroom exit doors and waited while the surly black security guard came over and opened the door a crack, just far enough for me to grab it without pinching my fingers and pull it open. By this time three kids who didn't have fifth period lunch had clustered around me, hoping to surge out into the crowded noisy lunchroom once the door was popped open from the inside.

"Man, you can't come in here," the guard told the denizens of the halls as I squeezed through the tiny opening he made with his body and the door frame.

"Come on, man, I got lunch this period," one of the kids whined. "I lost my ID."

"Hey, I'm with him," shouted another one as he tried to place his hand on my shoulder to illustrate graphically his connection with me.

"No way, man," said the guard. He then pushed the two kids back and closed the door. The boys now pressed their faces up against the glass on the door and made angry, bug-eyed faces at us.

"Thanks," I said to the guard. "Sometimes it can be a real hassle just getting in here."

He ignored my thanks and sauntered back over to the wall he had been leaning against. With a big yawn, he resumed his position.

The noise from the several hundred kids in that lunchroom was deafening. Many were yelling and wildly gesturing at one another. Five boys at the table next to me were rolling dice, shrieking crazily just before each die came to a standstill. The tremendous noise and excitement seemed to spur many kids on to even wilder displays of impulsivity.

Halfway across the room, I felt confused and vulnerable. Momentarily, I was aware that I was the only adult in a tumultuous sea of adolescent emotions.

FEAR OF VIOLENT, PRIMITIVE BEHAVIOR

My white friends, many of whom lived in Chicago's suburbs would quiz me often about the incidence of violence at Du Sable. I would tell them that violence at the school was not a regular occurrence—but it did occur with enough frequency to make anyone who could not relate to or understand riotous behavior uneasy. On any given day, a visitor to the school would most likely not witness violence. Sooner or later, however, the visitor would realize that there was an ever-present undercurrent of barbarity and hatred that could manifest itself at any time. For example, once I passed a student in the hall—a second later he was shot by another student. A black or white teacher in the halls could pass a group of males who, perhaps emboldened by marijuana or alcohol, would assume threatening karate stances and hurl obscene racial slurs.

As I have mentioned, the chaos and noise when students passed from one class to the next was at times overwhelming, even frightening. Students would run screaming down the halls, banging on lockers, slamming doors, and chasing and hitting each other. An open boys' washroom door would often reveal students standing in a thick haze of marijuana smoke. In the lunchrooms, emotions were frequently at fever pitch, and riots occasionally erupted. Fire alarms, with attendant rumors of fights, walkouts, or shootouts, would thwart the teachers' efforts to instruct from time to time.

Another disturbing aspect of the violence I witnessed at Du Sable was my own gradual realization that such events often aroused similar impulses within me. I, too, would have liked to aggressively "act out" my daily frustrations.

In a research study of the reactions of adults to aggressive, primitive behavior in children, Rosen (1963, pp. 261-62) discovered the same thing. Anxiety results not only from what the child actually does but from what the adult fears he might do:

He experiences strong <u>negative</u> feelings toward children who display characteristics which the worker
has rejected in himself. These characteristics may
consist either of direct primitive expressions of the
child's needs and feelings or of defensive patterns.
In the case of the former, the worker feels endan-
gered by the responses stimulated in himself.

<u>Example 1.</u> This particular remedial English class was, I
told myself, responsible for making this year worse than last. The
class had more than the usual number of rude, acting out kids—boys
as well as girls.

Today, we were reading aloud a play, <u>Five on the Black Hand
Side</u>, in our <u>Scope</u> magazines. Without <u>Scope</u>, we English teachers
would have been in real trouble—it was the only Board of Education
approved material that could hold for any time the interest of Du
Sable students.

A couple of the kids in this class had, two weeks earlier,
made a field trip with me and another teacher to see the movie
version of the play at a Loop theater. Now, they screamed loudest
for the lead parts.

"Jefferson, settle down and quit fooling around; otherwise
I'll give your part to somebody else," I said, trying to use his
eagerness for a part to my advantage.

"No. No. Don't give it to nobody else. I'll shut up," he
pleaded.

Finally, our reading of the play got underway. To prevent
us from getting too bogged down because of my students' inability
to read even simple material fluently, I took the narrator's part
and tried to keep things moving.

Halfway through the first act, Maurice had a long part that he
just could not read. My kids began to get restless. I was also
irritated at Maurice because he had clamored most for this part—
and now he couldn't handle it.

As I was coaching Maurice—trying to resist the urge to read
the part myself in order to get us moving again—Donald and Julius,
previously mumbling in low tones at the back of the room, suddenly
leaped up and started fighting.

"Donald! Julius! Cut that out," I yelled.

Understandably preoccupied with their battle, both boys ignored my initial command. I rushed to the back of the room and
tried to peel them apart. After a moment or so, I managed to get
them to stop and return to their seats.

"If this ever happens again, I'll send you both down to Sergeant
Smith," I warned.

"Well, he better never put his dirty hands on me again,"
Julius said, raising himself up in his seat as though ready to lunge
at Donald again.

"All right. All right. I don't want to hear any more talk like
that," I said. Inwardly, I felt anxious because of my own stirred
up, aggressive feelings and the dim, uncomfortable realization that
I, too, would like to behave aggressively toward this group of students. My class, I felt, considered the fight an acceptable expression of feelings. And for a moment, I almost imagined that I would
be a more effective teacher if I, like my students, cracked a few
heads when things didn't go my way.

Example 2. I was returning to my second floor classroom
following one of several false fire alarms that had interrupted
classes during the week. As usual, the majority of students poured
out into the halls but did not actually evacuate the building—electing
instead to stand shoulder-to-shoulder on the stairwells and wait
while frenetic administrators (and a few gung-ho teachers) yelled
and screamed for the building to be cleared at once.

In the hallway near my room I came upon a tightly packed
group of 200 or so excited students pushing and shoving each other
in an attempt to see what was happening. Immediately, I sensed
that an "incident" of some sort had just occurred during the tension-
filled minutes of building evacuation.

"What happened?" I asked a female student who stood next to
me.

"The principal got beat up! His face is all bloody!" she ex-
claimed hysterically. "He put his hand on a kid's shoulder and told
him to get on down the stairs."

For several days thereafter, I and my colleagues were deeply
troubled by this most recent outburst of violence at the school. If
our principal was not safe, we reasoned, how could we ourselves
ever feel secure in the same environment? Additionally, I wondered
what my principal—a bureaucratic systems man who heretofore had
neither sympathy for nor understanding of the stressors confronting teachers—would think as he completed the following Board of
Education procedures for reporting school violence, procedures he
had approved several months ago:

PROCEDURES FOR REPORTING VIOLENCE
OR OTHER ILLEGAL ACTS IN SCHOOL

In the event of related occurrences, teachers and
staff are reminded to follow the instructions as stated
in the Board Report 71-445, "Procedures to be used
for the Institution of Criminal Proceedings Against

Individuals Committing Teacher Assaults," and Board
Report 71-799, "Reporting Violence and Other Illegal
Acts in the School."

When an employee is the victim of an assault on
school property, it is the victim's responsibility to
complete an Employee Assault Report (six copies)
within 24 hours, and submit same to the office of
the responsible administrator. When a victim is
unable or unwilling to complete a report, the form
should be completed, using the best information
available, by the responsible administrator. The
administrator will ensure that an assault number is
obtained from the Office of School Safety and Environment by calling: 641-4497-98-99.

The assault report will be a six-part form. Dis-
tribution shall be made:

1. First four copies to the Office of the Department
   of School Safety and Environment, Room 262,
   228 North La Salle Street, Chicago, Illinois, 60601.
2. Fifth copy to District Superintendent.
3. Sixth copy to school files or engineer custodian's
   files.

The following kinds of assaultive behavior are to
be reported:

BATTERY

Assaults involving physical contact (Battery).
A person commits battery if he intentionally or know-
ingly without legal justification and by any means,
(1) causes bodily harm to an individual or (2) makes
physical contact of an insulting or provoking nature
with an individual.

These physical assaults are broken down by
severity of injury:
(a) Severe injury (hospitalized, grievous injury).
(b) Serious (received emergency or medical care,
    out-patient).
(c) Superficial (received treatment for minor
    injury).
(d) No injury (physical contact, no treatment).

ASSAULT

Assaults <u>not</u> involving physical contact.
A person commits an assault when, without lawful
authority, he engages in conduct which places another in reasonable apprehension of receiving a
battery.
On the "Assault Report" these types of assaults
are classified as "verbal assaults." Depending
on circumstances, it could include, "I will get
you," "I will kill you," "I will hurt you."

The administrator shall be responsible for
determining whether the Police (PO 5-1313)
should be called. Personnel are urged to bring all
criminal activity to the attention of the Police and
to cooperate fully in the processing of such matters in the courts. Police action may result in a
referral to the juvenile court or to the criminal
courts.

All copies of the Assault Report are expected to
be at the aforementioned locations within 48 hours
from the time of the incident. The Chicago Board
of Education Assault Report Form (DSSE-102) has
been instituted for the benefit of Board employees
and for the purpose of expediting reporting of of-
fenses which involve assaults.

ANXIETY OVER PERSONAL CLEANLINESS

While at Du Sable, I could not fail to observe that some students did not bathe and change clothes as often as we teachers
would have liked. This lack of personal hygiene I attributed, in
part, to the fact that 70 percent of our students were from families
receiving some form of public assistance. What I could not understand, though, was why so many of our students seemed bent on
making their school dirty and foul smelling. And, in terms of my
own inner struggle to cope with Du Sable, I am certain that the
students' proclivity for "messing" aroused anxiety related to my
own infantile struggle to adopt more mature standards of personal
cleanliness. In short, I did not want to be reminded of my own unconscious and ever-present infantile impulses to soil my surround-
ings.

Example 1. One day, I walked through the first floor lunchroom just after it had emptied of students. I didn't have to enter
the serving line to see what was on the day's menu. Dumped on the
table tops and on the brown tile floor were several helpings of
spaghetti with meat sauce, green beans, whipped potatoes, white
bread, and white and chocolate milk. Also on the floor lay a few
plain white cafeteria plates—smashed.

Example 2. About three or four times a year classes were
canceled so that teachers could meet at the school for inservice
training or to record grades on transcripts. On this particular inservice day, I happened to be walking alone through one of the more
remote hallways of the building. Now I had the opportunity to study
leisurely some of the damage wrought to the building by angry students. Several graffiti-scarred doorways in this hall bore evidence
of students' destructiveness. Heavy wooden door frames were
loosened, and gouges in the wood suggested that students might
have been armed with hatchets.

So extensive had this destruction been recently that the school's
daily bulletin frequently featured entries titled "Property Damage"
and "Broken Windows" that, as the following examples illustrate,
presented to faculty and staff a running tally of vandalism:

DAILY BULLETIN #104
Broken Windows:
Add 42 more broken windows to the grand total.

Property Damage:
3 urinals—smashed	$500.00
1 wash basin—smashed	$240.00
	$740.00

DAILY BULLETIN #122
Broken Glass:
Number of panels broken by vandals this month—20.
New total—1,139.

Vandalism:
3 toilet bowls broken and/or cracked—$300.00.

DAILY BULLETIN #177
Broken windows:
Number broken by vandals—17.

Property Damage:
| 3 Sloan valves—vandalized | $75.00 |
| 1 wall hung toilet—vandalized | $100.00 |

Near the end of this hallway, I caught the penetrating odor of urine from the doorway to room 104. I held my breath momentarily and rounded the corner. There I found the boys' washroom I had been looking for.

I entered and, much to my disappointment, found the facilities unusable. Two toilets were clogged to overflowing with excrement and toilet paper, while a large crack in the porcelain rendered the third inoperative.

ANXIETY GENERATED BY UNCONSCIOUS MEANINGS ATTRIBUTED TO BLACKNESS

If the lower-class school to which a teacher is assigned contains a significant percentage of black students, most middle-class teachers are apt to experience anxiety related to their students' race. It is an unfortunate reality that currents of racism continue to flow throughout American life. It seems that few white people in our society can be confronted with lower-class blacks without feeling some anxiety about what the experience of blackness symbolizes. (Many blacks in the ghetto even share in these interpretations.) Kovel (1970, p. 53) comments on the place of this anxiety in our culture:

> Indeed, since we all live in one culture, whose fantasies we at least partly share, and since this culture is obsessed with white-black racism, it would be hard to conceive of any American, no matter what his conviction or social role, who lived free from racial fantasy.

Kovel (p. 50) also suggests that a white American can "find an outlet for some of his infantile fantasies about dirt, property, power, and sexuality in his culture's racism."

I must admit, rather painfully, that when I was first confronted with groups of black students at Du Sable, I experienced anxiety the nature of which I am still not certain about. Perhaps, as Kovel (p. 66) asserts, the unknown, frightening contents of the id find their correlate in blackness:

> At this level we may understand that, spurred by the superego, the ego designates the id, which is unseen, as having the quality that comes from darkness; as being black. The id, then, is the referent of blackness within the personality; and the various partial

trends within the id, all repressed, make themselves symbolically realized in the world as the forms of blackness embodied in the fantasies of race.

I have seen many older, more sophisticated Du Sable students behave provocatively toward teachers as though they understand intuitively this anxiety a teacher may have. Some, it seems, even try to capitalize on the white man's fantasy and fear of what Jones (1968, p. 229) has termed the "black man as robber/rapist."

Example. Our faculty has just launched another of its periodic campaigns to prevent young men from wearing hats in the building. The incredible fervor with which many faculty members pursue the issue suggests that the business of hats may have a symbolic meaning more significant than the overt point of social etiquette or black pride. I sense that the concern over hats might in some way reflect teachers' anxiety about the sexuality of young black males whose manner of dress often clearly emulates that of the ghetto pimp. If this is true, then the forced removal of a hat might function, unconsciously of course, as a symbolic castration or denial of manhood.

It seems further evident that, for some teachers and administrators, the ability to make a student remove a hat demonstrates the teacher's superior strength. As the following sampling of notices regarding hat wearing intimates, some teachers receive an adolescent, macho satisfaction from making kids remove their hats:

SPECIAL BULLETIN
The wearing of head gear by some male students is being ignored by some responsible adults. (It is interesting to watch how students remove hats in the presence of some adults and put hats on in the presence of others. It is significant in that this may be a measure of respect.)

DAILY BULLETIN #155
Head coverings—some teachers are doing an excellent job of supervising students. Unfortunately not all teachers are doing their share. This is obvious as students are seen to react differently to different teachers.

DAILY BULLETIN #181
There is no reason why any student should be wearing head gear of any kind. If all personnel would

enforce this policy there would be no problem.
Mrs. _____ [the District Superintendent] has
given this top priority, so please act accordingly.

DAILY BULLETIN #76

Today is "Hats Off Day!" All teachers are reminded
to enforce the rule as a special effort today. Of
course, we do it every day also.

DAILY BULLETIN #83

Thank you to the teachers who tried so hard to make
this a successful "hats off day." I [i.e. Du Sable's
principal] walked around the first 3 periods and it
wasn't until the 3rd period that I saw students wearing hats, but only in 2 classrooms. Thanks!

DAILY BULLETIN #103

Please be reminded of the District 13 policy regarding
the wearing of outside apparel in the classroom—especially hats. Mrs. _____[the District Superin-
tendent] has stated that every teacher and every aide
must be vigilant regarding hat wearing.

DAILY BULLETIN #162

All students are to remove all hats, scarves, coats,
jackets while in the building. Classroom and division teachers are to explain to the students that this
is being done to develop pride and self-respect.
Teachers should use guidance techniques rather than
force so that the effects will be more permanent.

LACK OF PROFESSIONAL, COLLEGIAL SUPPORT FOR TEACHERS

A factor that added significantly to my anxiety while teaching
at Du Sable was the privateness, even loneliness, of my experiences
in the school. I soon discovered that my search for more effective
intervention techniques was not supported by professional, reality
oriented dialogue among teachers or between teachers and Du Sable's
administrative staff. In short, I found myself in a situation that was
not only irrational and unpredictable, but one that effectively dis-
couraged the use of analytical problem-solving skills for coping—
skills that are effectively employed in most other professions.

Instead, I had to rely on my individual experiences to suggest strategies for handling the exigencies of the classroom—and, as a result, "survival" in the situation easily became my paramount goal.

Example. At the end of an exhausting day, I read two bulletins from my principal. One memo included the following awkwardly
phrased exhortation for teachers to ponder:

> Some students are allowed to function in a manner that
> is commensurate with the negative image of the stu-
> dent erroneously held by some adults. "Teach each
> student as if he had an IQ of 120—adopt the attitude
> that "the student can learn and I can teach."

The other bulletin, titled "Please Think Children—Push for Excellence," concludes with the following: "Think positive! Be positive! We CAN do it! We will do it! We ARE good! We are GOOD!"

The inane pleas of the principal, his evident ignorance of
the pressures involved in trying to teach Du Sable kids day after
day, and his insinuation that any problems the school does have
result from teachers "not doing their jobs" or being unwilling to
"make sacrifices" makes me angry. While I would not want my
principal to lament the hopelessness of the situation at Du Sable,
I feel I have a right to expect more professional, realistic, and
supportive leadership. The principal's interpretation of the situation (while it might be a "politically" shrewd stance for a white
ghetto school principal to maintain) compounds the frustration,
guilt, and demoralization I and other teachers experience as a
result of our daily contact with students.

REFERENCES

Jones, L. Home: Social Essays. New York: William Morrow,
1968.

Kovel, J. White Racism: A Psychohistory. New York: Vintage
Books, 1970.

Piaget, J. The Moral Judgment of the Child. New York: Free
Press, 1965.

Redl, F., and Wineman, D. Controls from Within: Techniques
for the Treatment of the Aggressive Child. New York: Free
Press, 1952.

Rosen, J. "Personality Factors in the Reactions of Child-care Workers to Emotionally Disturbed Children." Psychiatry (August, 1963):257-65.

Wright, B. D. "Attitudes Toward Emotional Involvement and Professional Development in Residential Child Care." Ph.D. dissertation, University of Chicago, 1957.

3
DU SABLE STUDENTS:
SIX TYPES

Du Sable? Well, I think it's just
a—just a trip, really, in itself.
Cause everybody just—some of the
people just wild. And the teachers,
half of 'em all right, then again
half of 'em not. I know from my
four years experience at Du Sable,
it's really been wild and exciting.
For instance the lunchrooms, you
know, like they have riots and stuff.
Half the people not going, you know,
not comin' to classes, getting F's
and all that.

Jessie, A Du Sable High School
Student

MY first two years at Du Sable were terrible. As I tried to cope
intuitively with the stress of my job, I realized both the inade-
quacies of my prior preparation for urban teaching and the dearth
of research-proven, effective strategies for teachers in my plight.
Daily, I recognized that being a "good" teacher required much
more than subject matter competence—I knew I needed also to grow
in the skills of observing and interpreting the dynamics of interaction in my classes. Moreover, my continuing involvement in
psychotherapy and a strong desire to "make progress" in this

Portions of this chapter were first published under the title "The
Inner City High School," School Review, vol. 32, no. 3, May 1974.
© 1974 by The University of Chicago. Reprinted by permission of
the publisher, the University of Chicago Press.

sphere of my life made it increasingly difficult to blame my students for the problems I had while trying to teach them. No longer could I "act out" the anger I felt without knowing that I was doing my students, and myself, a disservice.

With this sense of frustration at my professional ineffectiveness and an inability to see order and meaning in my teaching situation, I decided to begin work on a Ph.D. in education at the University of Chicago in the fall of 1972. Initially, I was motivated largely by a desire to find out if some of the country's leading educators could provide me with the keys to greater effectiveness at a place as crazy as Du Sable. Any educational principles I acquired through my study, I reasoned, I would immediately "reality check" back at the school. Du Sable would be my "laboratory"—a laboratory where I would endeavor to integrate theory and practice.

I had the good fortune to have Professor Herbert Thelen for my first course at the university. During our many long chats about education, Herb would take my intuitive, unclarified assumptions about teaching and, with stunning elegance, clarify and enrich my original "hunches" so that I saw their relationship to known, predictable propositions about the educative process. Our ongoing dialogue caused me to shift from a narrow interpretation of the goals and methods of education to one that viewed education as a humane, purposeful activity designed to help human beings confront and interpret the meaning of their experiences.

With Herb's encouragement, I developed the habit of continuously interpreting and reevaluating my role as a teacher; and as I did so, I found out that I was involved in a personal, reflective inquiry into the meaning of education for my life. My experiences at Du Sable, I came to realize, had given me the initial impulse to adopt educative inquiry as a way of life.

At that time I also began to cope differently with the demands of my teaching assignment at Du Sable. Gradually, I became less concerned with the content of English per se and more concerned with helping students learn to learn, providing them with educative, growth promoting experiences. (Chapter 11 presents this personal model of teaching.) And the group investigation model I saw Herb employ in his own teaching, I began to use, with modification, at Du Sable.

One of the early topics Herb encouraged me to explore was how Du Sable students themselves coped with the demands of school. (It was a revelation to me that not only teachers, but students themselves, were in conflict with the Du Sable environment.) The remainder of this chapter, then, describes the many ways of life that Du Sable students developed in order to cope.

At an all-black, inner-city school such as Du Sable (and, indeed, at any school anywhere) student attitudes toward school are reflected in a variety of student "types." Each has its own style, its own way of resolving the conflict involved in choosing between getting an education for survival in a white-dominated society or embracing the nihilistic pathology available in the ghetto. This conflict, I found, dominated nearly every facet of Du Sable school life.

To determine my students' attitudes toward school, I once used my own observations made over approximately two semesters and compared these with the results of a projective test. The test involved interpreting a sketch of a classroom scene (Figure 1), telling what is happening and what the outcome will be. The sketch shows what appears to be a white male teacher with his back to the viewer. Before him are six black students of high school age. Three appear to accept the teacher's position of authority—among the other students, however, one has his head on the desk; another gets up from his desk while apparently making a comment to the teacher; and another is standing, holding aloft a piece of paper and saying something, perhaps directed to a fellow student.

FIGURE 1

PROJECTIVE TEST: PERCEPTIONS OF
A CLASSROOM SITUATION

Drawn by Roberta House Parkay

I asked each student to write a story based on the pen-and-ink sketch that represented typical classroom activity at Du Sable. I encouraged students to be creative and to write without concern for conventions of spelling and grammar. Finally, to provide a focus for their ideas, I suggested four questions:

1. What is happening in the picture?
2. What had led up to this situation?
3. What is being thought?
4. What will happen?

From my observations and my analysis of their projective stories, I was able to identify six student types and their number in my English class of 25 freshmen and sophomores: (1) conforming students (eight); (2) nonconforming students (two); (3) students who vary from day to day (six); (4) disruptive students (three); (5) withdrawn students (four); (6) marginal students (two). My hunch was that the same student types, in about the same proportions, would be found in any "average" class at Du Sable.

CONFORMING STUDENTS

Students who maintained positive attitudes toward school and teachers made up the largest group in my class. Because of personal convictions or parental and societal pressures, these students missed few classes and usually came prepared to work. Always polite to me and other students, this group seldom, if ever, criticized the class. Some were actively involved in class proceedings, and some were quiet and withdrawn but nevertheless conscientious and attentive. In general, conforming students appeared satisfied with teachers and the school.

On the projective test, some conforming students tended to see a functioning classroom: "I see a classroom of black students who are getting along with a white teacher. They all have respect for him and show a lot of intelligence by being disciplined. They are blacks who want an education in order to survive with a good living."* Others saw the potentially worthwhile class disrupted by uncooperative students:

---

*The interpretive stories used here are unchanged except for occasional standardization in usage and spelling.

I think they're having a discussion in a classroom. It looks like some of the students are not bothering to answer the question, while one is standing up raising her hand, one sitting is waiting her turn with her hand raised. One sitting is shouting out a possible answer, and a couple just don't know what's going on. To me it seems like the class is disorganized. What's going to happen at the end? I can see it already. Some will go out with new knowledge that will stick, some will go out knowing nothing at all.

NONCONFORMING STUDENTS

In contrast to the first group of students, my class had two nonconforming students. Though fairly bright, they were often very critical, sarcastic, and hostile toward me and their fellow students. In class, they either slept (or pretended to sleep) or punctuated the class period with well-timed groans and moans of disgust and boredom. Their ability to learn seemed severely limited by their hostility toward school in general and white teachers in particular. They considered any class discussion "just talk" and preferred busy work. Their main involvement usually consisted of complaining: "We never do anything in here," or "This class is boring."

In his interpretive story, one student suggested some of the hostility he felt toward me as a teacher and toward other students: "Miss MacTooney asked if anyone had any comments on the discussion from yesterday on drugs. Sam said, 'Yeah, I smoke dope just for the hell of it and if you ask me there's nothing wrong with it.' Voices: 'Man, you crazy!' 'He thinks he's something.'"

Another student, at times bitter and hostile, told a story involving disagreement, and, just as in class, she expected convenient right and wrong answers to very complex problems:

This is a classroom of sixth or seventh graders with a white teacher. They are apparently having a heavy discussion on racial rights. One student thinks she's right: however, the other student thinks he's right. Some students don't care one way or the other. But the majority are highly interested in the class. The outcome is that the teacher will probably bring things to order and he will probably make a statement saying that the first student is probably right.

STUDENTS WHO VARY FROM DAY TO DAY

In my class I had six students whose orientation toward school varied from day to day. One day these students would take an active, intelligent part in class; the next day they would be hostile, complaining, and disruptive; and the following day they might be passive, inattentive, and quiet. Rather than take class seriously, they tried to remain aloof or "cool," but if asked for their opinion about the class, each one was apt to say, "It's O.K."

One student, with a quick wit he unleashed on certain days, wrote: "Well, there is a teacher teaching sex ed. in his classes, and he is unable to get the kids' attention by just teaching out of the book and drawing on the black board. So now he's asking for two people (boy and girl) to demonstrate some positions." Students who varied from day to day really functioned as a barometer of my effectiveness; if I could reach this group I was as successful as Du Sable conditions would allow.

DISRUPTIVE STUDENTS

Three of my students responded to the demands of school by acting out their frustrations in a disruptive way. They were poor readers and had failed a number of classes. They often tried to block my efforts and those of any well-intentioned students. It was not unusual for me to have difficulty getting them into the room at the start of a period and, once in, getting them to sit down, open books, and stop talking and yelling. On bad days, a disruptive student would often try to turn my classroom into a circus, and, if he got the help of his classmates, he often succeeded.

One such student, a freshman who once halted my remedial class by spraying mace in the room, wrote a story that was punctuated with conservative notions of education: "I think the children are going wild. The teacher asks the class a question about the work. Some are doing it. Some are shouting. They raise hands all at one time. I think that is not a way to run a class. It's supposed to be like this. The teacher's supposed to ask a question about the assignment and one at a time they are supposed to raise their hands." Another also saw the classroom as a possible setting for disruption: "It looks like an English class and there are two people raising their hands. They're in back shouting if he wants to see a fight." Neither of these students, nor others who responded as they did, were bad; they simply had not had enough success in their education to begin to react differently to the conflict that school presented. Actually, their behavior seemed a

reasonable alternative to repeated failure. My main task as a
teacher, then, was to help them break out of the cycle of repeated
failure. If I could do that, they might no longer feel the need to
disrupt.

WITHDRAWN STUDENTS

In my class there were four silent, withdrawn students.
These students often did not attempt to answer if called on, or their
answers were barely audible. My withdrawn students came to class
faithfully and did their work, but it was difficult for me to notice
them much beyond their bodily presence.

One wrote an interpretive story in which the teacher's response to the class was much the same as his own: "In this picture
the school teacher seems to be telling the students to quiet down.
The class seems to be out of hand and the teacher is telling them to
raise their hands. If the class doesn't quiet down, the teacher
would just stop teaching." And, presumably, a withdrawn student
might also stop taking part.

MARGINAL STUDENTS

The last student type represents a life style and orientation
toward school that I could not know intimately. The model for this
type was the gangbanger who showed most clearly the pathology of
some who were trapped in the ghetto. My class had two of these
marginal students who, fortunately, never came to class. Another
group of marginal students, young people not enrolled in school
who came into the building to roam the halls or hang out in the
lunchrooms, I would also include in this group.

Marginal students harbored considerable rage toward those in
authority. Their "day at school" was often spent engaged in a cops-
and-robbers confrontation with all school personnel. Such students
might throw a chair at a teacher in the hall; start a plate-flinging,
chair-throwing riot in the lunchroom; gamble, drink, and get high
in the washrooms. In his appropriately titled Students! Do Not
Push Your Teacher Down the Stairs on Friday, Alan Jones (1972,
p. 50) describes the gangbanger's orientation toward school, making it clear that such "students," while not really a part of the
classroom, are of concern to the teacher: "There was always
somebody in those dark, musty corridors who could and would do
you bodily harm. Some of those gangbangers would like nothing

better than to tell their boys how they ripped off some honky teacher in school today. 'Man, you should have seen that white mother-fucker go down.' "

EDUCATIONAL GOALS OF ALL STUDENTS

While I noticed different responses to the conflict generated by attending school, most Du Sable students shared rather conventional notions about education. Regardless of actual behavior in class, they professed to want a class in which they could learn, "get their education"; a class in which students and teacher respected one another. Even though many students were unable to live up to the strict standards they set for themselves, I began to realize that the wise teacher could develop classroom procedures based on these student standards.

TYPES AS SELF-FULFILLING PROPHECIES

It is important to consider to what extent the behavior of inner-city students is a dramatic ritual that must be played out, especially in the presence of a white teacher. It often seemed that Du Sable students felt trapped by the labels the rest of society placed on them and were compelled to verify their accuracy. A few teachers told me that many of their students had all the reasons—low socioeconomic status, broken family, cultural deprivation—to explain away or to avoid responsibility for their disruptive behavior. As Mackler and Elkin (1967, p. 136) suggest, this negative identity is often the only one available to an inner-city student: "To be classified 'incorrigible,' 'stupid' or as culturally deprived is to set into motion a chain of self-fulfilling prophecies. With no other way of dealing with a rejecting environment one becomes incorrigible, dumb, culturally deprived, perhaps even feeling that a negative identity is better than none at all."

Even if a teacher understands the extent to which negative identity affects student behavior, there is often little he can do. Just as it is difficult for teachers to see beyond the labels attached to students, it is difficult, too, for students to see beyond the labels they have applied to teachers. It becomes almost impossible for both to step outside their roles simultaneously. On one occasion, for example, three of my freshmen remedial students were arguing and wrestling for possession of a pick. In a theatrical aside, one of the three turned to me and said, "You think we're crazy, don't you?" He saw both of us as having opposing roles that he, at that moment, was "proving." Similarly, one student's projective story suggested that black students might have certain roles to play in the presence of a white teacher:

> I think the picture is about a classroom of students
> and the instructor asked them a question, and he re-
> ceived several different answers, so they had a
> debate. And seeing that all the children were black
> and the instructor was white, it led to a serious thing
> when some students started fighting. One boy got hit
> in the mouth, while others were just sitting there
> feeling downhearted and sorry for themselves.

Each of the six student types described in this chapter indicates a dominant pattern in response to the conflict of school. For
the majority of students, some form of nonconforming behavior was
favored; for the minority, conforming behavior was selected. Yet,
I found that most Du Sable students were actually composites of the
six types; each student had the potential to respond to individual
incidents in the classroom in any one of the six ways I have described.

REFERENCES

Jones, A. Students! Do Not Push Your Teacher Down the Stairs on
Friday. New York: Quadrangle Books, 1972.

Mackler, B., and Elkin, P. "Urban Education in the North." In
Disadvantaged Child, edited by J. Hellmuth. New York:
Brunner/Mazel, 1967.

4

MISS MARTIN'S THIRD PERIOD: A STUDENT BEHAVIOR CLOSE-UP

The District Superintendent has
indicated that she has seen a lack
of teaching going on in many
classrooms.

Daily Bulletin #159, Du Sable
High School

OFTEN, my fellow teachers at Du Sable complained to me that
their students' main purpose while in class was apparently to resist, as much as possible, their efforts to teach. Likewise, from
the moment I and my students encountered one another in the
classroom, the flux of counter-educative events I had to contend
with was often confusing, if not overwhelmingly chaotic, in its
complexity. What any of us found in a given classroom was not a
cohesive, task-oriented group but several small, very strong,
often opposing subgroups that somehow the teacher had to rally
around the common goal of learning. In the words of one ghetto
teacher at another school, "The dynamics of the classroom are
overwhelming; they must be studied and solved before anything can
be taught and learned" (Silberman 1970, p. 445).

To begin to understand such events more fully than I might
through reflecting on my teaching alone, I once observed for a week
another Du Sable teacher—a teacher who I knew to be as "successful" as Du Sable conditions would allow. By observing a competent
teacher who actively taught her classes (rather than assigned "busy
work" to maintain law and order, a practice followed by many

beleaguered Du Sable teachers), I hoped to "untangle the web"—to use Adams and Biddle's (1970, p. 43) apt phrase—of classroom interactions.

The remainder of this chapter, then, recounts the flow of events during one 40-minute period—a period that was neither much better nor much worse than any of the others I observed during that week. My narrative focuses on the students' behavior; the teacher's actions are described when necessary to indicate the context of the student-student and student-teacher interactions.

THE TEACHER

The teacher, whom I will call Miss Martin, was white and had spent her entire six years of teaching at Du Sable. A graduate of the Master of Arts in Teaching program at the University of Chicago, Miss Martin was the kind of teacher one might observe in an effort to determine the characteristics of a "good" teacher. Obviously dedicated to helping her students learn, she seemed to have inexhaustible energy for trying out new techniques in the classroom. While other teachers loudly voiced their pessimism and frustration about their students' inability to learn from standard texts, Miss Martin was likely to be preparing her own instructional materials.

THE CLASS

The class I observed was a sophomore Essential English 1 class. At Du Sable, Essential students read anywhere from the first or second grade level to the seventh or eighth grade level, with most reading at about the fifth grade level.

Each of the 14 students who attended Miss Martin's class that day chose a seat from among the 27 movable desks in the room (Figure 2 indicates the seating pattern). To insure anonymity, I have changed the names of the seven boys and seven girls.

During my first visit, Miss Martin told her students that Mr. Parkay, also an English teacher at Du Sable, would observe their class for a week. She further added that I was sponsor of the school literary magazine, Write On, and students could submit their creative writing to me if they desired. Most of the students had no doubt previously seen me in the building and, I felt, did not consider me an "outsider." At any rate, the class proved to be so inner directed that I believe I was generally ignored.

FIGURE 2

MISS MARTIN'S THIRD PERIOD CLASS

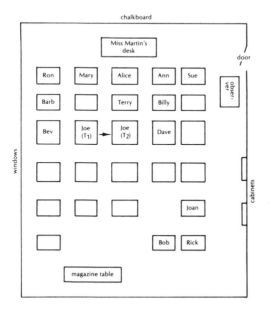

THE CLASS PERIOD

At 9:42 A.M., a loud bell signals the start of Miss Martin's
third period class; however, only six students are present. During
the next few minutes though, eight more students arrive one by one.
As these stragglers enter the room, they talk loudly, and without
restraint, to their friends.

"Hey, Billy! What's happenin', my main man." Terry and
Billy whack their open palms together and, with smooth, well-
orchestrated movements, run through the black power handshake,
their fingers intertwining expertly and effortlessly.

"Gimmie that pen," one boy snaps as he snatches a Bic pen
from a girl's desk. As the girl rises out of her desk to pursue her
stolen property, the boy tosses it back. Satisfied, the girl lets the
matter drop.

Three students leave their desks to get their journal folders
from a cardboard box on Miss Martin's desk. Miss Martin helps
them locate their journals and then directs them to retake their
seats. She also moves about the room passing out folders to other
students, some of whom sit at their desks as though waiting to be
served.

During these opening minutes of class, three boys wander aimlessly about the room. One, a tall, thin boy, presses his nose against the window, surveying the sidewalk two stories below. Just then a fat boy skips past and jabs him playfully in the ribs, rudely interrupting his dreamy state.

"Your mamma!" the tall boy yells as he makes an exaggerated lunge at the fat boy who is now giggling hysterically. With surprising agility, the fat boy now shuffles back and forth, boxerlike, enticing his classmate to combat.

"Dave. Joe. Sit down right now!" Miss Martin matter-of-factly corrects her students who, with admirable obedience, take their seats.

The third boy lopes around the entire circumference of the room. As he moves down the wall opposite the windows, he flicks the chains and padlocks that secure the room's two built-in cabinets. He catches Miss Martin's disapproving glance and then heads back to his seat.

"Good morning, people," Miss Martin officially begins at 9:45. She points to the chalkboard and explains the two topics for the day's journal entry (each class period is begun with a five-minute journal entry); "What was the most frightening thing that ever happened to you?" and "What did you do yesterday after school?"

As Miss Martin repeats the assignment and gives necessary directions, all but four or five students continue to talk in small groups about matters clearly unrelated to the journal writing assignment.

Several social interaction groups are quite evident at this time. In the back of the room, Bob and Rick chat and exchange an occasional comment with Joan who sits in front of them.

Near the center of the room, Terry, Billy, and Dave talk loudly and excitedly about an upcoming Muhammed Ali fight. All three are clowning—weaving, bobbing, jabbing, and ducking imaginary punches. Billy seems to be the leader in all this—Terry and Dave try their best to keep up.

Barb, Bev, and Joe form another talkative trio. Barb turns around in her seat and rests her elbow on Bev's desk. At this moment, all three appear oblivious to their teacher and unmindful of the task they have been assigned.

For those students in the front row, however, the journal entry is the main concern. Ron, Mary, and Alice write and occasionally look up at the board to recheck the day's topics. They do not talk to any of their classmates. Ann and Sue are also at work, though they exchange a comment every now and then.

Suddenly, Billy prods Ann in the back and makes an insult that I can't hear. Ann turns around, her tightly pursed lips indicating that she is ready for battle.

"You fat fool!" she snarls.

"You broad-assed chump!" Billy counters and then returns to his bantering with Terry and Dave.

Miss Martin talks softly with Ron and Mary at the front of the room. A moment later, she begins to move down the window side of the room, toward those students who still have not yet begun to write. The combined conversations of the three main social cliques are now quite loud. Their talk includes a great deal of clownlike nonsense.

At 9:48, the noise level has increased even more. "Let's please have it silent while we work on our journals," Miss Martin announces. Her tone is one of mild irritation. The talking continues, though perhaps not as loudly. Bill, Terry, and Dave continue to be the loudest.

Miss Martin continues, at 9:49, to move about the room to see how individual students are progressing with their work. Her plan seems to include interaction with each small group. Those students in the front row work silently while the rest of the class continues to talk in their subgroups, stopping occasionally for a perfunctory spurt of writing or a nonchalant glance at Miss Martin.

The chatter and clowning in Billy's group proves irresistible to Joe who changes desks at 9:52. Miss Martin works her way over to the four boys who now begin to direct many of their comments to her. There is a continuous outpouring of talk about the prize fight, color TVs, stereos, cars, and other material goods. Miss Martin urges them to direct their enthusiasm into their work. Obviously, she gets along well with all of them. With uncanny precision, the boys seem to calculate their foolish behavior both to escape work and to remain in Miss Martin's good graces. Their teacher's smiles indicate that they are very successful indeed.

At 9:55, Miss Martin returns the previous day's quiz on the metric system. (The Mathematics Department had scheduled a "Metric Week" during which English teachers were to spend a few minutes each period teaching the new system.)

Billy, absent on the day of the quiz, yells out, "I want to do the quiz!"

"You know you can't make up a quiz unless you bring an excuse, Billy," his teacher replies.

Billy beats his palms on his desk in mock anger. The more I observe Billy's antics the more he seems to fit the role of what Smith and Geoffrey (1968) call the "incumbent courtjester," with Terry, Joe, and Dave his attendant "clowns."

Disgusted with his low quiz score, Dave wads his paper up, rises out of his desk, and, executing a skillful hook shot, zings the paper ball into the corner wastebasket. Miss Martin, now at the back of the room talking with Bob and Rick, does not see this.

At 9:57, Miss Martin directs her students to turn in their journals. Only those students in the front row, however, comply with their teacher's directions. The others continue to be occupied with social talk or pointless fidgeting and squirming. Their inability or unwillingness to attend directly to Miss Martin's words is baffling.

Gradually, the other students begin to turn in their journals, and, amidst considerable noise and confusion, all the journals eventually end up in the box on Miss Martin's desk.

It is now 9:58, and Bob begins to sing a soul song currently popular on a black-oriented radio station. Billy and Ann exchange aggressive insults again. Miss Martin now stands in front of the room, near Alice and Ann.

"May I have your undivided attention?" she asks. "Would everyone look up here? Bob, up here."

Bob stops his singing. "What is we doing?" he whines. "You're always on my case. What are you saying—nothing—I hear you." His attitude is mildly belligerent, though he does begrudgingly start to pay attention.

Miss Martin holds aloft a small cylinder of ski wax from Europe and explains to her students that the weight is given in grams. Everyone now looks at the small green container in her hand.

"I'll pass it around for you to look at." Miss Martin offers the wax to Sue. Billy lunges half out of his seat and grabs it first, but immediately turns it over to his classmate.

Miss Martin then holds up an empty quart milk carton. "Here is something you see almost every day. A quart milk carton. It's almost one liter." She continues to review the basic units of measure in the metric system. She also informs her class that in a few moments they will have another quiz to improve upon yesterday's scores.

After their momentary involvement with the ski wax and the milk carton, most of Miss Martin's students cease attending actively and resume their subgroup conversations.

At 10:02, Miss Martin announces the quiz on the metric system. Only three or four students in the front row appear to respond to the announcement seriously.

Billy looks at Terry and says loudly, "You're crazy!"

"I need a pen," someone else blurts out.

"I need one too."

"Gimmie some paper."

Billy's group, apparently unmindful of the quiz, questions
Miss Martin about skiing.

"Do you know how to ski?"

"Did you ever fall and break a leg?"

"You skate? You roller skate?"

Miss Martin smiles but does not answer her students' queries.
Instead, she reminds them to pay close attention to the questions
she is about to ask.

"A meter is used to measure what?" she begins.

"What's that? Say it again." Several students don't hear the
first item that Miss Martin repeats before continuing.

"Number two. A gram is used to measure what?" It is now
10:04, and the room is almost completely silent as students write
their answers.

"Number three. How many inches in one meter?"

"What number's that?" someone asks.

"That was number three. Now, number four. How much is
one liter?" With the exception of occasional low snickering, the
remainder of the ten-item test continues without incident.

The quiz is over at 10:05, and students put finishing touches
on their papers. At this time Billy takes out a wallet-sized card
of conversion tables from English to the metric system. Miss Martin
watches Billy as he hunts for the correct answers.

"You know I'm not going to take your paper, Billy," she
reprimands.

Billy explodes with a loud guffaw. "You're not gonna take my
paper? Ooooh! Whoooo-eeee!"

Miss Martin collects the papers and then begins a review of
the quiz. She stands on the side of the room by Ron and Barb and
reads the questions aloud. With enthusiasm, her students shout out
answers in unison.

Billy and his sidekicks now demand to see the ski wax again.
A girl hands it to Billy who doubles over in his seat, pretending to
put on chap stick.

"For giant lips," says Terry.

"Elephant lips," chimes in Dave.

Miss Martin is now at the front of the room where she begins
to explain the "big project" of the term. She reviews the definition
of myth and discusses the different types. Those in the front row
watch and listen attentively; the remaining students, though, do not
pay attention. Billy and his buddies continue talking. Someone is
snapping gum quite loudly. Bob has resumed his singing in low
tones as he looks at a big Montgomery Ward catalog.

"Each one of you," Miss Martin explains, "will record one
of your journal entries on a cassette tape recorder. How many of
you have made a recording?" A few students raise their hands.

Terry is indolently rapping his Afro hair pick on his desk and on his head. Three students tap their feet while anxiously drumming on their desk tops.

Miss Martin now moves to the front chalkboard and begins to list previous journal topics as students recall them for her. The students in the front row watch and make suggestions for the list; the remaining fidget restlessly or stare off into space. Almost in unison, those in Billy's group suggest judo and karate. Then, from his seat, Billy playfully makes a couple of side kicks at Terry.

"Come on now, Billy!" Miss Martin warns. At this moment Bob has begun to hum in the back of the room as he looks at his catalog.

"How many of you would not be willing to form a circle and read aloud from your journals while I tape you?" Miss Martin asks. Most of her students raise their hands. Nevertheless, Miss Martin continues to explain the procedures for recording the journal entries. Meanwhile, Bob has begun to sing again.

At 10:16, Miss Martin suddenly stops talking and stands a moment in silence.

"How many of you understand what I've been saying?" None of her students respond. "All right, we'll go back through it step by step. Terry, you're not listening."

Three of Miss Martin's students sit with dull, blank stares on their faces, their chins cradled in their palms. Billy and his friends continue to fool around.

"That's mine! That's mine!" Billy moans loudly.

At 10:18, Miss Martin continues to solicit topics to put on the board. Again, she tells Billy's group to stop talking. They continue, though, to talk about karate, looking up occasionally to check Miss Martin's progress at the board and to gauge her anger.

Terry weaves and bobs in his seat and taunts Billy, "Try your luck, chump. Come on."

Billy grabs the front leg of Terry's desk and jerks it up a foot or so. Terry hops up and spins around and then plops back down in his seat.

At the back of the room, Bob continues to sing and thumb through his catalog. Other students sit and wait, knowing that the bell will ring soon. Joan puts her head on her desk. Billy continues to trade insults with Terry who again stands up, twirls around, and drops into his seat.

During these final minutes of the class, the talking and noise increase. Students seem to anticipate the bell's loud, intrusive clanging with a gradual crescendo of sound. The emotional effect of the rising noise level seems to spur some students on to even wilder displays of clownlike behavior. At moments, Bob's singing comes through loudly and clearly.

At precisely 10:22, the long awaited moment arrives. The dismissal bell rings and Miss Martin's third period students blast out of the room.

COMMENT

Perhaps the most obvious feature of Miss Martin's class was the fact that the aggregate of fourteen pupils was a cohesive group for only a fleeting moment or two. A "central group," to use Adams and Biddle's (1970) theory of communication structure, was generally nonexistent; instead, the students formed three "peripheral groups," and the remaining students not part of these cliques formed the "residue." Miss Martin seemed aware of this structure, as many of her interactions were directed at either an individual subgroup or an isolated student.

In one sense, Miss Martin's fragmented third period class might be taken as evidence of ghetto students' low sense of self-esteem. Her students didn't really take each other seriously, and most of them found it hard to restrain their individual impulses for the larger group's benefit. Collective effort in educational problem solving was seen as having no advantage over individual self-expression.

On the other hand, Miss Martin's students did take each other very seriously. Several of her students spent the period obviously jockeying for their position in the group, working through anxieties that arose from competition with peers, and exploring new found social capacities. The highest priority need for some of Miss Martin's students was to use the classroom as a place to further social relationships. And, short of exhaustive policelike dominance or the assignment of mindless "busy work," Miss Martin could not have eliminated such social interaction.

Restraint is one of the qualities essential for success as a student, and inner-city students typically have this quality in short supply. Students, as Jackson (1968, p. 18) notes, "must be able to disengage, at least temporarily, their feelings from their actions. It also means, of course, that they must be able to re-engage feelings and actions when conditions are appropriate." If, as in the case of Miss Martin's third period class, students are unable or unwilling to exercise this patience, the result is likely to be less learning for all. It is essential, as Joan Roberts (1970, p. 153) points out, that there be "joint agreement among all members that learning is the goal if maximal learning is to occur for any one of them."

It is common for school children all over to dislike going to school. The resultant conflict for the child, who may compare his plight to that of a prisoner, is not easily solved. He must come to grips with the tension between his natural impulses and desires on the one hand and the school's expectations on the other. In an all-black ghetto classroom such as Miss Martin's, however, these strategies are apt to be more visibly at odds with the teacher's expectations. I observed in Miss Martin's class students whose responses to the demands of school and society ranged from Billy's clownlike behavior or Bob's defiance to Joan's passive withdrawal or Mary's quiet, conforming obedience. Unfortunately, in an inner-city classroom it is often the lowest common denominator of student behavior that determines the classroom atmosphere and, ultimately, the amount of learning that takes place. And, as Smith and Geoffrey (1968, p. 154) suggest, "Children with marginal academic ability and interest, who might be able to maintain themselves in a classroom of more motivated pupils, find themselves seduced into a never-ending spiral of alienation from the school's general purposes and goals."

REFERENCES

Adams, R., and Biddle, B. Realities of Teaching: Explorations With Video Tape. New York: Holt, 1970.

Jackson, P. Life in Classrooms. New York: Holt, 1968.

Roberts, J. Scene of the Battle: Group Behavior in Urban Classrooms. New York: Doubleday, 1970.

Silberman, C. E. Crisis in the Classroom: The Remaking of American Education. New York: Random House, 1970.

Smith, L., and Geoffrey, W. The Complexities of an Urban Classroom: An Analysis Toward a General Theory of Teaching. New York: Rinehart and Winston, 1968.

5

THE STUDENTS
SPEAK FOR THEMSELVES

I use to come to class high. It
ain't no different cause you still
go see the same teacher. I do my
work whenever I'm high. Sometimes I do better, sometimes not.
To me, coming to class when high
ain't no better than coming like I
am now. Cause if I come to school
high when it's hot, I'll probably
feel better. If I was to come to
school sober now, I's probably
fall asleep. And if I was high, I
wouldn't fall asleep because I
won't be thinkin' about the hot
weather. You see, high sometimes make you concentrate—like
you gotta read a book and it's not
too interesting—like that. You
see, that's the way marijuana is,
but people don't know too much.

Bob, A Du Sable High School
Student

TO account for the crisis situation in inner-city education, it has
become commonplace to charge the educational system with failure
to meet the needs of minority group students. While there is no
doubt that change resistant ghetto schools, which reflect the subtle,

yet powerful, biases of the larger society, have, in effect, "institutionalized" failure, the fact remains that at such schools not all students fail to make adequate academic progress.

The extent to which a school's instructional program is able to facilitate maximal student learning varies greatly from pupil to pupil; within the same school and among students of approximately equal potential, some pupils experience success, others failure. Such differences in achievement suggest that what the learner brings to the school setting in the way of values, habits, expectations, and personal dispositions is one important determinant of academic performance.

While teaching at Du Sable, I had the opportunity to examine certain personality factors and dispositions characteristic of two types of students—those whose school experiences were characterized by learning and success and those whose experiences were characterized by minimal learning and failure. I wished to see if a relationship existed between these personality factors and achievement in school. I hypothesized that what a student makes of his school experiences is related to whether his personal orientation toward school allows, or precludes, conformity to school-determined norms for success. If a student perceives that his own values and life style are more or less congruent with the school's expectations of students, he is able to function with little conflict and can meet simultaneously his own and the school's requirements. On the other hand, if a student perceives that nearly every facet of his schooling fails to resonate with his own needs and expectations, he is apt to reciprocate with apathy, resistance to learning, and hostile acting out in order to thwart the educational mission of the school.

I began this inquiry by selecting eight students* from among those twenty-four enrolled in a junior English class I taught. As indicated by their ninth grade test scores (see Table 1), all eight students entered Du Sable with reading and math scores decidedly below national norms. At Du Sable, these students were placed in a "remedial" academic track for students at least two years below grade level.

On the basis of these test scores, we would predict that each student would perform about equally well in high school and none would be expected to achieve above average grades. However, as Table 2 indicates, three of these students went on to achieve above

---

*The names of these students have been changed to insure anonymity.

TABLE 1
NINTH GRADE READING AND MATH SCORES

| | Ninth Grade Reading | | Ninth Grade Math | |
	Percentile	Stanine	Percentile	Stanine
David*	2	1	5	2
Ann	18	3	17	3
Bob	24	4	2	1
Sue	15	3	13	3
Don*	5	2	10	2
Mary	29	4	6	2
Alice**	36	4	10	2
Jane	18	3	34	4

Unless indicated, scores are for the ninth grade Test of Academic Progress.

*Ninth grade Differential Aptitude Test.
**Eighth grade Metropolitan Achievement Test.

TABLE 2
STUDENTS' TWO-YEAR GRADE POINT AVERAGE AND
ELEVENTH GRADE VOCABULARY

	G.P.A. (A+5.0)	Percentage of "F" Grades	Vocabulary G.E. for Eleventh Grade
David	1.35	65	5.0
Ann	1.70	45	5.8
Bob	2.10	24	6.3
Sue	1.50	67	5.4
Don	1.44	65	6.8
Mary	3.25	0	9.1
Alice	3.40	5	9.1
Jane	4.35	0	8.3

Grade Point Average computed from a minimum of 20 quarter-unit grades in major academic subjects only.

average grades during their first two years at Du Sable. In addition, I gave all eight the vocabulary section of the California Reading Test, Level 5, Form A, 1970 edition, and found the same three students, Mary, Alice, and Jane (whom I will henceforth call the Achievers), to have vocabularies that, while still below grade level, were clearly superior to those of the other five.

The striking differences in achievement here and the relative "stability" of the students' rank ordering for success/failure both before and after two years of instruction at Du Sable cannot be attributed to the competencies, or deficiencies, of these students' teachers alone. Instead, as Jencks (1972, p. 256) contends, we must look to the students themselves for an explanation: "the character of a school's output depends largely on a single input, namely the characteristics of the entering children. Everything else—the school budget, its policies, the characteristics of the teachers—is either secondary or completely irrelevant." The achievements of one student and the failure of another, then, are to be explained through the complex reciprocal interaction of school, community, and family as they are interpreted by the psychology of the individual student.

To assess their values, needs, and dispositions, I interviewed each student for one hour, asking him about his perceptions of Du Sable, its students and teachers; his plans for the future; and his values in life. The eight students were not then in my class and appeared to have no anxiety about being interviewed—all seemed to respond to the interview questions openly, spontaneously, and usually, at length.

I chose the open-ended interview "case study" technique because it promised richer, deeper insights into students' motivations than might have emerged through the use of pencil-and-paper personality assessment instruments. What the method lacked in empirical certitude, I found, was more than compensated for by the flexibility it afforded me as I sought to "get at" students' true dispositions toward their experiences at Du Sable.

MEASURES OF ATTITUDE

In his summary of D. E. Levin's research on the prediction of academic performance, Getzels (1968, p. 517) states that:

Higher levels of performance tend to be associated with (1) social maturity in the school role, as reflected in better study habits and positive attitudes toward academic performance; (2) emotional stability; (3) cognitive styles involving greater flexibility in problem solving; (4) achievement via conformity; (5) achievement via independence, including more autonomy, more introversion, and less impulsivity.

While my interviews revealed that the Achievers' above average achievement was linked to the personal characteristics described by Getzels, I chose to analyze the interviews in terms of a series of dichotomies that seemed to stand out clearly in the behavior of Du Sable students. These dichotomies I formulated in light of my internalized, intuitive understanding of Du Sable student culture as I had experienced it over an eight year period:

1. impulsivity and affective action vs. thoughtful reflection;
2. "presentness" vs. realistic future orientation;
3. peer group conformity vs. independence;
4. nonconforming vs. conforming response to school demands;
5. negative vs. positive perceptions of authority;
6. self-contradiction and ambivalence vs. self-confidence and autonomy.

Impulsivity and Affective Action vs. Thoughtful Reflection

Within this dimension, the Underachievers—David, Ann, Bob, Sue, and Don—seemed to be influenced greatly by their moment-to-moment feelings. For many Underachievers, the classroom tends to be a bland, emotionless place whose necessary cognitive orientation fails to stimulate. The Underachiever is apt to feel bored, apathetic, and sleepy in class—in need of a high level of affective arousal to "feel alive." And when aroused, the Underachiever is apt to engage in, much to the frustration of his teachers, competitive interpersonal challenging with his classmates. In his study of high school students' attitudes, Thelen (1972, p. 123) describes quite well the Underachievers' orientation toward the classroom:

The fourth factor, accounting for about 4.3 percent of the data, appears to be a combination of rational consistency with needs to exploit one's peers. There is great preference for "telling" and rejection of "listening"; moreover, what one tells about is himself, his feelings, his opinions. Working together for a common goal is rejected, as is acceptance of responsibility for one's own progress. There is preference for activities involving the class as a whole (i.e., in which one is anonymous, can't be checked up on easily, and can avoid responsibility). The most attractive value is sensual enjoyment. This factor is negatively related to IQ, and tends to be found with lower-class boys.

The Achiever, on the other hand, tends to eschew the emotionality of his fellow students and instead holds himself personally accountable for meeting school-imposed requirements. The Achiever is also apt to have more insight into his own motives and greater ability to live up to his stated values.

"Presentness" vs. Realistic Future Orientation

The Underachiever tends to be rooted in the immediate moment and to "take things as they come." When asked about his plans for the future, the Underachiever is apt to speak vaguely of a number of possibilities, often responding with stock, middle-class answers; or he might entertain grandiose expectations, possibly to conceal his own insecurity about the future.

For the Achiever, the future seems to be thought of more precisely and in terms that bear some similarity to his present situation. The Achiever also sees education as preparing him not only to get a "good" job but to live life more fully.

Peer Group Conformity vs. Independence

The Underachievers, particularly those who are male, are often held in the strong grip of gang-oriented friendship groups. Though the Underachiever says he comes to school to "learn," he is very likely unable to resist the temptations offered by his crowd of friends or his "partners." In his study of the educational ethos of several high schools of which Du Sable was one, Thelen (1974, p. 146) similarly found that "in the inner-city general school (i.e. Du Sable), there is considerable conflict between interpersonal relations and work as the means to survival . . . the teachers see the class as a place in which learning activities are carried out whereas the students perceive it more as a milieu for interpersonal relationships." By concentrating on social interaction in this way, the Underachiever, I feel, is able to sidestep much of the anxiety that must accrue with continued below average achievement.

School for the Achiever is definitely a place where one can learn—if one wants to. The Achiever tends to be critical of his less academic, more impulsive fellow students. For the Achiever, the major conflict seems directed not at the school per se but at his classmates who, he feels, hinder his learning.

Nonconforming vs. Conforming Response to School Demands

The underachieving student tends not to conform to the expectations the school has of students. While teachers require students to attend classes, to be on time, to come prepared to work, to pay attention, and to be at least partially motivated to learn, the Underachiever resists complying with these requirements and views them instead as illegitimate incursions on his freedom.

In contrast to the Underachiever, the Achiever maintains positive, conscientious attitudes toward the school's role expectations for students. The teacher, so reasons the Achiever, may legitimately expect a certain amount of effort on the part of the learner. This difference in attitude is seen most clearly in the attendance rate of these eight students while enrolled in my class (see Table 3). Mary had frequent illnesses that caused her attendance to fit the pattern for Underachievers.

TABLE 3
STUDENT ABSENCES DURING A YEAR-LONG
JUNIOR ENGLISH CLASS

	Absences (Total Days=180)
David	50
Ann	42
Bob	18
Sue	57
Don	32
Mary	32
Alice	6
Jane	3

Negative vs. Positive Perceptions of Authority

The Underachiever is apt to view teachers with a certain degree of hostility and to feel that many teachers are not there to help
him learn. In this regard, it seems as though the Underachiever
is unaware of the role his behavior plays in provoking negative responses from his teachers.

While the Underachiever is often in open conflict with authority, the Achiever views teachers positively and feels they are doing
the best they can, given the kind of students they must teach.

Self-Contradiction and Ambivalence vs.
Self-Confidence and Autonomy

The statements of many Underachievers seem to reveal the
inclination toward self-contradiction and ambivalence, a kind of
internal disorganization or confusion about themselves. One has
the impression, too, that some Underachievers hold erroneous
notions about themselves in relation to the rest of the world or at
least are unaware of how their actions might appear to others.
Such confusion is most likely a reflection of the instability many of
them experience in their daily lives.

My analysis of the Achievers' interviews reveals greater
self-confidence and less ambivalence and indecisiveness about the
most appropriate course for their actions. The Achiever seems
to have greater emotional maturity and to have achieved more complete integration of the disparate elements of his personality.

THE STUDENTS SPEAK FOR THEMSELVES

The Underachievers

David

Seventeen-year-old David lives in the Robert Taylor Housing
Project with his mother, three brothers, and three sisters. His
father has not lived with the family for three years, but, says
David, "He still kick us down or whatever."
Speaking of the future, David reveals his high aspirations:

Well, I plan on being a big-time businessman, and ah—
going to school for a while, you know. Whenever I can
get out of here. Yeah—a big-time businessman. In-
surance policy or something like that, or president,

you know. See, I got to be president—of the office.
I'm thinking about going to Kennedy-King [a Chicago
public junior college] in August, and ah—it should be
very interesting.

A moment later, however, David modifies, and reduces, his expectations for life after high school:

If I could find a nice little—right at the moment, at
the age I am now—if I could find a nice little trade to
get into, you know, I go on and check it out. Elec-
tronics, you know. I'm kinda interested in engineer-
ing too.

His orientation toward Du Sable, he makes clear, does not
entirely revolve around education and learning. The excitement or
"wildness" that he feels he should condemn has, nevertheless, been
appealing:

Yeah, it's very exciting. It's all right, yeah. My
four years going here, you know, it's kinda hard
for me to keep away from it [the wildness]. Well,
it just came naturally, you know. I was just growin'
up, you know, and just being with the crowd. We
messed around the school. We play running around
the school, you know, running around in the school,
around the school—just being part of the crowd with
some kinda excitement.

And at Robert Taylor where David has lived for seven years, the
excitement is still valued: "It's just exciting in the projects. Just
wild, or whatever you want to call it. I—kinda like it, though. I
done really got used to it."
    Whether or not David attends his classes is based on concerns
of the moment rather than on long-term considerations. When I
asked him to account for his 50 days of absences for the year, he
said

It depends on, you know, how the day going for me or
something. I wake up in the morning—find out what's
happening. Then—just can't seem to make it [to
class]. But that's not regular. It wasn't ever regular.

Similarly, David's general orientation toward life seems to be one
of impulsive pleasure-seeking and affective gratification. His

answer to my question of what he likes to do shows clearly the
hedonistic orientation toward life that is so common for the Underachiever:

> Partying, messing around. Doing whatever's fair.
> Just being with the crowd. Whatever the crowd get-
> ting into. If you dig new peoples or whatever. Get
> in whatever they're getting ready to get into. Party-
> ing, you know, activity. That's having a nice time.
> But the main thing is—is the money. That's what
> makes the world go round. You gotta have that. I
> work and, ah—coupla womens come through for me
> every now and then, you know, but it's nothin' to
> brag on. It ain't what anybody else'd call it. It's
> just a nice relationship. I get high every now and
> then, too, you know. I don't make it no habit—
> reefer and a little beer.

While David does feel conflict between his life style and what
he senses is necessary for survival in a competitive world, he is
rather vague about his need for self-discipline.

> I feel that —that you're only up here (in Du Sable)
> for one reason. That's to try to get education. But
> if you think otherwise, the choice is you. You have
> to make your own decision on what you want to do.
> And the school itself, you know, the teachers they
> have a lot of things to do with it. But you know
> what's happening with you, so you gotta deal with
> it that way.

Ann

Ann, who has seven brothers and one sister, lives in an
apartment with her mother. The fatherless family is supported by
the mother's part-time salary and public aid.

While 16-year-old Ann plans to further her education, she
doesn't know where she'd like to go to school where she plans to
major in "everything." When I asked her what she liked about
school, Ann said, "Nothing. It's all right to come, but sometimes
I get tired. It's too hot to be sittin' in school. You're supposed to
have a summer vacation, not go to school all year round." (Du
Sable, at the time, was on a 45-15 year-round schedule. The
school year consisted of four 45-day terms, each followed by a
15-day "mini-vacation.")

I knew that Ann was bored in most of her classes, and so I pressed her to describe more fully what might be going through her mind at such times:

Some classes are boring. You just sit in there and
listen to the teacher. You go into class, and the
teacher, she'll be —first it'll be all quiet. She'll
be busy. Everybody'll be sittin' down lookin' at each
other. The teacher'll get up and say something.
They'll start [she sighs loudly] going on like that.
They'll start sighing and stuff. That makes it
boring.
Sometimes it be boring because it be hot outside, and
it be hot in here. You know, like you pick a subject.
That subject's going to be boring. Everybody just be
lookin' at each other and drifting around. Sliding
down in the chair and stuff like that. You can expect
it every year while you're in high school. Sometimes
I just feel like gettin' up and leaving. And I do, sometimes.

Ann's attitude toward her teachers is neither positive nor facilitative of her own learning: "They [teachers] are all right, some of 'em. You know, they have their attitudes, something like that. Some of 'em snap at you when you say something. But those're the main classes I don't go to. If I go, I don't say any-thing."

While Ann wants an education, she evidently goes to school more out of adherence to social cliches about education than out of internal conviction. She spoke of the need for an education the way many people say they need to get more exercise or to drink eight glasses of water a day:

I need an education. Everybody need an education.
I don't know why, but I need one. You just need to
learn. Learn about things that—like places you
never been. You might decide to go some day, so
it's best to go to school and know about it before you
get there. It wouldn't be right without it.

Bob

Bob is 18 and lives in Robert Taylor with his mother, father, five brothers, and two sisters. Two additional brothers are on their own. Neither Bob's father nor mother work, and the family is supported by public aid.

Like David, Bob's plans for the future, while they include some definite intentions, are rather vague and stereotypical:

Well, I'm trying to go to college and trying to take up
a business course. Course I'm gonna try to play some
sports, you know. Like baseball, basketball. I really
want to try to make it in the pros, really. But if I
don't make it in the pros, I got something to fall back
on like salesman or architect or, you know, like that.

As is common with the Underachiever, Bob notes that his classes have often caused him to feel bored and unmotivated. Daydreaming is one escape Bob has developed to avoid the boredom of ennui that so thoroughly pervades his life:

I feel bored a lot a times. I mostly feel bored when
it get hot like now, you know. In the late spring. By
wintertime or by springtime, I don't hardly feel bored.
I would be ready to come [to class]. Prepared to work
and do—. In fact, if the class was boring, I wouldn't
put my head down—I just be thinking a something, just
be daydreaming. That's what I be doing. You know,
I never—pretend like the class is boring—. I might be
staring like this [he stares vacantly off into space] but
I be daydreaming a lot. Like—only time I get bored is
when it's hot outside. That's the only time I get bored.

Like all of us, Bob wants to excel in the future, but his image of success, most likely shaped in the mass media, is one that few ghetto youngsters can hope to attain:

The most important thing in life is to be ahead. To be
somebody. To be successful. Like you might see
somebody you know a long time ago, and he might be
real popular. He might be a recording star, an
athlete, a doctor you'd hear of or read in the papers.
You know—have money, car, bank account—like that.

Bob's overall attitude toward Du Sable is negative and, tragically, he waits until his "time is up," hoping for a better life tomorrow:

When I get out of Du Sable, I don't want to come back.
Teachers're nice, but it's the way some of the students are. Plus the way the system is. You walk

down the hallways—hall guard tell you, "Go down-
stairs, so and so." For example, there's some of
the hall guards—some of 'em be pushing on you and
stuff—forcing you to do things you don't want to
do.
It's a nice school to stay here, but I wouldn't like
to come back after I leave it. I'd like to just forget
about it. 'Cause I did have some experiences I
didn't like over here. But I don't mind—I'm gonna
stay here till my time is up.

Sue

Eighteen-year-old Sue lives in the projects with her father,
one brother, and five sisters. Sue's mother died five years ago.
Her father is supervisor of their building, and Sue also works in
the same building.

Sue's comments about Du Sable are vague and contradictory,
and, like other Underachievers, she links her attitude toward
school and her achievement with such questionably relevant matters as the weather:

Well, I don't like the 45-15. It's all right, you know.
It's just that you got to go to school in the summer-
time, and it be too hot up in here to do work. Before
we went on 45-15, I liked it then; it was nice to me,
you know. I learned a lot. But now, since it's hot,
I don't like it.

Her teachers, according to Sue's perceptions, are not really
helpful, nor are they interested in her progress:

Well, some of the teachers, you know, they're all
right, but most of 'em got their little attitude when
you ask 'em something. They try to get all seddity
[act superior] and stuff. I guess they don't want to
be bothered at times. It seems like mostly when
you ask them for something, you know, most of 'em
just look at you. But, it's all right—.

Like most Underachievers, Sue frequently feels bored and
uninvolved in class. She prefers, as do the majority of Underachievers, to spend time in class writing (no more than copying
material with scribelike doggedness) rather than reading, an activity that evidently evokes considerable anxiety:

It just seems like there don't be nothing to do. You
just get sleepy and drowsy and stuff, and you be trying to find something to do, but, you know, you can't.
I like a class, like when the teacher—I like to write
a lots. That's what I like to do. But, you know,
when you read a lots it makes me sleepy and everything. When some peoples be readin', they be takin'
their time. And, you know, I believe I need glasses,
because it be hurtin' my eyes and I just get tired.

When I asked about the future, Sue's response was vague and
rather aimless before she latched on to a stock middle-class response: "Well, I haven't thought about that [the future] yet—. Well,
I want to be an airline stewardess—that's about all." For Sue, the
future seems devoid of any real possibilities. After she graduates
from Du Sable, she says, "First, I'd try to get me a good job to
start me off right. Then, I'd save me up enough money in the bank.
Then—I don't know. It's hard."
Much of Sue's aimlessness and indecisiveness about life is
likely the result of her very unstable, chaotic home background.
Of life in the Robert Taylor projects, she says:

I don't like it. It seems like it's dangerous up in
there. Everytime you look around somebody's shoot-
ing or killing somebody. Robbing or sticking up. It
make you feel like you're in prison with them bars
up. I don't like that.

Don

Don lives in Robert Taylor with his mother, father, four
brothers, and four sisters. His father owns two trucks that he
uses to deliver steel to factories in the city, and his mother is a
supervisor at a candy factory. The family, says Don, is "very
close."
Very personable and outgoing, 19-year-old Don is an unusual
Underachiever. What he lacks in academic ability, he seems to
make up for through his winsome personality and desire to succeed;
and it may be that in the ghetto culture one's personal elan is a
more valuable asset than academic talent.
Don's plans for the future are well cemented and involve
sports, his major pursuit while at Du Sable:

After I graduate August 29, I'm going to San Antonio
State College, and I'm going to major in business

administration. They're going to give me a baseball
scholarship, and a cat told me after the season if I
feel like playing a little football for him, I could do
that if I wanted to. But I guess I'll deal with that
when I get down there.

Don is critical of his fellow classmates who find school boring, yet I wondered if any teacher would be capable of allowing him
the kind of keen self-expression he seems to feel is necessary for
him to learn. In the following he describes how he would avoid
becoming bored in a class:

They put their heads down on the desk. All right—
if they participated in things that was happening in
class, it wouldn't be boring. And if they come all
the time like they supposed to, then you could make
a class exciting. 'Cause—in some ways, like you
can come to class and, you know, just psyche yourself out. Wow, this is the class! This is it! Hey,
yeah, I come here every day. It ain't like no other
class! They's why I can come and be me and have
a good time. I want to learn something. If you can
find a class like that, it'll turn out to be one of the
best classes you ever had. But, you know, if you
don't do that, the class, like they say, is boring.
You gotta put more of yourself into it, get something out of it.

In one class Don found boring, he tells how his need for affective
arousal and self-expression was satisfied—causing me to wonder
how his poor teacher handled the event:

The classroom was boring. 'Cause, you know, sitting there and everything. And, all right, we ran
across the book and everything. But then after we
ran across the work, didn't nobody do nothing.
They just sat there. Didn't nobody say nothing.
I said, "Hey, what's this? We at a funeral or
something? Somebody die? Hey, where the noise
at? Hey, like, you know, no noise. But you go out
in the hall, wow, all the noise you want! Playing the
music and everything." But, you know, everybody
just sat there. But then the noise—it started gradually growing and everything, you know. I was

making noise, keeping things going. Then everybody just started getting involved. And they felt
the same way that I did.

The Achievers

Mary

Seventeen-year-old Mary, who lives in Robert Taylor with
her mother, brother, and two sisters, presents one pattern of
ghetto school "success." She responds to the school's demands
with passive, withdrawing acquiescence. Achievers such as Mary,
while always attentive to their teachers' words and willing to do
their work, are so retiring and withdrawn that it is difficult for
their teachers to define them as real flesh-and-blood students.
Consequently, during my interview with her, she offered only the
barest indication of her orientation toward Du Sable.

Of the future, Mary is hesitant to plan much: "I was thinking
about going to college. But then I just think I'll go to a secretarial
school to be a secretary. I don't think I could make it through
college."

Mary did not wish to reveal to me her feelings about Du
Sable, saying only: "It's O.K. to me." She responded similarly
to my questioning about the school's teachers: "They're O.K.
I don't hate any of them." And the students: "They're O.K. I
have some friends here."

Mary, whose only comment about her feelings when in class
is that she feels "like a student," says the students' job is to
"listen to the teacher and learn what they can, because they might
need it further in the future."

In addition to enabling her to get a "good job," an education
is important to Mary because it will allow her to "better my life
in the future, and do what I want, and be what I want."

Alice

Alice's family came to the United States from British Honduras
about ten years ago. Alice now lives in an apartment with her
mother, stepfather, one sister, and two brothers. Her stepfather
is a carpenter and maintenance man for a Chicago hospital, and
her mother monograms clothing at home.

The oldest of the children, at 17 Alice is poised and pretty.
She speaks confidently of her future: "Right now, I'm going to
modeling school, and I plan on being a model and a secretary."
Later, she adds that she would like to "move up in business."

Alice's impressions of Du Sable, though initially negative, are now favorable:

> Well, the first time I was supposed to come up here, I didn't want to. The way people talk about it, you have a bad impression about it. But when you come over here and see what they try to do for you, and the way people are, you do get to like it. Right now I like it. I like the system that they have, and the teachers. I think the teachers are doing a pretty good job.

Alice is aware that most Du Sable High students differ from her in their dispositions toward school, and she doesn't hesitate to be critical:

> Well, some of them [the students] are all right, and some of them try to take advantage of the nice teachers. They want their freedom to do whatever they want to in the classroom. And I think that's wrong. If you come to learn you should be able to listen to the teacher and do what he or she tells you to do. It's boring to them because they're not participating in the work. They just come in and lay down, and they can do that at home. So I guess it's boring at home too. They just go home and sleep and not do anything.

At times, Alice's motivation to achieve comes into direct conflict with her fellow students' attitudes as she indicates in the following account:

> Today, one of the students said I was frantic, you know, cause I got through with all my work. I felt funny about it, 'cause here I am trying to do all my work to try and get an A because we're supposed to finish eleven units for this marking period. I'm really trying and they're putting me down because I'm ahead. They're not really trying, and they don't like to see people get ahead of them. I will go ahead, though. I'm going to be somebody to look up at. And if you just listen to somebody say "Oh, she's this and she's that," you shouldn't listen to that. You should make up your own mind and do whatever you want to do. Don't listen to what other people say.

Alice's drive to excel seems to be a stable part of her personality, and her aspirations for herself are not undermined by her actions—a form of self-destructiveness so common to the Underachiever. In short, she is willing to work hard to reap life's rewards:

> I just want to be me. I just want to know a lot. People not to look down on me, but look up on me. And I want to know a lot and do a lot of things. To do that you have to come to school and really work hard. That's the way I was ever since I was little. I always want to be ahead in life.

Finally, in commenting on the importance of her own education, Alice expresses a degree of insight and maturity infrequently found in Du Sable students:

> It's important for you to learn whatever you want to learn. They teach you different things that you want to know, so whenever you get older you can always look back on these things to help you do whatever you want to do.

Jane

Jane, who was adopted at birth, now lives with her aunt and older sister in the city. Her mother, father, and a 14-year-old brother live in a country house about 50 miles from Chicago. Until recently, the family had lived together in a Chicago home; the home, unfortunately, burned down. Alice's father is a retired janitor, and her mother works part-time taking care of children.

Influenced by her mother's work with children, Jane has definite plans for the future: "I would like to go to college and major in work with younger kids, maybe the handicapped."

Like Alice, Jane's first impressions of Du Sable were based on the school's bad reputation. She says, "I had doubts about it at first. Du Sable is bad. Those girls will get you in the bathroom and beat you up. But if you don't start off hanging with those kind of people, you won't end up like that." Because Jane was selective in choosing her friends, she now feels positively about her school:

> I think it's really a nice place. I mean most of the people try to put down Du Sable. But I say it's not Sable or anything like that. You can learn at any school. It's just the people. If they want to learn they can learn. A lot of the people say Du Sable

ain't nothing. Du Sable ain't this. I say, "Hey,
Du Sable has got some pretty nice people." I feel
that I can learn something. I have learned something. I've learned a lot from Du Sable. The teachers are pretty good here.

Jane is opposed to the Underachievers' attitudes toward school
and teachers, and she has not hesitated to let her classmates know
how she feels:

Well, they don't hardly come anyway from the beginning. And then they come out of class and say
that teacher didn't teach them anything. I say,
"Hey, you haven't been there, and then didn't try
to do anything the times that you did come. You
just went to sleep." I say, "Don't try to put down
the teacher. The teacher did try with you."
They're always talking about when they beat up somebody and what they did. How they went and got high
and everything. And that's not—especially for a girl
to put herself in that position—talking about how she
went and got high and she had a fight with somebody.
That doesn't even look right.

In addition to being influenced positively by her mother, Jane
has also found an "ego ideal" in an older woman who is studying to
be a nurse. She and others have encouraged Jane to achieve in
school:

She says, "Yeah, Jane, you're really nice." You
know, people tell me, "You know, you got a nice
disposition about yourself." I say, "Why, thank
you." They say, "You should go on ahead and finish
school and do whatever you're going to do. That
would be nice for you to come out of high school and
stuff. And Ma would really be proud of you."

Jane possesses an admirable degree of insight into her motivations and, perhaps more importantly, she has the willingness to
behave in accord with this insight. In the following, she comments
on a period when she felt like slipping into the behavior pattern
characteristic of the Underachievers:

I could say the last half of my junior year, no, the
end of it when our house caught on fire. That's the

only house I've ever known for us to live in. Like I
didn't care anymore about anything. I just really
wanted to give up on everything. But then I thought
about it. I said no, I shouldn't even be that way. So
this year I'm really going to try harder.

POSTSCRIPT: STUDENTS' CAPACITY FOR
CHANGE AND GROWTH

In the foregoing descriptions of the values and aspirations of
two types of Du Sable students, there is one dimension of personality
that I have not discussed, though I have long learned to respect it—
and that is the human being's capacity for change and growth. While
I have assigned these eight students to categories that in many ways
may be labeled "good" and "bad," I am not presumptuous enough to
predict what each of these young people is capable of becoming—to
do so would be miseducative in the deepest, most profound sense.
On the contrary, I respect and, in many ways, admire all eight of
these students as I have witnessed them trying to adapt to their
often confusing lives.
    Though I have willfully supported Jenck's assertion that "the
characteristics of the entering children" determine a school's output, there is the danger that this focus may be too narrow, thus
creating a stereotype for teachers to use against students. Instead,
teachers must accept and value their students as they are and encourage a vision of what they might become through continued
learning.

REFERENCES

Jencks, C. Inequality: A Reassessment of the Effect of Family and
    Schooling in America. New York: Basic Books, 1972.

Getzels, J. W. "A Social Psychology of Education." In Handbook
    of Social Psychology, edited by G. Lindzey and E. Aronson.
Reading, Mass.: Addison-Wesley, 1968.

Thelen, H. A. Education and the Human Quest: Four Designs for
    Education. Chicago: University of Chicago Press, 1972.

Thelen, H. A. The Educational Ethos of the Midwestern High
    School. Monograph. University of Chicago, 1974.

6

DU SABLE TEACHERS:
BURNOUTS, ALTRUISTS,
AND TECHNICIANS

I use sarcasm all the time in some
of my classes. It's the best technique I've come up with. It really
works in a situation like this. Oh,
I'm brutal in some of my classes.
Of course, I'm not with the sensitive ones—that would be cruel—but
with the ones that deserve it. . . .

A Female Du Sable Teacher

AS my years of teaching at Du Sable rolled by, I became increasingly interested in how my colleagues coped with extensive environmental stress. With the encouragement of my professors at the University of Chicago, I decided, then, to explore the topic in my dissertation study. For me, the problem held forth a twofold promise: not
only could I add to present knowledge of how ghetto teachers cope,
possibly even helping others such as myself adjust to their difficult
teaching assignments, but I could also explore further, and more
deeply, the effect that teaching at Du Sable was having on me.

I began my study with the hypothesis that an inner-city teacher's characteristic mode of coping with stress (and, subsequently,
his perceived level of job satisfaction and success) is directly related not only to the nature of his in-school experiences but to three
salient personality traits: (1) his level of energy for personal and
professional growth—whether he has a high or low "drive" toward
self-actualization; (2) his reality orientation—whether in his response

to stress he accepts, rejects, or is blind to the reality of his situation; and (3) his conceptual understanding—whether his belief system encourages him to view teaching as a humane, purposeful activity designed to help human beings develop through confronting and interpreting the meaning of their experiences, or whether it prompts him to view teaching as primarily an easy entry, high security profession or "job."

FOUR SALIENT DIMENSIONS OF TEACHING STYLE

The preceding personality traits, largely the result of the individual's unique life experiences, strongly influence the style of teaching a teacher develops. Four dimensions of teaching style, I feel, are salient for teachers working in a stressful environment such as Du Sable: (1) social or empathic distance between teacher and student, (2) indirect vs. direct teaching behaviors, (3) democratic vs. autocratic teaching behaviors, and (4) perceived levels of satisfaction and success vs. dissatisfaction and failure.

These dimensions of teaching style have extensive implications for the educativeness of a teacher's classroom. At one extreme is the teacher who reports a positive attitude toward the school setting and reveals democratic, indirect teaching behaviors. He tries to examine openly and honestly the nature of his conflicts with students and allows himself to experience emotional engagement with and empathy for even the most uncontrolled students. For such a teacher, ghetto teaching can serve as a catalyst for continued professional growth and personal integration at higher levels. Similarly, several educators have noted that job-related conflicts may "stimulate" some teachers to become more effective as human beings. Bettelheim and Wright (1955) and Bettelheim (1974) found that adults who worked with disturbed children at the University of Chicago's Orthogenic School were often able to achieve higher levels of integration by "working through" the anxieties aroused by patients' threatening behavior. In like manner, Schwartz (1974) contends that the "growth crisis" faced by teachers who must adjust to open classroom settings can serve as a springboard for self-actualization and further integration. Finally, Ekstein (1969) asserts that the various social and inner dilemmas faced by teachers may, if examined openly and realistically, function as growth crises that can lead to an enhanced professional identity and further self-awareness.

At the other extreme, however, are those teachers who, unable or unwilling to examine their role in the teacher-student battle, feel negatively about their teaching assignments and reveal teaching behaviors that tend to be autocratic and direct. Incapable of empathy with their students and alienated from their total teaching situation, these teachers are apt to find teaching at schools such as Du Sable a frustrating, unrewarding experience. As Du Sable administrators (and all the other inner-city administrators I've met) are not "enlightened" enough to offer teachers systematic professional help in coping with their job-related conflicts, these teachers may try to "defend" their beleaguered sense of self-worth by projecting some of these conflicts onto students. However, such a process only exacerbates further the teacher-student battle—as teachers commonly make use of various ego defenses, students must also protect their emerging, diffuse identities (Stein 1974). Thus, students, as well as teachers, can find themselves in anxiety-generating situations, with denial or distortion of reality often the only conceivable way to manage tension.

A PARADIGM FOR THE DEVELOPMENT
OF TEACHING STYLE

Beginning teachers assigned to a school such as Du Sable typically develop according to a rather general, predictable pattern. The new teacher, trained according to a middle-class set of expectations, encounters the school's environment and experiences shock or anxiety to which he has a unique reaction. This reaction, then, has certain consequences for the teacher's formal and informal relationships with students and faculty; and these consequences, "feed back" into the system, become part of the system's official and unofficial norms. We may view the relationship of these dimensions as in Figure 3.

The school is a social system, the specific characteristics of which are a function of the personalities of individual system members and the numerous other social systems that influence the school (Getzels 1969; Thelen 1974). Thus, a school develops a particular culture or way of life that encourages various teaching styles, or strategies, while it subtly discourages others. Through their teaching styles, then, teachers must develop behaviors that not only allow them to meet the institutionally prescribed requirements for their role but also allow them to cope with their job-related anxieties.

The stress and resultant anxiety felt by a teacher in a school such as Du Sable may be defined as an unacceptable, or extreme, tension generated by a felt incongruity between the teacher's image of an ideal situation and his perceptions of present reality. The precise amount of anxiety an individual experiences depends on how the stressful events are perceived (Dohrenwend and Dohrenwend

1974). In their adaptation to an unfamiliar culture, for example, some individuals may experience adverse effects, while others experience none (Hinkle 1974).

FIGURE 3

PSYCHO-SOCIAL FACTORS THAT INFLUENCE
THE DEVELOPMENT OF TEACHING STYLE

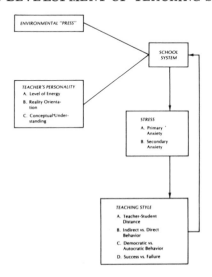

It may be necessary here to distinguish between objective anxiety and neurotic anxiety, both of which may influence teacher behavior. Objective anxiety is a rational, appropriate response to the perception of an external threat and is an expression of the instinct of self-preservation (Freud 1935). Examples of stressors at Du Sable that might cause the teacher to experience objective anxiety are instances of violence, student apathy, environmental press, dehumanizing treatment by pupils, administrative ineptness, repeated failure to achieve professional goals, and a lack of professionalism among colleagues. Neurotic anxiety, on the other hand, I will define as a disproportionate fear that, in part, is generated from within and is usually unconscious or only fleetingly available for conscious examination. Most neurotic anxiety originates in previous developmental conflicts the individual has not yet adequately resolved. Thus, stressors causing only objective anxiety in some individuals may, in others, also set in motion neurotic anxiety.

The anxiety teachers experience may be further distinguished as either primary or secondary. Primary anxiety results from the teacher's need to cope with actual conditions within the school, while these conditions, in turn, generate what I will call secondary anxiety within the teacher. The secondary anxiety I have noted within myself while teaching at Du Sable has included feelings of anger, frustration, powerlessness, lowered self-esteem, and guilt.

It is in response to both primary and secondary anxiety that styles of teaching emerge. Each teacher has to come to terms with the discomfort generated by the discrepancy between his life style and the conflicting reality of his students' life styles. Professionally, he has to find the terms on which he can be successful or, at least, can "protect" himself from a high level of anxiety and feelings of personal and professional inadequacy.

The particular style a teacher develops may be viewed as a reflection of the teacher's personality and his experiences within the school setting. Or, as Lewin (1954) asserts, behavior is a function of the person and his environment, $B = F(P, E)$. Particular styles of teaching, then, may range from regressive identification (or conflict) with students to professionally oriented inquiries to understand the situation.

THREE TEACHER STYLES

Through observations of and interviews with 21 Du Sable colleagues and the statistical analysis of extensive attitudinal and observational data that I have reported on elsewhere,* I have conceptualized three teacher styles or "ways of life" at Du Sable.

The first group of teachers—whom I will label the Burnouts—experiences the greatest amount of job-related stress and tends to feel frustrated, exploited, and ineffective while teaching at Du Sable. Burnouts, who tend either to fight Du Sable conditions or to take flight from them, express traditional, limited conceptual understandings of the educative process. They are also non-self-actualizing and prefer to maintain high social and empathetic distance between themselves and students. Burnouts frequently report that they have given up hope of teaching their students much of anything—their main objective while at school is psychic survival, "getting through" each day.

---

*"Inner-City High School Teachers: The Relationship of Personality Traits and Teaching Style to Environmental Stress" (Ph.D. dissertation, University of Chicago, 1978). A summary of this research (under the same title) also appeared in Urban Education 14, no. 4 (January 1980): 449-70. © 1980 Sage Publications, Inc. Reprinted by permission of Sage Publications, Inc.

The second group—I will call these teachers the Altruists—experiences a low level of job-related stress and is concerned with establishing open, warm, and humane relationships with students. Their personal values are most like those of self-actualizing individuals, and their conceptual understanding of the educative process is sophisticated and inquiry oriented.

The third group—I will call these teachers the Technicians—is characterized by strong feelings of effectiveness and overall job satisfaction. These teachers are task-oriented professionals who have a clear sense of what the job requires of them. They tend to depend on adhering to school and Board of Education rules and to hold personal values that are non-self-actualizing.

My analysis of the classroom behavior of Burnouts, Altruists, and Technicians (I used a slightly modified version of Flanders' Interaction Analysis Categories) did not yield any statistically significant differences among the groups. That is to say, all three teacher types spent most of their class time in the following routine verbal activities arranged according to their frequency: lecturing, asking questions, giving directions, listening to student responses, and occasionally criticizing students and/or justifying their authority as teacher. In spite of these rather standardized teacher-student verbal interactions, however, I noted considerable differences in the classroom climate established by each type. These differences were related to the degree of intimacy or conflict between students and teacher and to the general quality of observed interpersonal relations between teacher and student. Finally, my interviews with the 21 teachers revealed extensive differences in attitudes toward teaching at Du Sable.

In general, the classroom climate of the Burnouts emphasized the necessity of adhering to teacher-determined rules and revealed tension or conflict between teacher and students. In the interviews, the nine Burnouts told me that they experienced high levels of frustration and anxiety related to their work; they were frequently very scathing in their evaluations of students' abilities and the overall Du Sable milieu.

The classroom climate of the Altruists, I found, was characterized by warm, supportive teacher-student interactions and the absence of tension and conflict. Similarly, all five Altruists expressed accepting and caring attitudes toward their students and concern for their intellectual and emotional development.

My observations of the classroom climate created by the Technicians also revealed little or no conflict between teacher and student, but here the emphasis was on productivity and achievement rather than on authentic teacher-student relationships. During their interviews with me, the seven Technicians stressed the importance of having students cover and master predetermined course materials, and they expressed their belief that well-prepared, hard-working teachers <u>could</u> succeed at Du Sable.

Finally, to determine how pupils perceived the three teacher types, students in the classes I observed responded to a Student Opinion Survey. Surprisingly, the results of this survey indicated that each teacher, regardless of his teaching style, was judged favorably by the majority of students and not so favorably by a small minority. This finding caused me to speculate that (1) students tend to evaluate their teachers in a rather generous, stereotypical manner on criteria that are most likely not related to how much students actually learn, and (2) for any teacher, there are students suited to that teacher's particular style as well as students not suited.

REFERENCES

Bettelheim, B. <u>A Home for the Heart</u>. New York: Alfred A. Knopf, 1974.

Bettelheim, B., and Wright, B. "The Role of Residential Treatment for Children: Staff Development in a Treatment Institution." <u>The American Journal of Orthopsychiatry</u> 25 (1955):705-19.

Dohrenwend, B., and Dohrenwend, B. <u>Stressful Life Events: Their Nature and Effects</u>. New York: John Wiley and Sons, 1974.

Ekstein, B. "Psychoanalytic Reflections on the Emergence of the Teacher's Professional Identity." <u>American Journal of Ortho- psychiatry</u> 39 (1969).

Freud, S. <u>A General Introduction to Psychoanalysis</u>. New York: Liveright Publishing, 1935.

Getzels, J. W. "A Social Psychology of Education." In <u>Handbook of Social Psychology</u>, edited by G. Lindzey and E. Aronson. Reading, Mass.: Addison-Wesley, 1969.

Hinkle, L. E. "The Effect of Exposure to Culture Change." In <u>Stressful Life Events: Their Nature and Effects</u>, edited by B. Dohrenwend and B. Dohrenwend. New York: John Wiley and Sons, 1974.

Lewin, K. "Behavior and Development as a Function of the Total Situation." In <u>Manual of Child Psychology</u>, edited by L. Carmichael. New York: John Wiley and Sons, 1954.

Schwartz, R. L. "The Open Classroom: Growth Crisis for the Teacher." Elementary School Journal 74 (1974):326-35.

Stein, H. F. "Confirmation of the White Ethnic Stereotype." School Review 82 (1974):437-54.

Thelen, H. A. The Educational Ethos of the Midwestern High School. Monograph. University of Chicago, 1974.

7

THE BURNOUTS

I hate to say it, but I'm just too
good for this place. I'm not bum-
rapping it, but I didn't go to Chicago State [University]. I could
have and saved four or five thous-
and dollars on education. You just
can't bloom if the seed falls on
barren rock. It just withers. I
think I have a better opinion of myself—if given the choice—to choose
this place. I think this is a second-
class institution, and I don't think
I'm a second-class person.

A Burned-out Male Du Sable
Teacher

MY studies of the behavior and attitudes of teachers have long con-
vinced me that the most compelling (and often eloquent) way to present such data is to let the "subjects" speak for themselves. My
purpose in this and the next two chapters, therefore, is to make the
data I collected at Du Sable come alive by presenting two case studies for each of the teacher types: Burnouts, Altruists, and Technicians.

MISS WACKER

This teacher, whom I will call Miss Wacker, is a white female English teacher about 30 years old. She came to Du Sable five years ago because of a mandatory Board of Education faculty integration plan.

Miss Wacker is very frank and graphic in discussing her largely negative perceptions of Du Sable. Her manner of speaking is extremely rapid and nervous. When I asked her to describe her first year at Du Sable, she responded: "It was the worst year of my life—absolutely, utterly terrible." Miss Wacker was, however, able to endure the socialization process that all middle-class teachers must surely undergo in adapting to an environment such as Du Sable. She described succinctly the sort of "initiation rites" she had to withstand:

> I felt anxiety a lot more when I first started, definitely. Now I know more and more students and I've built up a reputation, too. Like your first year here they play the game, "Gee, I wonder how soon we can get her to quit teaching, see if she can handle it." You know, they know you're a new teacher and they'll drive you bananas your first year.
> Well, I'm here five years. I'm stable. The kids know me. They know that whatever they're about to do is not going to shock me, frighten me, or make me quit teaching on account of them. So they can't do anything to me that hasn't already been done, that would shock me.

Her comments about her professional development as an inner-city teacher describe how she has learned to withdraw from stressful confrontations with students. Quite clearly, Miss Wacker evidences the "burned-out" teacher syndrome:

> I've changed since I got into teaching. I'm tired. I'm more tired now; like I need spring vacation now. I'm exhausted now. I'm literally wiped out. I need to rest. I know at the beginning of the year—"Let's go get 'em, raring to go." And now it's—"Ah, shit, if they want to talk, let 'em talk." You know I'm losing control in my classes because I'm just too tired to fight with them. I'm just too tired to scream and bitch and fight.

In her comments about Du Sable students, Miss Wacker is particularly condemning. Moreover, her frustration is especially evident when she comments on the necessity of having to teach students on a remedial level without proper training herself and without adequate and appropriate materials:

> We all taught, four of us, in room 330, which is one huge septic tank. Four teachers yelling and screaming over each other's voices. The kids went bananas.
> Next year was really bad. I had two double-period basics. And this time I had bad groups. Large classes, 35 to 40.
> They had absolutely zero reading levels. I'm not qualified to teach that. I have a degree that says I can teach literature. What—one reading course and I'm going to teach A-B-C-D? I'm not a qualified reading teacher. I'd be the first one to say it. And I hate it. So boring, so boring for me.

In response to conditions at Du Sable, Miss Wacker has learned to cope through strategies that are clearly not in the best interests of students but which, nevertheless, lessen her job stress:

> I'm an easy-going slup. I don't like kicking kids out of class. I let kids come when they feel like it. Some teachers are hard and say, "If you're not here by five minutes after the bell, you're locked out," and boom, boom, boom. I can't. He comes in late, he comes in late. As long as they want to come to class. Fine. Keep coming. Keep coming. Better to keep coming than not at all. Even if they're 15 minutes late, maybe they can get something.
> They can actually be absent the whole 40 weeks as long as they do their assignments. They could get a C or a D. I know it's wrong. I feel myself it's wrong. Why should I pass him and the kids who come every day. Blah, blah. But it's easier on me. I don't like to fail students in the first place. I don't like giving F's.
> I'm easy. I'm very easy, 'cause I found it's easier on me. You fail them all, and they're coming at you hassling you. The kids that never come are hassling you.
> One kid I failed, he never came to class the whole year, right? He comes up to me and says, "You failed me 'cause I'm black. You a racist! You a racist, that's why you failed me." I said, "You know, you're right. But one thing puzzles me. There must have been 20

kids in that class I passed. Why did I pass them?"
He looks at me seriously and says, " 'Cause you thought
they was white."
I usually give them above the grade they should get. If
a kid actually deserves a B, he gets an A. If he actually deserves a D, he gets a C. This is why they don't
hassle me at grade time. They're always very satisfied with their grades. I have very few complaints.
It's easier on me. Look at those grades. B's and
A's. There's gobs of them, gobs of them. I'm
easy with those that come every day and do their
assignments.
Standards? I have no standards. This year I was going to try for spelling. I was going to take off for mis-
spelled words, right? And after ten weeks of circling
misspellings, I got tired of that. I said, "O.K., spell
it like you will. If I can figure it out again that's terrific." I don't take off for misspellings because you're
fighting a losing battle with yourself. If every teacher
in this school agreed to take off for spelling errors then
we'd have a chance. But you can't be the only one doing
it alone. If you are, you're knocking yourself out.
That's how I feel. I feel I don't have time to mark these
papers that carefully. I don't want to. I'm not knocking
myself out. I said, "Forget it."
I give easy tests, easy quizzes. I go over the test before the test. I take the test in my hand, read them the
answers in class, read them the test in class. It's
easier for me. I do what's easiest on my nerves. But
there's not much in the way of rewards or satisfaction.

In spite of the strategies she has developed for coping, Miss
Wacker is still subject to feelings of inadequacy and, perhaps, guilt
when she reflects on her inability to achieve the goals she has set
for herself:

I think I'm very ineffective. I don't know if I am or not,
but I feel like I'm not effective. I think I reach a few of
them, but that's about it. I feel like I'm ineffective because if there's 30 per class, why aren't I reaching 20?
How come I feel like I'm only reaching five or ten per
class? 'Cause that's the whole thing, you've got five
or ten paying attention, and that's who you teach to.
That's what I do. If they're talking in the back, I ignore
them, and I talk to the ones that are paying attention. I

teach the ones who want to learn and ignore the rest of
the shit. This is what happens, 'cause I don't know
what else to do.

In her relations with those Du Sable students who might behave aggressively toward her, Miss Wacker has developed a strategy that, no doubt, serves to increase, rather than to lessen, the
teacher-student conflict. Her stance is a good indicator of the
severe stress some teachers experience and the "irrational," or
at least unprofessional, adaptations such teachers are forced to
make:

> Now, if a kid threatens me, I say, "Ah, fuck off." I
> just swear right back, and they look so shocked by it.
> I say, "That's right, baby, so don't mess with me." °
> And when you show you're not frightened by it, they
> just back off. But when you're first teaching here, you
> don't know what to respond with. Now, after five years—
> "Ah, shit on you."

Miss Wacker openly admits that her commitment to teaching
as a profession is low. Furthermore, her motives for entering the
profession were based on parental pressure to acquire a marketable
skill in college:

> I don't believe I ever recall really wanting to become a
> teacher. My father just said, "If you're gonna go to col-
> lege and not work after high school, you're gonna get a
> teaching degree because it's the greatest job for a fe-
> male to fall back on." I didn't know what else I wanted
> to go into in college, so I went into teaching.

While she points out that teaching does have its satisfactions, these
are not related to interactions with students:

> Teaching is a hell of a job, but one: the hours are good.
> Even though I have to bring a lot of crap home with me,
> I can still do it at home, when I'm eating dinner, when
> I'm relaxing watching T.V. So you don't mind it as
> much. I'm not at the office any more. I'm in my car
> at three o'clock driving down the expressway. I'm still
> home at 4:30. And if I have work to do and I don't want
> to do it that night, I'll just do it the next night when I'm
> not busy. I still have that time to myself.

And vacations—[she hits the desk for emphasis with her
fist]. You cannot beat a teacher's vacations. There's
no job that gives you the kind of vacation—O.K., we
don't get paid summer vacations, but if I want to, I
can take two months off and do something with it. I
putter around the house for two months, and I love it.
So, I like the vacations.
Sometimes I like teaching if I have a good class and a
good day. But then sometimes I wish I hadn't gone into
it at all, 'cause it's really—it's aggravating at times.
Very aggravating.

The class Miss Wacker wished me to observe was her first
period senior English class. This particular lesson, which covered Shakespeare's Taming of the Shrew, was largely lecture, and
almost all student talk was in response to teacher questions as opposed to student initiated comments about the topic. My observations according to Flanders' Interaction Analysis categories revealed that considerable time during this period was devoted to silence (over 16 percent); in addition, though, there was considerable
"confusion" that occurred during teacher-student interaction (over
12 percent). These data, then, portray a teacher who spends most
of her time talking at students who are not always inclined to listen.

The manner in which this class began revealed the nonchalant
attitude of Miss Wacker and her students. At the 8:00 A.M. bell
signaling the start of class, only one student and I were present.
By 8:03, three students—but no teacher—were present. When Miss
Wacker finally arrives—at 8:07—seven students are present. I later
learned from Miss Wacker that she regularly enjoys a morning cup
of coffee in the cafeteria and, because her students are frequently
late to class, doesn't feel obligated to be on time.

"Take out a half sheet of paper and number from one through
ten for a true-false quiz," she says immediately upon entering the
room.

"I don't got no paper," a boy in the back blurts out.

"Beg, borrow, or steal," advises Miss Wacker.

She passes out the test and students begin immediately to work
on it.

"This is a private test, ladies," she warns two students whom
she suspects of collaborating.

"Ain't it time for our field trip?" one student questions.

"You guys are a trip." Miss Wacker's voice is light and
humorous.

She continues to give out quizzes and rapid directions as students continue to trickle into the room. By 8:16, 18 students are

present. Considerable talk and general noise and confusion occur unabated throughout the quiz. Very openly, students discuss the quiz among themselves. Occasionally, a student wanders about the room, perhaps to look out the window or to throw a piece of paper into the wastebasket.

At 8:21, Miss Wacker collects the papers, and a rapid question-and-answer review of the quiz follows. She reads the questions and individual students answer. Near the end of this review, it becomes apparent that a boy and girl in the class have been trading insults.

"I'm gonna jump on her, the bitch," the boy says loudly.

"Outside, Jefferson, then you can kill each other," Miss Wacker quips.

Only by ignoring considerable talk and confusion is Miss Wacker able to conclude her review of the quiz.

At 8:26, she plays a scene from Taming of the Shrew on a small cassette recorder. She is seated behind her desk operating the recorder and her students are to follow in their texts. The quality of the tape is very poor and, consequently, hard to follow.

As the tape plays, some students appear to pay attention, while others are openly involved in other pursuits. One student reads a comic book; another works on her shorthand assignment; and a third manicures her nails.

At this moment, Miss Wacker is noticeably "removed" from her students. Psychologically, she appears preoccupied with other matters—as the tape goes on, she stares vacantly at her students, apparently oblivious to their unwillingness to follow in their texts. Physically, Miss Wacker is also distant from her students. Her students are scattered around the back half of the room; the nearest is at least 12 feet away.

At appropriate moments, she stops the tape and summarizes the action or tells students to listen for developments yet to come. Her rapid-fire comments are given in a high, loud voice.

Near the end of the period, Miss Wacker passes out a dittoed sheet of questions and announces that class time will be given tomorrow to work on the exercise.

With three minutes remaining in the period, students and teacher prepare to leave. The atmosphere is one of relaxed, friendly social interaction as everyone "winds down" and waits for the dismissal bell.

Immediately after the class, Miss Wacker offers me her evaluation of the lesson: "This is my idea of a good class. Nothing unusual happened. I asked a few questions and they answered. Maybe I did too much talking."

The rapport that she has developed with these students is, she feels, the result of her "easy going" approach—an approach that she admits reflects her general state of nervousness and lack of preparation:

> I'm always nervous. You see I'm a nervous person.
> You see I smoke, talk fast. I'm a nervous wreck to
> begin with. I'm also nervous because I'm never pre-
> pared. I think I have a good relationship with most of
> them. There's a few in there I really don't care for.
> But most of them I get along with because I'm easy
> going.

At a later meeting we had, though, Miss Wacker was quite critical of these students. When I told her that the majority of her students (as revealed on a Student Opinion Survey I had students take) felt they had learned a "great deal" or a "fair amount" in her class, she is skeptical and, again, disparages her students' abilities:

> Now that's surprising. I've given them tests and that
> shows they don't know shit, 'cause I'm very easy and
> they're very lazy. I've gotten easier because they're
> so damn lazy. If you try to work 'em too hard, you
> don't get anything at all. I mean, I don't know how
> some teachers get it, but I try and I get nothing. So I
> say to myself, I'll be easy, and I don't give a shit.
> It's actually less aggravation for me now. I just do
> it my way and ignore what's happening.
> You try to work 'em hard and they just ignore you, and
> that's even worse. As far as I'm concerned, they've
> learned nothing all year. I don't know what I'm expect-
> ing from them. Who knows, the teachers probably said
> the same things about us when we were in high school.
> We didn't learn nothing, and we thought we were learning
> something.

MISS CHANDLER

Miss Chandler is a young black female mathematics teacher who was completing her first year at Du Sable when I visited with her. Before coming to Du Sable, she taught about a year each at two other all-black Chicago public high schools.

Miss Chandler, herself a graduate of an inner-city high school in Chicago, is openly critical of conditions at Du Sable—conditions

that she judges to be worse than at any other school she has
worked in:

> In comparison to the short time I've been teaching, I
> think this is the worst. In comparison to them [other
> schools] and Du Sable, there's a tremendous differ-
> ence. I didn't have the headaches there like I have here.
> Maybe it's 'cause the kids are so old. I have a lot of
> kids I think should have been out quite a few years ago.
> And this year it's just a thing where there's nothing on
> their minds other than sex, pot, and you name it—but
> everything except the subject matter. So there was a
> tremendous amount of difference.

Like her fellow Burnouts, Miss Chandler reports that her job
is very frustrating and stressful. Her criticism of the school's
milieu is sharpest when she discusses Du Sable students and their
abilities:

> Hey, let's face it, we've got rotten apples all over.
> The largest problem that I have with these kids is
> their retention. And I feel personally the only reason
> that they have a retention problem is because they don't
> want to do it in the first place。
> And many of the things we do the child will just bluntly
> say—and I've had several of my students say that—"You
> do try, but I just can't remember that。" It's nerve-
> wracking. It's not that it hasn't happened before, but
> not in such a vast number—that they come to class just
> like they would go to a nine-to-five job, no paper, no
> pencils, no book, no anything.
> And I think this was the first shocking thing when I
> started teaching, to see kids sit up and take no notes of
> any kind and just sit there and watch you and then say,
> "Well, you know, I really don't understand," or "You
> don't give notes—." I'm showing all of these thousands
> of examples on the board. What else is this but notes?
> I'm not putting it there for me.
> Their study habits are atrocious. They're ridiculous,
> really, because they don't have any study habits. Even
> if they catch on, they catch on for that first 40 minutes,
> and when they leave they never pick it up again till the
> next day.
> Then, of course, I do have the problem where a lot of
> them can't read.

In her response to teaching conditions at Du Sable, Miss Chandler has developed certain strategies for coping. Her adaptions parallel those revealed to me by other Burnouts. These teachers first experience "shock" at students' behavior and very low achievement levels. Next, the teachers try to develop appropriate intervention techniques; and finally, realizing failure and frustration, they "withdraw" emotionally from the situation and reduce efforts to change students' attitudes toward learning. At this point, day-to-day psychic survival becomes the teacher's priority. As Miss Chandler puts it:

> I don't worry about those that don't come. It took me half a year to decide to do that. But I just stopped worrying about those that don't come.
> I think when I first started teaching I had a few students that said, "You don't really care about us. You forget what kind of students we are, and you really aren't trying." And I was breaking my neck!
> I said to them over and over, "You don't have photogenic minds." But yet they come and they sit and they look, and they do the same thing in another class. Something is wrong someplace. I've tried to retrace myself, but you can only retrace yourself for so long, and then you have to look at the other side of the coin too.
> If you don't get involved, teaching is not very difficult. The more involved you are, the more difficult it is.
> The only thing I can say is—when one is ready to learn, one will learn and not before. I don't care what it is. The only thing I did was, rather than worry myself to death over it, leave it alone. You do what you can, and you leave it totally up to the rest of them. You keep doing the same thing or you present new ideas that will reinforce the old ones in hope that they will grasp it.

Miss Chandler's commitment to teaching as a profession is low. She views her work at Du Sable as a "job," and she has yearnings, though rather vague, for a new position. With her low level of energy and without a clearer statement of professional goals, my hunch was that Miss Chandler would likely remain in teaching—becoming increasingly pessimistic and/or burned out with each passing year.

During my observations, Miss Chandler's classroom behavior consisted largely of lecturing and asking questions, though these activities were frequently punctuated with rather abrasive verbal exchanges between herself and her students. The dominant classroom atmosphere was one of friction between teacher and student. This antipathy, though, seemed to have its humorous side, too; and I suspected that Miss Chandler and her students had reached a tacit agreement wherein both were now able to ventilate, within limits, their frustration during a class period.

The particular lesson I observed focused on how to compute distance if given the rate at which an object travels and its time. After the bell signaling the start of class, students continue to trickle into the room, most talking loudly with their friends and engaging in silly behavior. On the blackboard, Miss Chandler writes material that her students are to copy.

"If you're smart, you'll copy this," she warns. "Did you hear me tell you to start copying the material on the board?"

Gradually, the noise level diminishes and most of the 17 students present begin their work.

Miss Chandler spies one girl primping and rearranging her hair.

"I think you'd better copy it, Miss Harris! Where's your paper? I'm waiting on Christmas. Don't say anything when you get an F."

The chastised Miss Harris slings her books and purse on the floor and, with an unmistakable scowl of contempt for her teacher, begins her copying.

Miss Chandler's tone of voice is strident and insistent as she continues to confront students reluctant to begin work. A huge, slow moving boy who enters late is told to go back to his previous class for a tardy pass. He resists—more through lack of energy than defiance—and Miss Chandler threatens, "Maybe Mr. Prokop [the assistant principal in charge of discipline] can give you ten lashes across the butt."

She returns the previous day's papers and proceeds to review the material in question-answer fashion. As this interaction proceeds, both teacher and students interject aggressive comments aimed at the other—students moan and grumble about the demands their teacher places on them, and Miss Chandler complains about her students' lack of ability and motivation.

Confusion builds, crescendolike, in the classroom until Miss Chandler stops her explanation of the material.

"Please, you're driving me crazy, slowly but surely."

"Why, you crazy?" a girl in the back blurts out.

"You sit there like on Hollywood and Vine and don't copy it down," Miss Chandler retorts with an exasperated sigh.

She finally gets her students back on task, whereupon she writes more information on the board. Many students again grumble and complain about the work they are called upon to do.

"Why do I hear all this talking?" Miss Chandler whines. "I'm gonna put down an F for a smart mouth."

"No you won't," says an exceptionally bold student—a rough-looking little girl near the door.

"Yes I will, sweetie," Miss Chandler shoots back.

With ever-present verbal sparring between teacher and students, work continues. There is, however, a certain playfulness evident in the remarks of both teacher and students. My hunch (one that Miss Chandler confirms later) is that earlier in the school year teacher and students probably confronted one another in greater earnestness before subsequently working out the present pattern of interactions that allows both to discharge tension as the class proceeds.

Miss Chandler continues her lecturing on the rate x time formula. A few students now begin to talk among themselves about matters clearly not related to the lesson.

"Jesus Christ," complains Miss Chandler. Singling out one of the troublemakers, she continues, "Lorette, shut up, girl."

The class continues with the lesson. Yet, after a moment, these same students begin talking again. In their favor now, however, they are also apparently copying the material on the board as well.

"I hope you're copying this down as much as you're running your mouth," Miss Chandler says, ceasing for a moment her writing on the board.

"I'm tired of writing," whines a boy in the front who has now sprawled across the top of his desk in mock exhaustion, gingerly nursing his right hand as though the overworked appendage were about to fall off.

"Tell me something else new," his teacher responds, unimpressed at his suffering.

"It's two o'clock, time for the bell," says another boy. (My watch, a model noted for its accuracy, shows 1:50.)

"Don't lie, Jeffery."

"We need a break," moans Jeffery.

"You have a break next week with spring vacation, what more do you want?"

"I'm sick of you," Jeffery mumbles and trails off with what might have been an obscenity.

"I'm tired of looking at your face, too," counters Miss Chandler.

Jeffery now mimics his teacher who continues to exhort him to return to his work. Finally, though, Miss Chandler drops the issue and returns to the board work and her lecture. Minutes later, the bell signals the end of the period.

As I mentioned above, Miss Chandler's relationship with these students was even more tempestuous at the start of the school year. During our postobservation interview, she described the evolution of her way of working with this class:

> Listen, you may not believe it, but that's my better
> class. But when I first started, that was my worst
> class. I had about fifty students to begin with, if not
> more. And when I first arrived on the scene I
> was hoarse every day. I had grown women in the
> class.
> The first week or so it took the whole period—well no,
> I won't say the whole first week, but close to it—it
> would take me a whole period to take the attendance
> primarily because I didn't know anyone. It [sic] was
> so many of them, and they were loud and boisterous,
> rude. You name it, they were.
> The first day it wasn't so bad because I had about
> three or four women in the class and they were all
> absent the first day I took it over. The second day
> when these three or four came in, God, I lost all con-
> trol. I let this happen for about two days; and then the
> second day it happened, I put them out.
> Anyway, after I put them out, I ended up telling Mr.
> Prokop that, "Hey, one house with four women is too
> many. Now one of us has to go—either them or me."
> Like the first day I couldn't even give my own rules
> and requirements. It was just horrible!

COMMENT

In a sense, the teaching style of Miss Wacker and Miss Chandler represents one successful adaptation to a stressful teaching environment, for their approach to teaching does enable them to cope with the day-to-day exigencies of the inner-city classroom. Beyond this tolerant stance, however, I feel that teachers who maintain this style of teaching do so at great cost to themselves and, of course, to their students. Such an approach to teaching, through ways that are both overt and covert, perpetuates the teacher-student battle that is common to inner-city high schools, and it forestalls the possibility that effective solutions will be found to the ongoing crises in these schools.

8

THE ALTRUISTS

I like the students here. If you tell
them to take their hats off, they'll
do it without so much—. They
might look at you—see who you
are. But they'll do it. And even
students whom I don't know or
don't have in classes seem to garner some kind of respect.

An Altruistic Female Du Sable
Teacher

Unlike their burned-out Du Sable colleagues, altruistic teachers prize their relationships with students. While they see as clearly as anyone the resistance most kids have to learning, Altruists are more able, and willing, to empathize with the troubled adolescent.

When confronted with a pupil aggressively acting out his emotional frustration, for example, such a teacher would tend not to react defensively or with hostility. Instead, he would bring the situation under control and then diffuse the student's anger by patiently listening to (and accepting the validity of) the student's perceptions of school life—much as an effective social worker might do.

The two case studies that follow illustrate well the humaneness and compassion of the altruistic teacher. It should be clear that these teachers are not sentimental bleeding hearts who, till the bitter end, claim to see the world through rose-colored glasses.

99

Instead, they are strong, mature, and well-integrated individuals—unafraid to show love in a hate-filled environment.

MRS. ELLIOTT

Mrs. Elliott is a middle-aged black English teacher who came to Du Sable 15 years ago. Prior to that, she taught at an elementary school in Alabama.

Unlike the Burnouts, she feels comfortable teaching at Du Sable. Though fully cognizant of conditions that exist within the school, she is not upset about them:

> The general chaos in the building does not bother me.
> I'm not frustrated by that. I clear my end of the hall
> and teach my class. So I don't worry about that.
> I really think the school as a whole should be a little
> more closely something or the other. We should be
> able to get things done, but we can't.

When she speaks of Du Sable students, Mrs. Elliott is positive and feels the quality of students is improving:

> Maybe next year we'll have a better group. Because
> it seems to me they are getting better. The atmo-
> sphere was really good at the beginning of the year,
> and students were just with it or something.

Even with former students, she maintains close, caring relationships:

> Now I get long distance calls from colleges where the
> kids have gone asking me to help them with this para-
> graph or explain this to them. "I remember we had
> this, but I forgot what you said." Just them calling
> back is good, especially after they hated me so much.
> I demanded a lot from them. I think I'm the winner
> after all.
> I have so many students like that who really come
> back. I'm part of the woodwork around, they say.
> It seems like every student who comes back seems
> to remember that Mrs. Elliott is here, and they
> come in and look on me, which is kind of nice.

During her 15 years at Du Sable, Mrs. Elliott has witnessed many changes in the student body. In response to these changes,

she has maintained an open attitude and a willingness to learn from
her students. As she told me:

> Your strategies change from time to time, and your
> problems change from time to time. Since the early
> sixties we had a different brand of student here. The
> late sixties we had a totally different brand of student
> here. That was the child who preached relevance.
> Give us blackness. Give us love.
> They were demanding things of us which really made me
> get out and look for this business of relevance and what
> we were asking for. So, I took suggestions from them.
> I'm willing for that. Whether I follow through on their
> suggestions or not, I let them think at least they're be-
> ing heard, and I really try.
> The main thing I try to do is allow them to tell me
> sometimes. I think my idea is to let the student help
> us plan for them. The required teachings can be done
> in so many different veins. I have just about come to
> the conclusion that students can help us a lot. An idea
> might be to let them tell us sometime—get us scouting
> around to find things and present it their way, if that
> gets the point across.
> I have learned to allow them to help us motivate them
> by asking them what they are interested in. "What do
> you want to do, and how do you want to do it?"

Unlike the Burnouts, her commitment to teaching as a profession is obviously genuine and springs from sources deep within.
"I'm very satisfied with teaching itself," she says. "I never wish
I hadn't gone into teaching. I remember my third grade teacher,
and then I wanted to be a teacher."

Mrs. Elliott's self-expressed educational philosophies were
quite evident when I observed her conduct a discussion of Francis
Bacon's essay "Of Love" with a group of senior students.

At the start of this class, she makes several announcements
regarding a field trip the class is to make on the next day to a
Chicago university.

The discussion of Bacon's "Of Love" begins when Mrs. Elliott
invites her 15 students to give their impressions of the selection.

"I didn't like it," a boy in the front unhesitatingly volunteers.

"I acknowledge your right not to like the work, Stanley, but
could you be a bit more specific and tell us just why you feel as you
do?" his teacher says, probing gently.

Stanley goes on to explain that he finds the author's ideas
about love far-fetched and unrealistic. Mrs. Elliott nods her head

empathically and asks occasional questions aimed at clarifying Stanley's position.

Following Stanley's explanation, several other students volunteer their, usually positive, impressions.

Next, Mrs. Elliott lectures briefly on how various notions of love are presented on the stage. All her students appear to pay attention; several spontaneously make their own comments or ask questions. At one point, the discussion is quite lively and humorous. Though I find this exchange between Mrs. Elliott and her students confusing and hard to follow, I know that everyone is involved and actively thinking about the discussion topic.

Mrs. Elliott now has a student read aloud from the essay. At appropriate points, she interjects comments or asks for a definition of a word from the text.

"Who are the 'stars' worth loving today?" she asks, referring to a passage just read.

"The Jackson Five, Bruce Lee," a boy in front proposes.

"Muhammed Ali and James Brown," shouts another boy from the back row.

The lesson continues to move along smoothly, alternating between close readings of the text and lively, often humorous, discussions aimed at making interpretations and drawing parallels with modern life. During these interactions, students pay attention or participate actively and express their opinions.

One barometer of student interest and involvement is evident when the dismissal bell rings and the discussion continues—with no loss of energy.

Mrs. Elliott's comments about these students and her relationship with them reveal the depth of her caring:

> Attendance is exceptional in that class. I very seldom have anyone absent. And they really try hard to do whatever is assigned them to do.
> At the beginning of the year they were afraid of me. I seem somehow to have a name as being a tyrant or something. But once they get in there and find I'm fair—. They always know what I'm expecting of them.
> At the beginning of the year, I make out a syllabus, not just for the office, but for them also. I give them a list of things that we plan to cover and everything that is required of them. Whenever I give the date, they usually have it ready.
> We get along very well. I don't have any discipline problems. And this class gets to class on time.

I think they are really concerned about themselves
and about how I think about them, because they are
constantly saying, "We're not your favorite class."
But I love them. I love them all. And I think they're
not frightened of me any more. I think they really
seriously want to learn, and I think they realize how
they have been cheated to an extent as far as knowledge or as far as information—through the years.
They really see, it seems for the first time, how really little they know—or how much they have not learned
and should have learned.
I don't really pat them on the back too much, but un-
derneath I'm really proud of them, and I think they
feel this. They have a sense of something—communication that is not verbal.

MISS CUMMINGS

Miss Cummings is a young white English teacher who has been
at Du Sable for one year. Two years before she came to Du Sable
she taught at a high school in Australia. Her student teaching was
done at a racially-mixed school on Chicago's North Side.

Like her altruistic colleagues, Miss Cummings' teaching
style is based on humane, open interpersonal relationships with
students.

When she first came to Du Sable, Miss Cummings experienced
little stress. The anxiety she did feel was related to the school's
large size—a factor that she felt mitigated against closeness among
staff.

I think the first thing that really hit me was the fact
that I had come from a smaller school where we all
had one staff room. We all had the same lunch, that
kind of thing. It was kind of a close thing. We did a
lot of sharing. If somebody had an idea and it sounded
good, we'd do it. Here, it was like there were so
many people. I really didn't feel it was as open—like
the other school in Australia.

That she experienced no traumatic period of adjustment may
have been related to her self-actualizing tendencies and the self-
confidence she developed in her overseas teaching assignment. As
she told me:

I think having taught two years helped my confidence.
As far as I was concerned, I was here to teach, and I
figured I could just about handle anything that would
come up.
I had to teach subjects I was never prepared to teach
when I was overseas. I had to teach Australian history which I knew nothing about. And so I just found
that I could depend on myself to do it, and I think that
helps. Once I knew I could do it in this situation, I
said, "Well, I can handle that, maybe I can try something else." The fact that it was a city school and a
black neighborhood didn't bother me.

Unlike the Burnouts, Miss Cummings feels that Du Sable kids
are not to be blamed for conditions at the school; instead, teachers
themselves are responsible for improving conditions:

To blame it on the kids—you can't. For one thing,
they don't know what they're supposed to do. It's up
to you to train them, to mold them into what students
are supposed to be like.
The kids themselves want to see learning, and I feel
that's half my battle. The other half I have to do is
simply make it important to them. I think a lot of
teachers don't have that situation; that's probably why
they get frustrated.

The strategy she has developed to cope with the needs of her
students shows the emphasis she places on personal relationships
between herself and students:

If students are willing to respond when asked or if
they're responding voluntarily, then I think it is important for me to listen to what they're saying, to
make sure the other people are listening. I always
tell them, "Never ask a question unless you have
some idea of the answer. I ask questions even though
I might know the answer because I want to hear what
your answer is." I think that's important for them,
'cause I think if they felt no one was listening, then
why should they bother answering? "She's made up
her mind, she knows exactly what it's all about. So
why's she asking us, she knows it?" You let them
know you're not infallible and you don't expect them
to be either.

Her commitment to teaching as a profession is strong and it represents a significant part of her identity. However, she admits that her inability to measure the effect of her teaching on students is one unsatisfying aspect of teaching:

> A teacher's next to <u>God</u>. I've always thought it was.
> I mean I wanted to do it, so I became a teacher. May-
> be if things hadn't worked out as smoothly as they
> turned out, I would have gone into something else. But
> I'm glad I went, I'm glad I gave it a try. There's some-
> thing about education that's so interesting—.
> It seems like maybe I am missing something, though.
> Maybe there's more to it than just marking papers and
> entertaining in front of the classroom. I worry about
> whether learning is going on, and how do you mark
> that? How do you really know? I guess growth is sat-
> isfying; you want growth. But it's just that sometimes
> it can be unsatisfying in that you're never really sure
> where you're standing.

I had the opportunity to observe Miss Cummings lead a discussion of <u>Macbeth</u> with a group of above-average juniors. As her
students enter the classroom this period, Miss Cummings chats in-
formally and comfortably with several of her pupils.

"Jefferson, I like that shirt you're wearing," she says to a
tall handsome boy, noticeably aglow in his silky flowered shirt with
a crisp, high collar.

"Man, Jefferson sure is clean today, ain't he?" chortles another student as he vaults over his desk and lithely drops into his
seat.

Miss Cummings' transition from this casual interaction to the
actual start of her discussion is smooth and effortless. She and her
14 students are now seated in a circle.

"Before we continue our reading of the play today," she begins, "let's just quickly review the three terms that we use in talking about any work of literature. What are they?"

Clearly eager to please their teacher, four students respond
almost in unison. "Character, setting, and plot."

"O.K. Let's take the characters first. Who are the important ones we've met? And how would you describe them?"

She pauses briefly while her students think.

"Sherman, can you give us a character?"

"Macbeth. He's an army general."

"Whose army is he in?"

"Duncan's army, I think," answers Sherman. "He's the king
of Scotland."

"Right. Very good, Sherman."

Enthusiastically, though politely, students continue to give brief descriptions of key characters in the play.

Now Miss Cummings turns to the play's setting. "Where and when does the play take place?"

"Scotland in 1606," offers Reggie, a small boy sitting just to the left of his teacher. His timorous voice suggests that he is uncertain about his answer.

"Well, you got the location right, Reggie. The play does take place in Scotland, but it was written in 1606."

"I think it's supposed to take place around the ten-hundreds," offers another student, a tall willowy girl with pigtails.

"Very good, Shelly. The play actually begins in 1040 and ends in 1057. Now, who can summarize very, very briefly the plot up through Act Three?"

Sherman unhesitatingly volunteers and gives a credible, easy-to-follow summary of the first three acts.

"O.K.," says Miss Cummings. "Now Act Four takes us all to the witches' haunt. It's thundering outside." In a progressively softer, wavering voice, she continues to set the mood. "Something awful is about to happen."

The reading commences, with all students paying attention to what is obviously difficult material for them. As her students read the witches' parts, Miss Cummings prods them enthusiastically and good-naturedly.

"Come on, witches, you're putting on a spell. Make it sound like one."

> Round about the cauldron go:
> In the poisoned entrails throw.
> Toad, that under cold stone
> Days and nights has thirty-one
> Swelt' red venom sleeping got
> Boil thou first i' th' charmed pot.

With the next part, Miss Cummings enjoins all her students to participate.

> Double, double toil and trouble;
> Fire burn and cauldron bubble.

Throughout the lesson, Miss Cummings pauses frequently to clarify the meaning of selected passages. The atmosphere in the group is relaxed and informal, and her voice is unhurried and conversational. She creates a true sense of group involvement and

cooperation by frequent references to "we" and "us"—and by her
ability to listen very carefully to the self-expressed opinions of
students.

After the class is over and the students have left, Miss Cummings comments proudly on their performance. Here, she shows
an enthusiasm for teaching and an acceptance of students that she
no doubt communicates daily to her classes.

> They are a really beautiful class. They'd be the class
> I'd be most proud of. You could have sat in on any
> class, but they're just the best. They're quiet; they
> want to learn—they may not always understand what is
> going on. We do a lot of explanations, "What did this
> guy really say—."
> As bright as I think they are, their reading scores don't
> measure up to that brightness. They do the work.
> They're willing to try and give things a go. I just feel
> that there's some accomplishment in that class, that
> there is really some learning going on.

Her further comments suggest that all her students respond
positively to her warmth, her student centeredness, and her authentic desire to help students learn:

> I've just found my classes nice to teach, and therefore
> that really makes you want to come in every day and
> teach. Teach—not yell and throw books around and
> play those silly games they end up playing. "You stole
> my pencil." "He took my book." "He's got my ruler."

One of the most revealing commentaries on a teacher's effectiveness are the comments students make about that teacher. And
in this regard, three of Miss Cummings' students with whom I
chatted stressed how their teacher makes them feel comfortable
while in class.

The first, a small quiet boy who admitted to struggling to
maintain passing grades, put it this way:

> I feel that this teacher has helped me a lot. She is
> not as impersonal as some of the teachers in our
> school, and she makes learning very enjoyable.

Another student, a thin hyperactive girl with an irritatingly
loud voice—whom I imagined capable of becoming involved in a
battle royal with just about any teacher—said:

I feel very relaxed in class. She doesn't front you off
or get smart with you like other teachers often do with
you. She tries to help you with your problems if
there's some reason why you can't make it on time.

The third, an attractive girl with a winsome smile and a pleas-
ing manner, said:

She is a really nice and down-to-earth type person, and
I like her a lot. She is my favorite teacher this year
and is very nice to talk to. She is also very warm, understanding, and considerate towards her students. I
like her method of teaching very much. I also have to
say I learn a lot out of her class the short time I've
been there.

COMMENT

The style of teaching modeled by Mrs. Elliott and Miss Cummings is one that promotes positive teacher–student relationships
and the growth (both academic and emotional) of students. Yet such
a style is not easily mastered. To be an altruistic teacher in a setting like Du Sable—to help students achieve healthier attitudes toward themselves and toward learning—requires strength of character and a measure of daring. One must dare to establish genuine
relationships with students whose culture conflicts with one's own.
For without such relationships, teacher and students easily find
themselves adversaries—locked into an endless battle in which all
that is learned is how to defeat, perhaps even destroy, the other.

9

THE TECHNICIANS

I'm here to teach certain material.
The book's supposed to be covered
in 40 weeks, and I go through it.
I think if you have a teacher in the
classroom that knows what he's
doing, you can get it across. The
students are really going to respond fairly well.

A Technician at Du Sable

To be a technician implies that one is an expert in a specific
technical process—a process that calls for the employment of certain skills for the purpose of achieving a predetermined outcome.
Should unforeseen problems arise in pursuit of this outcome, the
technician has within his repertoire of competencies those problem-
solving skills that will eventually lead to successful completion of
the task.

I knew several teachers at Du Sable whom I would say had a
"technical" approach to their work. Unlike their burned-out colleagues who are anxious over their perceived lack of success at
teaching, Technicians expect their students to be successful. Toward this end, they know just how much their students learn, or fail
to learn, in their classes. And in instances of the latter, they usually know what to do about it. They use a wide variety of materials
and activities that they have worked out and tested in previous
classes.

109

Technicians not only feel confident about their ability to meet the challenges of ghetto teaching; they also report high levels of job satisfaction. The Technicians I interviewed and observed have, I feel, a realistic picture of conditions within the school. Yet this reality appears not to upset them; rather, it provides them an opportunity to demonstrate their competence in a difficult situation.

In the two case studies that follow, the Technician's strong task orientation is evident. In short, each of these teachers knows the job that needs to be done, and they know how to go about doing it.

MR. LAZARUS

Mr. Lazarus is a white male in his late fifties who has taught French at Du Sable for two years now. In appearance and background, he struck me initially as out of place in a school such as Du Sable. The distinguished, white-haired teacher has a professorial air about him that increases upon hearing him refer in a heavy accent to his 11 years of teaching in European schools or, rather humbly, to his additional knowledge of Latin, Greek, Sanskrit, and Russian.

Mr. Lazarus' personality and the influence it has on his teaching style is perhaps best revealed through a quote from Horace that he told me summarizes his philosophy of life: Nil sine magno labore vita dedit mortalibus. (Fate has willed to man nothing but hard work and toil.) To that end, Mr. Lazarus feels that students must learn to strive and work hard in order to better their lives.

Coming as he did from European schools, it is not surprising that he experienced some anxiety in adjusting to a school such as Du Sable. However, through discipline and hard work he was able to make a satisfactory adjustment. The biggest change he had to make, as he reports in the following, was to modify his expectations of students:

> The difference is great (i.e. between Du Sable and
> European schools). Also, I think there were different
> times, different era, when I did teach in Europe. Dif-
> ferent social environment. Maybe different background
> of the students also. It was quite an adjustment needed
> to work over here. I had to change some of my tech-
> niques I used in Europe.
> I did face some problems, some individual students. I
> was trying to apply same methods I used in Europe, like
> friendly persuasion first and then coming in contact with
> the parents, and then in some difficult cases I had to go

for help at the school management, the assistant principal for discipline problems.
The one thing which was the most different was that I had not to demand so much. The level of the demand, of the information which I required from the students had to be diminished greatly. Changed greatly. Now I came to the conclusion that I can't expect as much from the students in the Chicago area as I used to get out of those in Europe. I think this is one of those basic things I had to realize, then I adapt myself to the new reality—adjust myself to the new reality, cutting down the demands for information.

Through his efforts to adjust, Mr. Lazarus was able to minimize greatly the anxiety he felt in his new teaching environment. And of the present he says:

As far as myself is concerned, I feel at home at Du Sable. I feel at home as far as my colleagues are concerned and the students. I feel I am doing something useful.

Not only does Mr. Lazarus have positive feelings toward Du Sable students, but he reveals considerable understanding of the forces that can influence the behavior of disruptive students:

I have confidence in my students, and I feel that the students have confidence in me.
I have, I don't know why, a certain kind of idealistic view toward the young generation. There is good material, only bad examples—either at home or outside the home in the society—which spoil some young individuals.
Now, those students are problem students in my opinion, and they just break down the progress of others. But I feel this is the only solution a society can afford today, putting them in the school, in the same classes, not forming separate classes of those retarded students, putting them in the same class with the risk of hurting better students. I feel that this is the way. It depends on what angle you look at it from. Looking from the human angle, putting them in a specific class, like in one group, would be like hurting their feelings, that they belong to a lower group of the society.

In describing the strategies he has developed to cope with Du Sable students, Mr. Lazarus shows considerable insight into the educative process. Also, he makes clear how he, like other Technicians, relies upon a specific set of procedures that minimizes disruptive behavior and maximizes learning:

> Each individual teacher, in my opinion, trains, if this is the right concept to be used, or teaches the students to behave, to adjust to one's methods, techniques, procedures, and requirements. He then induces the student into the general or common atmosphere in that classroom society.
>
> Now as far as the procedures and the techniques of the approach: I noticed that these students like to work more under guidance, under direction than those in Europe. Those were more independent, maybe with that sense of independence already coming from the family. These require more guidance, more direction.
>
> I give much more writing, over here, copying and then explaining one item by another, just keeping their attention. Their span of attention requires activity, otherwise they get distracted. They don't like to read from the book so much as the European students did, but if you guide them step by step, they are busy all period and they do my work. Some students are motivated, they try very hard. Some lack of ability; still they work hard.

The classroom behavior of Mr. Lazarus represents a significant departure from the behavior of either the Burnouts or the Altruists. My observations of Mr. Lazarus' combined French II and III class, for example, revealed that he talked over 80 percent of the time (according to Flanders Interaction Analysis Categories) and the students spoke only 5 percent of the time. Moreover, almost 80 percent of his talk consisted of giving directions—an indication that his approach to teaching is to structure very highly the learning environment of students.

Prior to the start of this particular period, Mr. Lazarus has covered the entire front and side blackboards with review sentences in French. Several stacks of dittoed worksheets are spread out on the teacher's desk. These are given to students as they enter the room.

Several students enter talking loudly and fooling with one another. One boy, short and roly-poly, swoops into the room singing and dancing. His friend, a tall, thin basketball type, follows him eating a sandwich.

"My, my. This sure do taste good," the friend exclaims. He smacks his lips loudly while passing the sandwich temptingly close to the short boy's nostrils.

"Gimmie bite, chump," says the other boy as he makes a half-hearted swipe at the sandwich. The tall boy holds the food aloft in his right hand and with his left pushes his friend away.

"Hey, hold on, baby. Can't just nobody eat this here sandwich! This ain't no ordinary quarter-pounder—no pale-faced cracker food. This here is a genuine, deluxe barbecue chicken sandwich made by my auntie. Ya dig?"

In the meantime, Mr. Lazarus is a blur of activity. Very rapidly, he moves back and forth handing out dittoes and occasionally assigning a student to a particular seat. He also takes attendance and gives some students make-up work.

The noise level and confusion in the room is still considerable as Mr. Lazarus himself begins to read the sentences on the board. He goes through the sentences quickly, all the while instructing his students to pay attention and to follow mentally his translations.

" 'The husband and wife walked down the boulevard.' Notice the use of the past tense.

"Jessie, pay attention. Attend to the board here. Deborah, we are working up here. 'I am unable to go to the store with you.' "

Following the fast-paced review of the board work, Mr. Lazarus directs his students to begin working on their dittoed sheets. This command is met with a considerable outcry of student resistance.

"Why do you want us to do that, man?" asks one student, a scowling, narrow-eyed boy in the front row.

"What we got to do?" blurts out another student.

Mr. Lazarus appears to handle these and other student complaints largely by persevering and pressing on with his instructions until eventually everyone understands what to do. He does not respond directly to any of the challenging remarks made by students. His approach seems to work, for eventually all students are busy working on the assignment.

"Translate into English the sentences in section one. There are eight of them. Write directly on the worksheet. Do not use your own paper.

"Look at sentence number one, everybody. Recall the examples we worked on yesterday. Translate these in just the same manner. Remember how the past tense is formed. I will take off if you use the wrong tense. So work carefully."

For the remainder of the period, Mr. Lazarus paces rapidly back and forth across the front of the room as he "talks through" the four-page exercise. Nearly all his statements are in the form of directions for students to follow.

Every two minutes or so he asks students if they have any questions about the work. When a student does have a question, which occurred frequently during this period, Mr. Lazarus walks over to the student and, before answering, repeats the question for all to hear.

In spite of their initial reluctance to work, students all seem involved now and intent on finishing their assignment. Occasionally, one student asks another a question related to the task at hand. Unlike the beginning of the period, there are now no complaints about Mr. Lazarus' teaching methods.

At the sound of the dismissal bell, students hand their papers to their teacher who is stationed at the door. Following my observation, I am left with the impression that Mr. Lazarus, true to his philosophy of "hard work and toil," has indeed been very active during the period and has expended a great deal of energy helping his students learn.

Of this class, Mr. Lazarus says simply that they have been "trained" to meet his demands:

> I do work with those students for the second year.
> They are trained by me already, and they have tried
> to adjust to my demands, my requirements. And we
> get along.
> Also I stress, emphasize specifically, that I require
> attendance if they want to pass. And also I require at-
> tention in the class. Not killing the time, not looking
> for a social hour, but for working—coming to work.
> It takes time probably, and it takes patience until the
> teacher achieves that level at which he feels at home
> in the classroom and feels he can do the job. Be a
> responsible, useful teacher.

Turning to teaching in general, Mr. Lazarus reveals a solid commitment to the profession. Teaching now gives his life a sense of meaning and fulfillment he was unable to find in other pursuits:

> I feel that I get a satisfaction. I feel that I am a useful
> member of the society. I feel this is the field in which
> I could accomplish—I could contribute more to the
> society than in any other field. In industry I felt al-
> ways like outsider. I did work hard there. I was

always on the job cutting steel at Chicago Rivet and
Machine company, but there was no inner satisfaction,
just working for living. Over here I am working for my
living, earning my living, but also I feel I am doing a
job which is good to the American society.

MR. WATSON

Mr. Watson is a young white male mathematics teacher who
has been at Du Sable for six years. Prior to coming to Du Sable,
he spent a half-year at an all-black vocational high school on Chicago's West Side and a year as an eighth grade teacher at a school
in a changing neighborhood on the South Side.
When he first came to Du Sable, Mr. Watson, like all of his
colleagues, underwent a period of adjustment until he was able to
reduce greatly the anxiety he felt:

I think, at least for me, the first year was the rough-
est. But I think in general that's true for any teacher,
'cause students have to get to know your face and name
before they identify you with the school; otherwise,
you're an outsider. The treatment you get is rougher
than it would be otherwise. The years have steadily
improved since then. That was the worst year I spent
at Du Sable.

He also comments on how he has been able to maintain his commitment to do the best he can in a difficult situation, making clear his
task orientation and his desire to do a good job:

I don't think I've lost, say, the spirit or the zeal to go
out and try to teach the students, which I think a lot
of teachers have lost after maybe five or six years.
I don't think I've lost that. And, like I said before, I
think I'm doing a better job because I'm more experienced at it now. I can get through better.
When you look around, you see teachers that have
really lost the desire to teach. There's a lot of
burned-out teachers. There's teachers don't do anything around this school except read newspapers, do
crossword puzzles. Look around, you'll see the ones
doing crossword puzzles eight hours a day.
It's almost like everything I've ever done. I just took
pride in doing it well. If I do something, I want to do

it well. And the only way to teach well is, if you got a
desire to do it, you come prepared, go into the classroom, do a good job. That's what I do.

Mr. Watson also credits his success at Du Sable to his ability to
adapt to new situations:

> I think a lot of the teaching around here is being able to
> fit in with the students, at least being acceptable to
> them. A lot of it is learned. I've always been pretty
> good at adapting. I can just pretty well adapt to wher-
> ever I'm at. There's a lot to learn in a school like
> this.
> Some teachers won't learn to adapt at all. They don't
> learn things from the school. They don't adapt.

In his perceptions of students, Mr. Watson is realistic,
though he does not condemn students as do the Burnouts:

> These kids will never be perfect. You give them a
> hundred first grade problems and they won't get
> them all perfect. It's just a matter of concentration
> or something that they lack. I call it educational
> maturity. I don't think they have it.
> Like we give our final exams—and problems you know
> they can do, they have no concept of how to attack them.
> Problems they did during the year.
> The way I think about it is, you wouldn't take a second
> grader and give him a final exam on what he had in
> second grade, 'cause he just doesn't have the educa-
> tional maturity to put all that together at one time.
> And I think our students are pretty much the same.
> They haven't developed the educational maturity to
> take a final exam. They're not the level a second
> grader is, but they're not on the level of the high
> school students in the suburbs either.

As is characteristic of the Technicians, Mr. Watson focuses
his attention on getting students to master his course material
rather than on developing close relationships with them. And,
whatever the academic past of his students might be, he is confident that they will learn in his classes:

> I think the students have gotten more out of my courses
> each succeeding year. That's the main purpose of it,
> I guess, is what they get out of the course.

I observed Mr. Watson teach a basic mathematics class during ninth period, the last period of the day. As students enter the classroom, Mr. Watson returns homework assignments from the previous day. With surprisingly little confusion, and a virtual absence of horseplay, students each take a calculator from a cardboard box on their teacher's desk and then sit down.

"Do you got my paper from yesterday, Mr. Watson?" a boy asks immediately upon entering the room.

"You betcha, Julius," his teacher says with animation. "Keep it up. Keep it up." He hands the paper over to a grinning Julius.

Mr. Watson's 15 students are all seated now—pencil, paper, and calculators at ready. Without instruction, they direct their attention to their teacher who sits on the edge of his desk at the front of the room.

"Let's begin today with a quick review of what we've already learned about using calculators.

"Remember, your calculator only gives the right answer if you push the correct keys in the correct order. Also, you should have some idea of the size of the answer. This will help you spot errors. What do we call this?"

"Estimation! Estimation!" a boy in front yells immediately, as though leading a football cheer.

"Righto, Sammie. Very good. We need to estimate the answer before using the calculator. To estimate the answer, round off each number in the problem so that you have only one digit that is not zero."

Mr. Watson moves to the blackboard and quickly writes several three-, four-, and five-digit numbers. He then goes through the numbers one by one as students, with great excitement, tell him what the rounded numbers would be.

Next, he writes four five-digit multiplication problems on the board. He good-naturedly restrains his students from immediately entering the problems into their calculators.

"Wait. Wait. Hold up there," he says, waving his arms in exaggerated alarm. "First, we need to estimate for the answer, then you whiz kids can go for the answers."

He manages to get most of his kids to work at solving the problems through estimation, though a few students—as evidenced by their Cheshire cat grins—have obviously already solved the problems by calculator.

After students have estimated their answers and compared them to the calculator-derived answers, their teacher turns to the problem of using calculators with fractions. All students watch as Mr. Watson writes 12 5/6 and 7/8 on the board.

"You can't key numbers like 12 5/6 and 7/8 on most calculators. So what do we do?"

A girl in back of the room, just in front of a small bookcase
filled with a few math textbooks and stacks and stacks of dog-eared
dittoed worksheets, blurts out, "You change 'em to decimals."

"Excellent, Ruby. Exactly. We need to change the fractions
to decimals, and we do it like this."

He holds a calculator aloft, keyboard facing his students, and
shows his class how 12 5/6 is changed to 12.833.

"Now let's find out how to add a percent. Suppose you buy a
pair of jeans for $14.50. The sales tax is 5 percent. How much do
you pay?"

"We gettin' these jeans at Smokey Joe's?" a boy near the window quips. Several of his fellow students giggle.

"I don't know, Marvin. Do they have good prices?"

"Man, that place is a rip-off," says another boy.

"No it ain't," Marvin shoots back.

"Where is Smokey Joe's?" asks Mr. Watson, apparently
seriously interested. "I never heard of it."

"Downtown on State Street. Across from Goldblatts and all
them pawn shops," says Marvin.

"Well, then, let's say we're getting these jeans at Smokey
Joe's. On sale for $14.50 plus 5 percent tax," says Mr. Watson,
calmly and skillfully getting his class back on task. "There are
two ways to solve this problem. One has two steps, and the other
has one step."

"I got it. I got it," exclaims a girl up front. "They'd cost
$15.23?" Her voice rises as though asking a question.

"Are you asking me or telling me?" her teacher asks.

"I'm telling you—they'd cost $15.23," she says, slightly
miffed at having to repeat her answer.

"Good, Annie. Now tell us how you got that. Did you use the
one-step or the two-step method?"

"I think I used—uh—two steps. I got 5 percent of $14.50, and
then I added that to $14.50."

"That's right. Annie used two steps. Now, can anyone solve
this problem in just one step?" With this challenge, Mr. Watson's
students are quiet. Several stare at the walls or ceiling as they
search within for the correct procedure.

Suddenly a student, a heavyset girl who has heretofore been
quiet, gasps, "I got it!" She bends over her tiny calculator and
painstakingly enters a couple of numbers. "I got it," she exclaims
again.

"O.K., Patrice, how did you do it?"

"You multiply 14.50 by 1.05."

"Exactly," the teacher says, a broad smile crossing his face. "Multiply by 1.05 and you add 5 percent to the price. And you only have to use one step."

Mr. Watson takes his students through two more story problems—one involving the purchase of a stereo; the other a week's worth of groceries.

Mr. Watson then passes out a three-paged dittoed handout titled "Check Your Calculator Skills."

"Spend the rest of the period working on these problems. Raise your hand if you have any questions, and I'll come around to help you. I'll take up your papers at the end of class."

For the remainder of the period, students are busily, and quietly, at work on their assignment. Not even the sounds of kids playing ball two stories directly below on the street distracts them.

Mr. Watson spends the rest of the period circulating about the room, answering students' questions and monitoring their progress.

At 2:46, the dismissal bell rings. Just before he dismisses class—students do not run out of Mr. Watson's class at the first sound of the bell—students are given a homework assignment in the text and reminded about a forthcoming test.

During our postobservation interview, Mr. Watson commented on his students' high level of motivation and on how his relationship with the class had evolved during the year:

> Things have gone fairly well with this class. There are only 21 students on my roster in this class. Or twenty some—a couple of them never come—they just never come. But the rest of them really—for the most part—have tried fairly hard and done pretty well. I usually start out a lot tighter with discipline at the beginning of the year and then sort of loosen up as it goes along. So that by this time of the year I may joke with the class a little bit. Whereas, in the first of the year I don't joke with them too much.

COMMENT

We have now looked at three kinds of teachers—Burnouts, Altruists, and Technicians—and how they respond to environmental stress. Of these three, the style of teaching employed by the Technicians (Mr. Lazarus and Mr. Watson, for example) is perhaps the one most often associated with "good" teaching. If we consider (during this era of the back-to-basics movement and a backlash to the permissiveness of the 1960s and 1970s) what ends are sought as a result of the teaching-learning process, the predominant zeitgeist seems to be that the school's major purpose is to transmit knowledge and skills—and only incidentally to enhance the student's self-image. Toward this end, the Technicians have developed the most effective strategy—a strategy that emphasizes productivity, achievement, and getting the job done.

Yet, I think a case can be made for a model of teaching that employs, when appropriate, the approaches of both the Altruist and the Technician. I believe that inner-city students do learn best in highly structured classroom settings where their step-by-step progress is monitored by strong authority figures. However, many ghetto students are so emotionally blocked by hate, fear, and constant anxiety that they need teachers sensitive enough (and strong enough) to help them work through their feelings before they can function in a classroom that is exclusively academic and achievement oriented. In the following chapter, then, I describe the personal model of teaching that I developed to provide my students with some of the educative experiences they needed and to provide myself with the means to go beyond the burnout which I knew, after four years at the school, was beginning to take over my life.

10

BEYOND BURNOUT:
A PERSONAL MODEL OF
TEACHING FOR THE GHETTO

There's not a damn thing you can
do except try to stay alive when
you walk into that classroom.
You do that by being tough as nails
and hoping no one calls your bluff.
These kids come from a tough environment. They respect tough
people. If you're not tough then
you'd better forget about teaching
here, because these kids will turn
your classroom into a living hell.
. . . I'm just giving you my philosophy on teaching in the ghetto.
Take it or leave it.

Alan Jones, Students ! Do Not
Push Your Teacher Down the
Stairs on Friday

As I coped intuitively with Du Sable conditions over the years,
I found that my own personal model of teaching was beginning to
emerge. My psychotherapy revealed to me weekly how my life experiences had shaped my self-concept and how this image of myself
could either promote or hinder my own learning and growth. It was
easy for me to see, then, that many of my students also wrestled
with distorted self-images and that this all-consuming battle often
left little motivation and energy to learn. I also came to feel that

beneath students' aggressive acting out was a plea to be understood—and to be loved.

As a result, I underwent a transformation in my approach to teaching. Gradually I became less concerned with the content of English per se and more concerned with helping my students get beyond their emotional blocks so that they could learn how to learn. My primary goal while teaching came to be the creation of a group climate in which listening, sharing, and thinking would occur. I would listen to my students; they would listen to me and to each other; and as much as possible, we would think together on commonly perceived tasks or problems. I measured the success of my classes by whether or not a meaningful student-teacher dialogue had occurred. Often this dialogue amounted to a cultural trade off—my students had a lot that they were able to teach me, and I, of course, had a lot that I was able to teach them.

With each new group of students, I assumed that this dialogue would be achieved only through a gradual process. Through mutual interaction and the daily give-and-take of the classroom, something important would happen for all involved. What usually emerged was a shared group awareness or consciousness, a sense of "us." Without this feeling of cohesiveness, I found, the group's productivity would be low. Little that was meaningful would take place, and improved attitudes toward the self and toward learning would be unlikely.

I was also concerned with the quality of this educative dialogue; my students needed to be stimulated and challenged. Thus, I would often deliberately emphasize abstract, hard to grasp subjects such as the value of literature, the nature of art, the worth of education rather than the memorization of facts followed by routine question-and-answer periods.

In addition to the influence my psychotherapy had on my teaching style, I was guided (and at times sustained spiritually) by the models of teaching proposed by three well-known educators. Herb Thelen, through his writing and through my lengthy visits with him at the University of Chicago, continued to influence the way in which I tried to promote personal and group inquiry in my classes. In the works of Carl Rogers I found confirmation for my emerging style in the classroom—a style that tried to facilitate the growth and becoming of whole persons. Lastly, William Glasser's Classroom Meeting Model gave my students and me a vehicle for discussing reasonably the many problems that might arise in class—problems with attendance, acting out in class, cheating, irrelevant texts, and so on.

The model of teaching that follows does not provide a step-by-step sequence for the teacher to follow; it provides, instead, several rules of thumb that can guide the teacher as he makes decisions regarding his own teaching behavior and the sort of instructional environment he wishes to create. This strategy suggests for the teacher both a way of "being" in the classroom and a framework through which to interpret the experience of teaching in the ghetto. It is not a model of teaching for the timid or fainthearted; it requires that the teacher experience the risk of establishing genuine relationships with students whose culture conflicts with his own and of becoming involved in the education of whole persons.

FOUR VARIABLES IN CLASSROOM METHOD

Teachers are the single most important factor in determining the group's cohesiveness and its ability to direct its energies to learning. Teachers, more than anyone else, have the greatest power to manipulate the classroom environment. While they cannot control the effects of poverty and racism, there are four vital areas in the classroom that they can control. (1) In spite of hefty board of education curriculum guides, teachers can determine much of the content of their classes and the relevance of the curriculum. (2) Teachers' attitudes toward students are important factors in determining the emotional climate of a group. The amount of support teachers give students enhances or limits learning. (3) A great many methodological choices are open to them: teachers decide to emphasize discussion and not lecture, they make this requirement and not that, they delegate responsibility to one class and not to another. (4) Teachers can be unaware of the true nature of their classes or they can be guided by an understanding of group dynamics to develop an awareness of how a class perceives itself.

Toward a Meaningful Curriculum

Of the four classroom variables that any teacher can manipulate, subject matter is particularly important to the ghetto teacher. Without material that students consider relevant, meaningful, and involving, even the most knowledgeable teacher will fail.

In the curriculum for ghetto schools, it is common for teachers to set goals for their students in terms of improving certain skills, such as raising abysmally low reading scores and filling in gaps in basic knowledge. These deficiencies are real and the larger society requires certain competencies for success, but inner-city teachers must realize the necessity of first engaging students in terms of their own needs and experiences and then moving on to raise their achievement levels. What this means for the teacher is that he accept his students, "their language, their dress, and their values as a point of departure for disciplined exploration, to be understood not as a trick for luring them into the middle class, but as a way of helping them to explore the meaning of their own lives" (Friedenburg 1964, p. 33). The inner-city school's failure to educate adequately is due in part to the teacher's unwillingness, or inability, to relate to his students. Although we will continue to see during the 1980s a proliferation of black-oriented materials such as black literature of high interest and low vocabulary, attractively presented reading programs, reworkings of American and world history to emphasize black achievements, various multimedia units on drugs, prejudice, art, communication, and jobs, none will work if the gap between teacher and students remains or widens.

In spite of genuine attempts to meet students on their own ground to present meaningful material, an inner-city teacher may fail to reach a considerable portion of his students. The present norms for teacher behavior in a ghetto school are similar to those in any other school, and a teacher cannot go too far in trying to reach certain students. Most likely he will fail with some and have limited to moderate success with others. In all probability, the "gangbanger" whom we met in Chapter 3 learns nothing except perhaps that he is a social misfit. A student who is disruptive or nonconforming gets very little out of class; most of the work he does is very perfunctory. A withdrawn student never seems to get involved with his education in spite of the hours spent sitting in class. In the main, the teacher's efforts will be directed to those students who are conforming and to those who vary from day to day. If these students are reached, others with different orientations toward school might become interested.

What did Du Sable students find interesting and meaningful? While I discovered nothing to guarantee success, I did find students interested in racism and prejudice, the oppression and unfair treatment of any group, and the philosophy and attitudes of white, middle-class America. Many of my colleagues chose to ignore these issues, content to say that such concerns were not in the curriculum and that they were not social workers or psychologists. (I did, incidentally, discover that ghetto teachers actually have more freedom in regard to selecting curriculum than teachers in other schools; administrative pressures to adhere to a standardized curriculum are not too great as long as the teacher indicates he can cope with the situation, and parental pressures are almost nonexistent.) Teachers who had such feelings were probably better off ignoring these issues. But I did find it helpful to relate the content of English to these concerns or to my students' perceptions of life. I could present material of surprising difficulty to my students if

I related it to where they were at the moment. I came to disagree
with many of my fellow teachers who felt that their main job was to
bring material down to the students' level. More precisely, I felt
the art of teaching involved trying to place subject matter within
the students' collective frame of reference.

To find out how my students were responding to material, to
see if we were thinking along the same lines, I usually began our
discussions by asking an open-ended question that seemed appropriate in terms of my understanding of their experiences. Then, if I
felt we could profit by further exploration of the material, I would
"teach" them what I knew about it.

I also found it helpful to deal openly and directly with the way
students saw and responded to the content of my classes. If I could
accept the validity of their negative responses, my students often
tried to teach me what they understood about the material or expressed an interest in learning in spite of their initial feelings.

I recall, for example, a class in which we watched a sound
filmstrip on a black symphony conductor, Dean Dixon. I found
Dixon's comments on his life interesting and the musical passages
moving. My class apparently did not. Three students talked in low
voices, two more had their heads on their desks. When the filmstrip was over, the room was silent; to speak seemed a violation of
the room's quiet.

"Don't you think classical music is kind of sissy?" I began.

A few hands shot up. "No. No. It's just different. You're
stereotyping."

"How is it different?"

"It's harder to listen to."

"It's more complex. It's got more parts in it."

A lively discussion on classical music followed and we were
able to draw parallels to some poetry we had read.

In another class we had just read Dostoevski's The Thief
aloud, and I was doubtful my students could relate to the story.

"How many of you have had something stolen?" I asked.
About half the class immediately raised their hands.

"My coat."

"My radio got ripped off."

"Now, think about what Dostoevski says. How can this guy
who had a pair of pants stolen, say that an honest thief stole them?
Do you think there is such a thing as an honest thief?" Here, I was
able to relate the story to my students' experiences before we began our discussion.

I was acutely aware that my students were interested in me
as a member of white society. This interest, I found, could be
turned to educational advantage if I showed that I was as interested

in learning about my students as they were in learning about me. In one class, for example, we had been discussing militant black poets when the importance of different groups empathizing with each other was introduced.

A student asked me, "What's in the minds of these white racists who don't want blacks bused to their schools?"

I thought for a moment. "Well, they say they're worried about overcrowding in the schools. But I think they're also worried about blacks moving into their neighborhoods."

"Do you know any prejudiced people like them?" he asked. The room was silent; everyone was interested.

"Some."

"Well, since we don't get a chance to talk with them, you'll be our key. Maybe you can find out what's on their minds."

My students' conventional ideas about education included an almost universal desire to "get an education." Many of them saw this as their hope for a better future.

Because of this desire, I would, from time to time in my classes, reflect on our progress as a group engaged in getting an education: What did it really mean to be educated? How did we know when we were getting it? What was left after we returned books, finished taking tests, and discarded old papers?

I also had students on occasion fill out various end-of-class evaluations that I tabulated and fed back to the class, a procedure that allowed us to work out goals together and let the class see that the power to change could come from the group.

The teacher who tries to adapt the content of his courses to students' needs in the manner I have described will meet with some disappointments. Just as individual students develop patterns of behavior to cope with school and life, an entire class can have a dominant style. In fortunate instances, the class purpose is learning, and its style coincides more or less with the teacher's purpose. In others, the group's purpose may be to thwart the teacher. The teacher can also be ineffective if his class has goals that replace learning as the primary goal. And it is possible for a group of students to be so enveloped in apathy that they have no guiding purpose.

Teacher Attitudes

A teacher's attitudes toward his students, the way he feels about them, and the mood or emotional climate he sets in the classroom determine the amount of energy the group, or individual members, must expend in battling the teacher. The more the teacher is able to minimize or sidestep the emotional aspects of the teacher-student battle, the more energy and time will remain for learning.

At schools such as Du Sable it is often difficult to assess a teacher's attitudes. Many teachers, experiencing the sort of "culture shock" I described in Chapter 2, find themselves in conflict with their students on nearly all levels and feel justified in holding negative attitudes toward them. It then becomes difficult for a teacher to see beyond the abuse he may receive from a portion of the student body—a contemptuous slur mumbled in his presence, a provocative shove going through the lunchroom crowd, a door slammed in his face by two students. This situation is made more tragic because ghetto students generally are in need of experiences with adults who have positive attitudes toward them. What happens instead is a standoff, with teachers and students demanding respect from each other. The only possible way out of this destructive cycle is for the teacher, as the person with the most power and, hopefully, the most wisdom, to give the first clear indication of respect while making it clear that respect is expected in return. It is a great step forward when a teacher is able to avoid confrontations and help students see that cooperation and mutual respect bring their own rewards.

Defensiveness vs. Understanding

A model of teaching for the ghetto must help the teacher reconcile his personal and educational values with the conflicting reality of his students' life styles. It must provide that teacher, if possible, the terms on which he can be successful, or, at least, can protect himself from a sense of failure and professional inadequacy. Unfortunately, the model of teaching that emerges most effortlessly in response to this conflict is one based on a defensive attitude, a stance that "protects" the teacher by projecting only negative characteristics onto groups of students. Such a model, of course, greatly limits the possibility that students learn and grow.

There is, however, another attitude that is apt to prove more educative and growth promoting for the student—and for the teacher. Through applying a model of teaching that emphasized increasing my understanding of the complex dynamics of the ghetto school, I was able to increase the educative moments in my classes as well as make sense out of my experiences. The understanding I achieved was both intuitive and rational; what I did in the classroom was determined by what I felt intuitively would "work" and by the more thoughtful, detailed knowledge I had about my students. Furthermore, the understanding that guided my teaching was dynamic, not static. As I never felt that I had the understanding of Du Sable, my model of teaching retained a protean, adaptive quality to it. In essence, my model involved the ongoing process of interpreting and reevaluating the role of the teacher. Or, more accurately perhaps, the model was itself an educative, reflective inquiry into how to teach in the ghetto.

Empathic Listening

One of my major concerns while in the classroom was to empathize with and to understand my students' perceptions of their school experiences. Rogers (1974, p. 107) suggests that this attitude can encourage learning and growth:

> When there is a sensitive empathy, however, the reaction in the learner follows something of this pattern, "At last someone understands how it feels and seems to be me without wanting to analyze or judge me. Now I can blossom and grow and learn."

Through nonjudgmental understanding of my students' opinions (though I would later give my opinions, too), I believe I lessened the hostility many of my students felt toward teachers and school. While I did not quite agree with my students' explanations of why school was boring or irrelevant to their lives or why some of their teachers were mean or lazy, my listening to them and understanding them did pave the way for new insights and attitudes.

It is also important that a teacher demonstrate that what students say is important and can have an effect on what happens in class. One of the most frequent student complaints I heard while at Du Sable was that teachers did not want to listen, they only wanted to talk.

Listening to students does not have to be only in reference to class work. I had students explain to me a wide variety of their out-of-class pursuits, from electric guitars to computers. My interest indicated not only that I felt my students were important, it also placed me in the role of learner and gave me the opportunity to demonstrate the importance of asking questions and thinking.

Realness

The longer I taught at Du Sable the more _real_ I became. Gradually, I moved from the formal rigidity and distance characteristic of most teachers toward informal spontaneity and realness with my students. My increased informality and nondefensiveness, I discovered, led to a greater appreciation of my students as people and to a wider range of emotional reactions that I would reveal in the classroom. In addition, as Rogers (1969, p. 106) contends, realness is a quality that facilitates learning:

When the facilitator is a real person, being what he is, entering into a relationship with the learner without presenting a front or a facade, he is much more likely to be effective. . . . Thus, he is a person to his students, not a faceless embodiment of a curricular requirement nor a sterile tube through which knowledge is passed from one generation to the next.

Because I no longer denied my appropriate feelings of anger, humor, happiness, and even boredom when in class, I was less apt to deny my students their right to be human too.

When a teacher is not listening he is very likely talking, and the realness of his words is especially important. Ghetto kids are astoundingly quick to see pretense or phoniness in their teachers, and the extent to which they cooperate is determined by whether or not they believe their teachers "talk straight" with them.

In addition to the emotional valence of the words he uses, a teacher should consider his choice of words. Students respond to a variety of levels of usage, depending upon the current mood of the class. At times, I found that a request using a street idiom would get cooperation quickly and easily. At other times, though, if I sensed that students were "with" me and were stimulated, I would escalate the level of my vocabulary and see if they could keep up.

I also found that words could be used dramatically in the classroom. Frequently I would use lead-in sentences such as: "I'm going to ask you something that probably nobody has ever asked you before—." "We're going to do something very unusual today, so I want everyone to pay close attention—." "Now, what would you say is the one most important—."

On a few occasions I created a different kind of drama and successfully confronted classes on a verbally aggressive level. As one aspect of interpersonal relations among my ghetto students was ribbing or the "put down," I would use this approach to reemphasize my position as group leader.

Acceptance

I also found that my students' growth and learning were enhanced if they felt accepted while in my classes. While I communicated to my students rigorous and clear standards for behavior and achievement, they had to know also that I accepted all of them—even those who were unable to meet these standards.

My students' behavior often seemed designed to confirm their expectation that a middle-class teacher, especially one who was white, would have only negative attitudes toward them. I therefore learned the importance of being able to check, whenever possible, any impulse to act out the anger and frustration I felt at my students' unwillingness to learn. To do so would have only furthered the teacher-student conflict. I do not mean to suggest that I was weak or permissive, however. I made it clear at the start of each class that I respected students and that I expected the same in return. Besides, I was certain my students could tell the difference between an undisciplined—and ultimately destructive—permissiveness and firm discipline based on a caring for and acceptance of students.

Teaching vs. Therapy

The facilitation of students' learning was always the object of my teaching at Du Sable. However, I became aware over the years that I had grown in my ability to offer students warm, supportive, and, hence, "therapeutic," experiences. My psychotherapy had progressed so that I was beginning to recognize, and to come to terms with, some of the deeper conflicts in my own life. And this growth enabled me to respond to my students in ways that helped them begin, at least, to work through the conflicts and anxieties that blocked their learning. I could see, for example, that my acting out in therapy the anger I felt toward significant others in my life (and, behind that, the pain that came from feeling unloved) was no different from the anger and the hurt that many of my students felt because of their life experiences. I began then, quite consciously, to respond to my students' anger in the same way that my therapist responded to mine—nondefensively and with understanding and love. I want to make it clear, however, that I did not practice psychotherapy with my students—to do so would have been an unethical, unprofessional invasion of their private lives.

The importance of being close to and involved with students I found confirmed in Glasser's (1969, p. 19) conception of Reality Therapy:

> Reality Therapy says that teachers and students must become involved; that when students are involved with responsible teachers, people who themselves have a success identity and can fulfill their needs, the students are then in a position to fulfill their own needs.

To the extent that I was able to be warm, genuine, and supportive, then my teaching was "therapeutic" for students who had not had positive relationships with an adult and, at worst, of no consequence to those who had. Furthermore, if I could give the lie to those few students who were driven by a consuming, almost paranoid, hatred of white people, then such an experience would be "therapeutic" and might lead to insights similar to one James Baldwin (1971, p. 24) was able to make as a student:

> My favorite teacher happened to be a black lady; then, later on, a white school teacher who was a Communist. . . . She fed us and took me to the theater and things like that. And she was the first human being to sort of move out of that kind of monolithic mass that is composed of the landlords, the pawnbrokers and the cops who beat you up. She gave me my first key, my first clue that white people were human.

As a final caveat, I do not wish to emphasize too strongly the therapeutic dimension of my model of teaching, for, as Richard Jones (1968, p. 84) asserts, "teachers have tended with discouraging regularity to be intimidated by these methods. They have seen in them, however mistakenly, the need to be on trained and experienced terms with the 'mysteries of the mind'." If a teacher can just artfully and honestly present his students with learning experiences based on his sensitive understanding of their lives, he need not concern himself directly with therapy—after all, it is up to each student to decide privately what the experience means to him.

Teacher Methodology

A teacher's methodology concerns what we might call "visible" teaching techniques—what the teacher actually does. While a teacher might be limited in his ability to establish interpersonal relationships, to show a sense of humor, or to create an interesting teaching style, there are a few easily understood methods that will increase his influence with students.

I found that I got more out of my students and held their attention more if I were visible in the classroom. For me, this usually meant standing and moving about the room or sitting at a student desk in the middle of a semicircle. By using room space ingeniously and altering seating patterns, I found, much could be done to make classes more interesting for both me and my students.

I also found it interesting to reverse roles and delegate my position to a student or a small group of students. I think my students learned from seeing me in the role of student-participant, and I was better able to understand the student's role. A variation of this is for the teacher to enter the group and let the subject matter or the task occupy the position of authority and attention.

As each school year progressed, I tried to place more and more of the responsibility for learning on my students. This did not mean, however, that I abdicated my responsibilities as leader. I simply made it clear that worthwhile classes depended on students meeting their obligations.

In the area of discipline, for example, I was able to rely on students to help maintain certain standards of classroom behavior. Believing that discipline must ultimately come from within rather than from without, I let my students handle as much of the discipline as they could. If a few students happened to be talking or disturbing a class, I was often able to stop what I was doing and wait until someone else in the class asked the students to quiet down so we could return to the matter at hand. Most students agreed that proper conduct was their responsibility more than mine.

The inability of ghetto students to break off intergroup communication is well known (recall our visit in Chapter 4 to Miss Martin's third period class). Any teacher unable to use this (really, rather natural) urge to talk will have a very difficult time indeed. It therefore seems axiomatic that a teacher try to provide for group discussion or small group buzz sessions almost every day. Without this opportunity, students will either continue to talk or slide into silent apathy, ignoring, in either case, the teacher; only the unusually motivated will pay attention.

Group Dynamics

Perhaps the main concern of the ghetto teacher is to get a given class to see itself as a group. As I have already stated, what I was often faced with in a class was not a smoothly functioning group but several small, very strong, often opposing, subgroups that I somehow had to rally around a common goal. I had to build up the group so that individual members would look to the entire class rather than to their subgroup for satisfaction.

I often felt that the low self-esteem of inner-city kids was reflected in their fragmented groups. It was hard for many of my students to subvert their individual will for the group's benefit if they did not believe that their collective effort was more effective than their individual efforts. In short, they did not seem to take each other seriously nor think they could accomplish much as a group. Often, if I was asked a question and, in turn, asked if anyone else in the class knew the answer, some students would become irritated and accuse me of being evasive. Apparently, they thought I was the only one to be listened to and taken seriously.

My approach to ghetto teaching had as one of its major goals the creation of a classroom environment characterized by a cohesive group oriented toward listening and thinking and, hopefully, toward inquiry into mutually agreed upon problems or questions. Such an atmosphere, however, is not easily realized in a ghetto school. By withdrawing or by supporting each other in small groups, ghetto students are able to discount the teacher and thereby avoid the anxiety brought on by years of below-average or failing academic performance.

In spite of my students' tendency to resist instruction in this way, I found that I could encourage the gradual emergence of group cohesiveness if I truly listened to what my students were saying and if I indicated my willingness to participate in an honest teacher-student dialogue that, while it might not be directly related to the content of English, was in some way educative.

At this point, some may wonder what I intended for my students to get out of my classes. Two things. First, I wanted each student to feel good about what happened to him while in my class; I wanted him to feel that he was successful. Some students so seriously doubted their ability to succeed that, even with passing grades, they would ask me if they weren't failing! Thus, I tried to discover on what terms, with what materials and methods students could learn successfully. I saw no virtue in adhering to a Board of Education curriculum if it only served to make frustrated students flee learning.

Second, using their experiences as a point of departure, I wanted my students to:

- learn how to learn and come to have some notion of what it means to be educated;
- learn to judge the implications of their behavior and to become responsible for their actions;
- learn to inquire into the world beyond their immediate environment;
- and learn how to seek some understanding of the chaotic, hostile world many of them experienced daily.

One way I was able to promote personal or group goals in my classes was to give students the opportunity to identify what was important to them and then try to shape our activities in terms of those goals. This sort of cooperative educative inquiry Dewey (1938, p. 85) had advocated in Experience and Education:

> The way is, first, for the teacher to be intelligently
> aware of the capacities, needs, and past experiences
> of those under instruction, and secondly, to allow the
> suggestion made to develop into a plan and project by
> means of the further suggestions contributed and or-
> ganized into a whole by the members of the group.
> The plan, in other words, is a co-operative enter-
> prise, not a dictation.

I found that mutually agreed upon projects were not only more meaningful for my students, but they also enabled students to learn that
their input could make a difference.

I recall, for example, one class that, when asked "What is
worth learning about?", generated the following list:

1. Black plays.
2. Drugs and their effect.
3. Colleges and tests.
4. This class.
5. How far can black men go in politics? Can there
   ever be a black president? Which blacks are
   qualified?
6. Dope, sex, pimping, and conning.
7. What is happening in the black neighborhoods, and
   where do they get their language?
8. Racism—its causes and ways to remove it from
   society.

Based on concerns expressed in class, we had several interesting
discussions, and some English assignments I was able to relate to
these interests.

While I found that lists of goals such as the above were easily
compiled, willingness to act on these goals was not always assured.
Because my students were generally deficient in the basic skills
(primarily reading) and the attitudes and experiences needed to sustain inquiry, identified interests were often discouragingly short
lived—usually enough to sustain only one or two class discussions
and very little inquiry. In short, it was often very difficult to get
students beyond the high emotions characteristic of the early,
interest-arousing stages of inquiry.

But even waning interest, I found, could be approached in an
educative manner. By using Glasser's Classroom Meeting Model,
I was able to deal openly and honestly with the way students saw and
responded to the content of my classes. Classroom meetings, according to Glasser (1969, p. 122), are:

. . . meetings in which the teacher leads a whole class
in a nonjudgmental discussion about what is important
and relevant to them. There are three types of classroom meetings: the social-problem-solving meeting,
concerned with the students' social behavior in school;
the open-ended meeting, concerned with intellectually
important subjects; and the educational-diagnostic meeting, concerned with how well the students understand the
concepts of the curriculum.

Classroom meetings allowed me and my students to exchange
thoughts and feelings on a variety of subjects. I held problem-
solving meetings on student participation in walkouts and riots,
police brutality in the ghetto, gun control, inappropriate behavior
or acting out in my classes, and ways to make my classes less boring and more educative.

Another way to further personal and group inquiry is for the
teacher to be alert to what his students are doing, what they are
talking about, and what they are reading. If a teacher is willing to
listen carefully to students and take note of those instances during
which he feels intuitively that genuine personal inquiry is taking
place, he is better able to provide the kind of education students can
become involved in. The most fruitful discussions I have been involved in, ones characterized by listening and thinking, occurred
when I allowed topics of interest to emerge from the group. These
discussions covered a wide range of subjects not thought to be within
the province of English: dreams, love and marriage, racism, abor-
tion, and education. I did not stifle these expressions of opinion,
for my task was not to control student expression but to encourage
the kind of expression that would improve learning.

As an example of how the deeper, real concerns of students
can be used to energize group inquiry, I recall a senior English
class in which we had been investigating the nature and causes of
prejudice. On this particular day, I began by confronting students
with a film that I thought spoke rather frankly about different types
of prejudice—racial, religious, economic, and so on. Following
the film we had a discussion during which my students, hesitantly
at first, began to reveal some of the issues the film had aroused.
With a spirit of genuine interest and concern, a few students began
to ask me direct, perhaps outlandish, questions:

- What would you do if you married a white woman and
  later learned that she was prejudiced against blacks?
- What did you think when you first saw a black person?
- Would you marry a black woman?

- If two planes, one carrying twenty white women, the other twenty black women, were going to crash and you could save only one plane, which one would you save?
- Do you have any friends who are prejudiced against blacks?
- What do your friends say about blacks when all of you get together to play bridge?
- Would you vote for a black president?

In spite of the absurdity of some of the questions and the fact that they were designed to "put me on the spot," the session was extremely valuable. Eventually, the class and I decided to continue our investigation by reading Baldwin's The Fire Next Time and Richard Wright's Black Boy. Had we read these books without at least confronting some very real concerns on the part of students, I am afraid our work would have been superficial, if not hypocritical.

FACTORS THAT LIMIT THE IMPLEMENTATION
OF A MODEL OF TEACHING

One of the dangers of formulating a model for teaching is that it can create the illusion that teaching is a simple, straightforward activity—if one only follows, step-by-step, the model. The protestations of the behaviorists aside, teaching is not that simple!

While at Du Sable, I was aware of four school-related factors which worked against my implementing the teaching model presented in this chapter. These factors, I contend, also contribute to the generally low morale often found among ghetto teachers.

Students' "Inability" to Learn

First, I must admit that, at various times, I entertained the notion that no matter what strategies I employed in the classroom, I could not increase the amount of material my students learned. And, as I revealed in Chapter 2, I have even felt that my students so thoroughly resisted instruction that they were "unteachable"—at least as far as a middle-class curriculum was concerned.

Such ideas have found their most articulate and persuasive spokesman in Edward Banfield (1968, p. 142) who sees lower-class values as the primary obstacle to educating youth from the lower class:

Class-cultural factors largely account for the conspicu-
ous difference between the slum and the suburban school.
Each school has a class character imposed upon it by
the social setting in which it exists; this, and not staff
inefficiency, racial discrimination, or inequitable pro-
vision of resources, is the main reason for the virtues
of one and the defects of the other. The implication is
one that reformers find hard to accept—to wit, that no
matter how ample the facilities of the school or how
well-designed its curriculum, no matter how able,
dedicated, and hardworking the teachers, no matter
how free the atmosphere of the school from racial or
other prejudice, the performance of pupils at the lower
end of the class-cultural scale will always fall short
not only of that of pupils at the upper end of the scale,
but also of what is necessary to make them educated
workers.

Elsewhere, Banfield (1968, p. 157) reaches another conclusion that
many ghetto teachers, given their intimate daily experiences, might
accept: "High school, it seems fair to conclude, cannot possibly
'educate' those young people whose class culture strongly disposes
them not to learn."

In spite of the logical appeal of Banfield's argument, however,
I felt that what I did in the classrooms of Du Sable did make a difference. Had I not believed that, I would have joined the ranks of
the burned out, reducing even further, I am certain, the number of
young people whom I would be able to reach.

Lack of Support Within the School Environment

A second factor that made it difficult for me to implement my
model of teaching was the fact that the Du Sable ethos offered almost no professional or psychic support for teachers who wished to
use a highly personal, student-centered approach to teaching. (Chapter 14 discusses the need to create professional, problem-solving
atmospheres in ghetto schools such as Du Sable.) When I encountered strong resistance or hostility in my students, for example, I
was most aware that the school offered neither support nor protec-
tion. When I felt that my approach to teaching confronted directly
the hostile "edge" of my students' collective culture, with no prob-
able relief to the tension between me and my students, I would often
"retreat" to more traditional methods rather than push my students
to new insights and run the risk of destroying any positive feelings
that might remain between us.

Difficulty of Promoting Genuine Inquiry

Thirdly, I found that the achievement levels, the personal experiences, and the modes of inquiry of most of my students were painfully inadequate for the kind of inquiry I would like to have had occur in my classes. In his study of the educational ethos of several high schools, of which Du Sable was one, Thelen (1974, p. 129) similarly found that lower-class culture makes a poor base for educative inquiry:

> The bland, traditional, certification-oriented middle class operation simply doesn't fit the culture of poor people. What results is an image of confronting demands whose difficulty mobilizes (in the ideal) the classroom into a partially realized community. But these aspects of community tend at most to be tolerated as "adjustment mechanisms" rather than being capitalized on to develop a genuine group-and-individual inquiring way of life.

Lack of Collegial Support

A fourth factor, one that seriously saps the ghetto teacher's energy, results if colleagues criticize the teacher's quest for a better way of doing things. These cynics are apt to state emphatically that <u>nothing can be done</u> educationally unless far-reaching social and economic changes are made throughout the land. They teach, subtly insuring that their expectations come true, and gain release from frustration by making witty, incisive remarks about the gross inability of their students, the myopic tunnel vision of administrators, and the crumbling educational superstructure of which they are part.

CONCLUSION

In addition to the above factors that mitigate the teacher's ability to implement the model of teaching I propose is the painful realization that the cynical teachers mentioned above are partially correct. Significant change in schools such as Du Sable has to involve a remaking of U.S. society, and, at the moment, that is unlikely. Until that moment comes, then, it is doubly important that each teacher have the professional honesty and the courage to assess the effect of his classroom methods on students and to continue his quest to develop and to implement a model of teaching that will enhance students' learning.

REFERENCES

Baldwin, J., and Mead, M. Margaret Mead-James Baldwin: A Rap on Race. Philadelphia: J. B. Lippincott, 1971.

Banfield, E. The Unheavenly City. Boston: Little, Brown, 1968.

Dewey, J. Experience and Education. New York: Macmillan, 1938.

Friedenburg, E. Z. "An Ideology of School Withdrawal." In The School Dropout, edited by D. Schreiber. Washington, D.C.: NEA, 1964.

Glasser, W. Schools Without Failure. New York: Harper and Row, 1969.

Jones, R. Fantasy and Feeling in Education. New York: New York University Press, 1968.

Rogers, C. Freedom to Learn. Columbus, Ohio: Charles E. Merrill, 1969.

Rogers, C. "Can Learning Encompass Both Ideas and Feelings?" Education 95 (1974):103-14.

Thelen, H. The Educational Ethos of the Midwestern High School. Monograph. University of Chicago, 1974.

11
THE ENGLISH
OFFICE: TIME OUT!

If it weren't for my friends in the
English Department, I wouldn't
stay in this god-forsaken school.
But we stick together, we support
each other. We're all going
through the same shit, you know.

A Du Sable English Teacher

FROM 1974 through 1978, I was chairman of Du Sable's 25-member
English department. As chairman, I had both the opportunity to be
more influential in trying to improve the instruction Du Sable kids
received and, because I found myself closer to the decision-making
sources of power within the school, the opportunity to increase my
understanding of the English department as a subsystem within the
larger unit of the school.

    This chapter, then, draws on those experiences and examines
teacher behavior and attitudes that contributed to the maintenance
of the English department as a psychosocial system. It is my
hypothesis here that conflict (with himself, students, administrators, other departments, other teachers, and the surrounding environment) characterized nearly every facet of the English teacher's
professional life at Du Sable. Consequently, the dominant motivation of the English teacher, and of the department as a system, was
to cope with the situation in a way that reduced, or at least managed, the tension that arose from this multidimensional conflict.

For years I had recognized that many English teachers, my-self included, had come to view the department office, room 260, as an oasis in a desert of doubt, cynicism, and hostility. By enter-ing room 260, we could, for one brief period, call "time out" to the teacher-student battle that raged throughout the classrooms and hallways of Du Sable.

METHOD OF STUDY

My study of the English department spanned several weeks and was conducted from the vantage point of participant-observer. I also had my departmental colleagues complete a 14-item question-naire designed to elicit their dominant perceptions of the English department. These 14 questions follow:

1. How many years have you been teaching? How many at Du Sable?

2. Where do you realize the most satisfaction daily?

English Office, Room 260	Classroom	Other Department Offices	In Halls	Other

3. Where do you realize the least satisfaction?

English Office, Room 260	Classroom	Other Department Offices	In Halls	Other

4. What do you feel is your level of job satisfaction?

Very Low	Low	Rather Low	About Evenly High & Low	Rather High	High	Very High

5. What are your feelings toward the administration?

Very Favorable	Rather Favorable	Neither Favorable Nor Unfavorable	Rather Un-favorable

Very Un-favorable

6. What are your feelings toward the students at Du Sable ?

    Very   Rather   Neither   Rather Un-
    Favorable   Favorable   Favorable Nor favorable
                         Unfavorable

    Very Un-
    favorable

7. Are you on the transfer list [i.e. a list on file at the Chicago Board of Education of teachers wishing to be transferred to other schools] ?

8. How often do you seek advice from other English teachers regarding teaching methods, materials, etc. ?

    Never   Almost Never   Sometimes   Very Often

9. What are your feelings toward other English teachers as a group of colleagues ?

    Very Un-   Rather Un-   Neither Favorable   Rather
    favorable   favorable   Nor Unfavorable   Favorable

    Very
    Favorable

10. How much do you feel your students learn from you?

    A Great   Quite   About Average   Not Too   Almost
    Deal   a Lot   Much   Nothing

11. Through special training, new instructional materials, etc., do you feel that English teachers could do a more effective job of instructing our students ?

    Definitely   Perhaps   It's Hard   Probably   Definitely
    Yes   to Say   Not   No

12. How do you think the administration views the English department ?

    Very   Rather   Neither Un-   Rather Un-   Very Un-
    Favorably   Favorably   favorably Nor favorably   favorably
                         Favorably

13. How would you rate the cohesiveness of the English department members?

Very Low	Rather Low	Neither High Nor Low	Rather High	Very High

14. Approximately, how many periods per week do you spend in the English office?

15 or More	10	7	5	3	None

Finally, I interviewed the members of the department and invited them to make their own analyses of the English department as a psychosocial system. These interviews were open-ended, though they focused on the following seven questions:

1. What characterizes a "good day" at school for you?
2. What characterizes a "bad day" at school for you?
3. What "rewards" (personal, emotional, status, etc.) do you hope to get out of your job?
4. In regard to the above question, what "forces" tend to prevent you from obtaining these rewards?
5. Would you say there are any unwritten "rules" that govern the behavior of teachers within the department? By this I mean mutually agreed upon standards of behavior (not administrative rules) that English teachers tacitly agree to follow. What are these rules?
6. Is there conflict (rivalry, competition, etc.) within the department? With other departments in the school?
7. Since you began teaching at Du Sable, have you had to make "adjustments" of any sort. Describe.

The data that I collected in the preceding manner (what Becker [1958, p. 656] has termed "quasi-statistics") I will now use to construct a general theoretical model of the English department as a psychosocial system. As various dimensions of this system are described, the teachers themselves will also comment occasionally on the same phenomena.

THE SOCIAL STRUCTURE OF THE DEPARTMENT

While I was chairman, the department was a biracial (11 black and 14 white) group of individuals whom I judged to be from the same broad culture—a culture whose members could be identified by a common professional language and similar beliefs regarding the value of education. On the other hand, the group was heterogeneous in regard to age, sex, socioeconomic background, and ethnicity.

Teachers everywhere lead highly structured daily professional lives, and such was the case with English teachers at Du Sable. Each teacher was responsible for five 40-minute class periods of English during a nine-period day; the only exception was the department chairman who had four classes.

In addition to five classes, each teacher had a "self-directed" period, a "conference and preparation" period, and a lunch period—three "free" periods that could conceivably be spent in the English office. For one period a day, teachers were also assigned to a "duty"—patrolling the hallways, monitoring the lunchrooms, working in the attendance office, and so on. (My questionnaire revealed that nearly two-thirds of the department's teachers spent from ten to fifteen periods per week in the departmental office.)

Within the department, all members officially held positions of equal status—however, the position of department chairman carried with it a slight increment in status (though more titular than real). In addition, teachers with seniority usually taught the older, and somewhat more capable and tractable, students; these teachers, then, possibly enjoyed more status within the department.

Thus, the department's social structure was greatly influenced by scheduling "regularities" beyond the control of anyone in the department. With whom one shared a room, when one had "free" nonteaching periods, and what levels one taught doubtless facilitated the emergence of certain social relationships while it precluded the emergence of other social combinations.

THE "BOUNDARIES" OF THE ENGLISH DEPARTMENT

Because all English teachers were concurrently included in other subsystems within the school (teachers were involved in other groups according to their nonteaching duty assignments, teachers had friends in other departments, teachers formed car pools that cut across departmental lines, and so on), the "boundaries" of the English department were not always distinct. They were often diffuse and "overlapped" with the boundaries of other subsystems within the school. The "density" of the English department as a system therefore changed continuously. For example, the system and its "components" were most in evidence at departmental meetings with all members in attendance and least in evidence when teachers were spread throughout the building discharging their professional responsibilities that, at any given moment, might or might not be related to the English department per se.

The English department, at its most fundamental and apparent level, then, was a group of 25 teachers, all of whom had highly regulated roles and fairly predictable movements in time and space. The boundaries within which these movements occurred were set by Board of Education policies and enforced by administrators within the building. These boundaries remained constant, with the exception of minor changes, for the duration of a school year.

TWO FUNCTIONS OF THE ENGLISH DEPARTMENT

Clearly, the "official" function of the English department was to educate students. To help each student achieve to the best of his ability was the institutionally prescribed and consistently maintained mission of the department as a system. While individual teachers differed regarding the feasibility of achieving this goal, all teachers saw the department as more or less concerned with facilitating and supporting the instructional efforts of English teachers in the classroom. Through the department, for example, teachers received instructional supplies and information regarding various procedures important to their day-to-day existence in the classroom. Feedback as to whether the department was "on course" with respect to its official function (i.e. support of instruction) came from several sources: departmental members themselves, students, administrators, teachers in other departments, and parents.

The second function of the department, I found, had to be inferred, for, as Glidewell (1973, p. 58) asserts, "groups often behave in accord with some implicit rules of exchange which participants do not understand and cannot articulate." This "unofficial" function, acknowledged to varying degrees by teachers, concerned the reduction or management of tension and anxiety that arose from job-related stress. This stress resulted from conflicts that occurred in three general areas.

First, as I have maintained throughout this book, teachers were, with different intensities, in conflict with their students' dominant culture. In daily contact with resistant, perhaps hostile, attitudes (what one black female English teacher described to me as "balk—pure, unrestrained, unmitigated balk"), English teachers experienced a high level of frustration and anxiety. As they assessed their performance in the teacher-student conflict, then, they had to admit that day after day they met with only limited success. Despite their efforts (and most of the teachers in my department had high expectations of students and they worked very, very hard at teaching), teachers usually saw few signs of substantial student achievement. Annual standardized reading tests, for example, revealed that, as the majority of students spent time in school, the number of grade levels they were behind in reading actually increased.

Secondly, English teachers experienced, again to varying degrees, conflict with the administrative staff whose directives frequently ordered teachers to do a job their firsthand experiences told them couldn't be done—at least if they followed administrative procedures. (Chapter 13, for example, reports on an ill-planned, three-year innovative experiment that the administration spearheaded and teachers, along with students, soundly rejected.) My questionnaire, for example, revealed that only one-fourth of the English teachers held favorable attitudes toward the administration, and less than one-sixth of the teachers believed the English department was viewed favorably by the administration. One teacher, talented and unusually successful at getting kids to shape up and produce in her classes, summarized for me her view of the department-administration conflict: "The administration symbolizes the Board of Education and a lack of concern for teachers. You have to learn how to put up with shit—administrative, Nixonian crap."

I sensed that some teachers, however, might have been ambivalent in their attitudes toward the administration. Attraction might have been mingled with their hostility. Administrators had a virtual monopoly on the scarce resources of status and power within the school, and these resources they preferred to keep within their ranks rather than distribute among teachers. Administrators were also envied because they were no longer in the classroom and therefore did not experience intense, daily conflict with students.

A third conflict teachers experienced occurred within. They had to cope with the discrepancy between their professional ideals or standards and the reality of the classroom. Similarly, Gordon (1957, p. 40), in his analysis of the social system of a suburban high school, found that teachers can experience role strain as they struggle to minimize the discordant elements of their work:

The structural context of the school presented the
teacher with the task of continuous integration and adjustment of conflicting expectations. There was a
considerable range of adaptation among teachers in
their capacity to harmonize the conflicting tendencies. There also was a great range in the amount
of personal anxiety teachers experienced in relation
to their efforts to carry on the teaching function.

As they worked to live up to their image of themselves as professionals, then, English teachers experienced anxiety and a per-
sistent threat to their self-esteem. As one teacher, a perceptive
white male, put it: "You always feel guilty in a school like this.
We don't talk about what goes on in our classes. We don't know
what to do. It's as though we share a collective guilt."

"INPUT" AND "OUTPUT" COMPONENTS OF THE
ENGLISH DEPARTMENT AS A SYSTEM

Figure 4 illustrates the relationship of the English department
to certain "input" and "output" variables. In addition to constant
"pressure" from the larger environment surrounding the school,
input into the system came from two general sources: the school
as institution or suprasystem within which the department was embedded, and the students themselves. Similarly, output was of two
sorts: the officially recognized product of student achievement,
and the "unofficial" product of social interaction designed to reduce tension brought on by the situation. While the system's output
of social interaction and tension-release activities was not recognized as a "legitimate" output according to the original design of the
system, many teachers recognized the importance of releasing
tensions. One teacher, for example, admitted to me that: "I don't
like the kids. It's terrible when I have to leave the office and go to
class. It prevents me from being with friends."

Though Figure 4 does not indicate it, the English department
received considerably greater input from its environment than it
returned as "transformed" (i.e. educated) output to the environment. As Glidewell (1973, p. 7) notes, this imbalance is wide-
spread among educational systems:

Perhaps the most clear and compelling evidence of
the sparse immediate output from educational subsystems lies in the everyday experience of the mil-
lions of parents who have asked their child, "What
did you do at school today?"

This disparity between the degree of input and immediate output is the result of several factors: (1) student achievement or growth is often realized not in the present but in the future, (2) the department (as is true with nearly all systems of public education) was virtually powerless to alter the input it must "transform," and (3) the output of instruction (as any of us can immediately discern if we reflect upon our own experiences as learners) is often not easily observed or measured.

FIGURE 4

INPUT AND OUTPUT OF THE ENGLISH DEPARTMENT

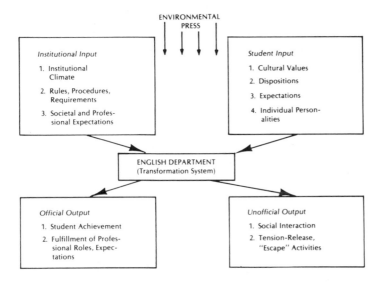

FUNCTIONS OF CONFLICT WITHIN THE SYSTEM

That English teachers experienced conflict within themselves and in their interactions with students and administrators did not mean that these areas of stress threatened the viability of the department as a system. In fact, as Coser (1956, p. 31) points out, conflict may be essential to the maintenance of a system:

Groups require disharmony as well as harmony, dissociation as well as association; and conflicts within them are by no means altogether disruptive factors. Group formation is the result of both types of processes. The belief that one process tears down what

the other builds up, so that what finally remains is
the result of subtracting the one from the other, is
based on a misconception. On the contrary, both
"positive" and "negative" factors build group relations. Conflict as well as cooperation has social
functions. Far from being necessarily dysfunc-
tional, a certain degree of conflict is an essential
element in group formation and the persistence of
group life.

Furthermore, conflict served to clarify and solidify group boundaries in a way that strengthened group identity and awareness of
separateness. One teacher with whom I spoke, for example, described how conflict strengthened the internal cohesion of the
English department and furthered individual commitment to the
system: "Nobody in school likes us [i.e. the English department].
In their eyes we're a bunch of lazy no-goods. We have to stick
together."

BEHAVIORAL MANIFESTATIONS OF CONFLICT

Coser (1956, p. 41) postulates three possible ways through
which conflict may manifest itself in behavior that occurs within a
system:

(1) direct expression of hostility against the person
or group which is the source of frustration, (2) dis-
placement of such hostile behavior onto substitute ob-
jects, and (3) tension-release activity which provides
satisfaction in itself without need for object or object
substitute.

Within the English office, tension-release activities and the dis-
placement of hostile feelings rather than direct aggression (though
I did observe this behavior on a few occasions) constituted the
main "safety valve" for discharging accumulated tensions. Consequently, behavior in the office included not only activities related
to teachers' work as professionals but a good deal of bitter complaining or joking about the common plight of English teachers.
Students, administrators, parents, and the Chicago Board of Education were alternately under attacks of varying intensities. One
teacher, a white female, typified the tension-release behavior that
occurred in the office when she confided to me that:

The principal has killed free communication with his
personality, the way he handles things. The administration is six stupid people doing stupid jobs. They
have to puff themselves up to make themselves feel
O.K. Their jobs have nothing to do with education.
They don't serve anybody but themselves.

Humor, which veiled deeper hostile feelings, was also used
to reduce tension. One teacher, a white male, explained to me
how humor helped him cope with stressful aspects of his work:

The only way to get through the day here is to make
a joke about it. If you take the job seriously, it'll
grind you up and spit you out. Compared to the rest
of the world, Du Sable's a laugh a minute. You gotta
see it that way. Everybody—the kids, the principals,
the teachers—even the janitors—is crazy around
here. And if they're not quite crazy yet, they will
be soon. So, you see, all you can do is laugh about
it.

Humor such as this teacher expressed, it seems likely, allowed
teachers to minimize their involvement with and commitment to
teaching at the school. Additionally, the covert message conveyed
by their behavior was that the demands of the role were beneath
their capabilities.

"REWARDS" WITHIN THE DEPARTMENT

Most of the rewards sought by English teachers were of the
sort commonly recognized as "legitimate." Teachers hoped to
see their students grow academically and emotionally; they hoped
to get positive feedback informing them of their effectiveness; they
wished to achieve a measure of power and status appropriate to
their perceived level of competence; and, finally, they wished to
be rewarded financially for their efforts.

Of the foregoing "rewards," only financial compensation occurred with sufficient regularity and intensity (though the Chicago
Board of Education has entered the 1980s with weighty financial
problems that periodically imperil teachers' biweekly paychecks).
Other, more personal and professional, gratifications often proved
elusive, and "substitute" rewards had to be sought through the
interpersonal exchanges that occurred within the department. As
one teacher, a white female, put it:

> I find it satisfying to know the people [in the depart-
> ment]. If it weren't for the people, I wouldn't stay.
> I can talk about things that bother me. I get help,
> too, in dealing with problems involving the kids and
> the administration. Most of my friends are here.
> I get a lot of strokes. They approve of me.

This promise of mutual aid and support was mentioned often by
teachers and, no doubt, accounted for the major attraction the
English department had for its members.

NORMS AND VALUES

Within the large, cohesive core group that regularly frequented the English office, there was a group norm that supported
the risk taking necessary to create an atmosphere of openness,
trust, and psychological closeness. I noticed a moderately high
level of personal disclosure that existed among many teachers (this
level of disclosure, however, was stabilized so that very personal
problems and what one was really doing in the classroom were not
discussed). Furthermore, participants, if they wished to remain
in this close-knit group, were expected to reciprocate in a way
that maintained and enhanced the group's "cultural" values of
openness, trust, and the offering of mutual aid. And, as one
teacher pointed out to me, acceptance by the group depended upon
one's having survived his rites of passage as a ghetto teacher:

> The English department is the closest department
> [in the school]. We're just like a family. Some
> people try to get in right away, but they're not ac-
> cepted. They have to go through the same things.
> We have a sort of humor, and they don't know the
> basis of our humor. They're imitating.

During my observations, I also noted that each individual felt
free to interpret administrative rules as he wished, without fear of
departmental pressure to conform. In this regard, several teachers admitted to me that they did not go to their duty posts, that
they took "sick" days off when they were not sick, or that they were
regularly, and willfully, late to class. The violation of some of
these rules, I felt, offered teachers not only a way of reducing
commitment to the larger school system, but also a way of pas-
sively resisting or internally sabotaging the operations of the
school itself.

Finally, the English department permitted a wide variety of individual adaptations to the psychic demands of the job. Several teachers told me that they felt no departmental norms to behave in prescribed ways; instead, they were confident that they would be accepted as they were. The range of behavior I observed, therefore, ranged from risque joking and adolescent horseplay, to hostile denunciations of administration and students, or to tearful, emotional outbursts.

I believe, too that membership in the department was "therapeutic" for some teachers, as it supported them in their struggle to cope with a stressful situation and the personal conflicts this stress may have aggravated or set in motion. One teacher, for example, explained to me how membership in the department facilitated her growth in a way that was more personal and private than professional:

> My friends [in the department] accept me the way I am. We've been growing together. We've helped each other grow. I couldn't have come as far as a person. The department has been a ground where I could try myself and not feel scared or rejected.

DEGREE OF INCLUSION IN THE DEPARTMENT

As I have indicated, teachers within the department varied in regard to the level of job-related conflict they reported and the extent to which they viewed those outside the department as the "enemy." My questionnaire also informed me that those with the highest level of conflict with the environment frequented the office most often, while those least conflicted seldom visited the office. This correlation illustrates further the way in which conflict contributed to group formation, and it suggests also the possibility of a "group myth" or an unconscious desire to perpetuate certain (i.e. negative) interpretations of the situation.

Furthermore, teachers varied in regard to how involved they were in the daily operations of the department (though I am certain that those with low inclusion and involvement were committed to other "systems" throughout the school). Membership ranged from those who were deeply and personally involved in a common exchange of opinions and emotions, to those who were involved by role only, and, finally, to those who were in conflict with the department itself, as the following male teacher informant admitted to me:

I'm on the outs with the faculty, but it doesn't bother me. I learn more from my students than I do from the department, and that's sad. Rewards in the department? Right now, I don't feel I get any.
I'd classify myself—some say I'm disruptive, radical—as innovative. If you try that, you're on the outside looking in. Yet I'm on the inside with the students. I know their needs. I think of myself as different, and I know I don't belong. I'm out of place with the majority.

COMMENT

The study of subgroups within a school setting, including the nature of colleague relations among staff members in a particular subgroup, can extend our understanding of how a school functions. In this regard, Hargreaves (1972, p. 402) argues that:

The social relationships of teachers form an important part of being a teacher; it is the teacher's colleagues who in many ways control his induction into the profession. The teacher's conception of himself, his values and attitudes to many aspects of education . . . may be influenced by his relationship with his colleagues and his superiors and thus influence the teacher's behavior in the classroom and his relationship with pupils.

Through our increased understanding of the English department as a psychosocial system, then, we can now appreciate more fully the limits, and the possibilities, of the educative process as it occurred at Du Sable.

REFERENCES

Becker, H. "Problems of Inference and Proof in Participant Observation." American Sociological Review 23 (1958).

Coser, L. The Functions of Social Conflict. Glencoe: The Free Press, 1956.

Glidewell, J. "A Social Psychology of Laboratory Training."
Mimeographed. University of Chicago, July 15, 1973.

Gordon, C. The Social System of the High School. Glencoe: The
Free Press, 1957.

Hargreaves, D. Interpersonal Relations and Education. London:
Routledge and Kegan Paul, 1972.

12
THE ADMINISTRATION: WHITE PRINCIPAL, BLACK SCHOOL

I am amazed at the lack of understanding of human nature which is often displayed by the administration of this school. I am tired of being forced, of being sent disciplinary notes, and of being told I have a choice when I feel there really isn't one.
I feel forced to do things which I consider to be worthless and often insulting. I'm afraid to express my feelings because of retaliation. I don't like the tension that I feel. I like to have a voice in affairs which affect me so greatly. Teachers are people—people have feelings—feelings affect job performance.

A Social Studies Teacher at
Du Sable

IT was the second day of the second semester, fourth period. Two thousand Du Sable students and their division teachers waited in the auditorium for the assembly to begin. Rumor had it that the theme of this assembly would be a return to law and order.

Du Sable's principal, whom I will call Mr. Krimbill, stood onstage behind the podium and looked around the packed auditorium, scanning row-by-row the noisy students on the first floor before squinting up into the balcony to gauge the situation there.

Division teachers stood in the aisles, looking around uneasily, like scared new kids on a tough block, to see how well their colleagues fared at controlling their charges.

Du Sable's district superintendent, a starchy, angry looking middle-aged black woman who herself had graduated from Du Sable an unknown number of years ago, was stationed in front of a set of double doors near a corner of the auditorium. Arms folded across her big bosom, she stared out at the scene with a steely, disapproving gaze. At that moment I realized that the kids had been pretty astute to have nicknamed her "the General." Her office was in the high school building, and every so often in the morning I would pass her in the halls—my "Good morning" ignored 50 percent of those times and acknowledged by a gruff "Hello" the other 50 percent.

Krimbill now moved the microphone attached to the podium nearer to his mouth. In a surprisingly soft yet self-assured voice, as though daring students to challenge his authority, he began, "Will division teachers look around and see who is wearing head gear."

Several students let loose with ear-splitting whistles. Howls of disapproval and booing followed.

"Man, you not gonna touch this hat!"

"That man crazy. Who he think he is?"

"Touch my hat, chump, and I'll knock you on your broad-assed, snow white butt."

For a second it seemed as though our principal's opening remark would trigger pandemonium. Thank God, I thought, as I looked up and down my two rows of students, none of them happened to be wearing hats.

Here and there, a few division teachers motioned to students to remove their hats. A black male science teacher in the back of the auditorium, unable to get a girl to remove her "head gear," a rather dopey-looking black felt hat with a small peacock feather in it, escorted the defiant girl out of the auditorium. Mr. Krimbill looked upon this show of teacher determination with a thin smile of approval.

"Welcome back to Du Sable," Krimbill continued. "For those of you who are new, I am Mr. Krimbill, principal of the greatest high school in Chicago."

Again, bedlam threatened to break out. Half the kids seemed to agree with their principal, and they screamed and stomped their approval.

"Yeah, we number one."

"Right on, we is the greatest."

"You right this time, Krim."

The other half, equally energetic and vociferous, felt just the opposite.

"Fuck you!" a kid several rows behind me yelled.

"Man, this raggedy old place ain't shit."

"Come off it, man, this ain't Disneyland," a math teacher right behind me mumbled.

Undaunted, Krimbill pressed ahead. "Remember what Reverend Jessie Jackson says, 'What the mind can conceive and believe, the mind can achieve.'" This attempt by their white principal to rely on the words of a black charismatic leader to make them shape up brought forth even more anger from the uproarious students.

"Du Sable High School is you," Krimbill went on. "You are Du Sable High School. What people say about Du Sable they say about you. What people say about you, they say about Du Sable."

His audience began to quiet down now. As he rolled on, Krimbill slowly became more animated.

"When people bad-mouth Du Sable, stand up straight with your head held high and show the bad-mouthers they are wrong."

Occasional snickers and whistles still continued to be heard.

Krimbill now turned to the matter of kids making suggestions to improve the school.

"It is our feeling that each student has a stake in his own education and that he should be involved in decision making. This does not mean, however, that a few vocal students should declare themselves self-styled leaders and dictate to all students. But rather it means that each student should voice his own opinion and ideas through proper channels and should hold his representative responsible for the presentation of these ideas and opinions."

"Man, where does this joker think he's at?" the math teacher behind me snorted. "Some North Shore hotsy-totsy high school? New Trier? Winnetka? These kids don't give two shits about proper channels."

"Each student should work for change," Krimbill continued. "Not just for the sake of change, but because change will bring about better education. Change, however, must take place within the framework of the law, as we know it, and not outside the law."

"There it is—law and order," the teacher behind me muttered.

"Now, looking ahead to this semester, our emphasis will be on appearance, attendance, and achievement. Appearance—attendance—achievement. First of all, appearance. Mr. Prokop will now review our dress code with you."

The term dress code was a catalyst. The kids erupted into a roar of disapproval, knowing full well that this semester was beginning with an administrative crack down, and the dress code was the first order of business.

Prokop, Krimbill's right-hand man—especially when the going got rough (and right now the going was rough)—walked up to the microphone. He was a tall, big-boned black man whose full title was Assistant Principal in Charge of Administration and Pupil Personnel Services.

"May I have your attention," Prokop began.

Because of the noise in the auditorium, I strained to hear what he was saying. I leaned back in the rickety wooden seat I was now in and wished that I was someplace quiet. I glanced at the gray plaque high above center stage. In bold raised letters it said, PEACE IF POSSIBLE: BUT JUSTICE AT ANY RATE." Du Sable at that moment, I thought, was failing dismally at both missions.

"May I have your undivided attention, brothers and sisters? Let's show some pride. Right now, I'm ashamed to be black." Prokop's voice cracked with emotion. He seemed either on the brink of bursting into tears or exploding with anger. I couldn't tell which.

Division teachers, myself included, began to get up and patrol our small sections of the auditorium, gesturing to students to sit down and shut up.

"I want it quiet, now!" Prokop roared from the edge of the stage, projecting his booming voice to the far corners of the auditorium without aid of microphone.

Order was gradually restored, and Prokop went on in a clear, stentorian voice. "Some of you may think dress codes are obsolete. But let me tell you, young men will not wear hats in the building—even if we have to go to court and be told to desist.

"If you went to see a doctor for an operation and he came out with a hat, purple shirt, yellow pants, five-inch heels, and a blasting radio, you'd run for the nearest exit. Am I right?" Prokop was gathering momentum now.

"And, young ladies, you can not go around with exposed bodies without inviting trouble. You know what I mean.

"When I have parents who come up here with their daughter to tell me a young man grabbed her, I say to them: 'Ask yourself, what was she wearing?'"

For an additional 30 minutes, and with no greater success at convincing Du Sable students that their policies were for their benefit, Krimbill and Prokop outlined the remaining components of their get-tough program: an elaborate, unwieldy system for teachers to keep track of class cuts and tardies; a definite grade of "F" for those students absent ten or more days; and the use of student study agreements keyed to specific behavioral objectives.

During the assembly, I felt, as I am certain many of my colleagues did, not so much that the new policies were unfair (God
knew we needed to make a stand of some sort), but that they were
presented to students in a manner that was guaranteed to antagonize
and to promote even further the teacher-student conflict.

In the remainder of this chapter, then, I will look at the role
that Du Sable's principal and administrative staff played in contrib-
uting to, and perpetuating, the sort of school climate I have described in the preceding chapters. My discussion is based on the
rather obvious fact that, in any school, the principal is the person
who influences most the organizational climate. In addition, there
is ample evidence that the quality of a school's administration—with
pupil backgrounds held constant—is positively linked to student
achievement (Weber 1971; New York State Office of Evaluation Performance Review 1974; Brookover and Lezotte 1979; Kean et al.
1979; and Venezky and Winfield 1980). My purpose here, as it has
been throughout this book, is not to blame any one group for Du Sable
conditions but rather to extend our understanding of how the actors
in that drama—students, teachers, and administrators—interacted
in such a way as to create the milieu that I experienced for eight
years.

For a principal to be an effective leader in any situation, and
at troubled schools such as Du Sable in particular, he must make
a fivefold commitment. He must (1) promote and maintain professional relationships with teachers (2) demonstrate educational
leadership, not only skills in management, (3) demonstrate daily
his own excellence in teaching, (4) support teachers, and (5) communicate openly and authentically with his faculty.

PROFESSIONAL RELATIONSHIPS WITH TEACHERS

The conditions necessary for professional, problem-solving
relationships to exist between a principal and his teachers are, I
feel, the same as those that ought to exist between teachers and
students. Both dyads, principal-teacher and teacher-student, are
essentially teaching-learning relationships and have as their optimum outcome mutual respect and a deeper understanding of the
"subject" being "taught." Just as a teacher looks upon his class
roster at the start of a year with the hope of establishing educative
relationships with students, so ought the principal look at his staff
roster with the hope of establishing relationships and extending
teachers' understanding of "the subject"—in this case, teaching.

If, during inservice meetings and everyday dialogue with
teachers, a school's principal reveals himself to be insensitive,

unable or unwilling to think thoughtfully about and read widely in
education, and unable to build up group morale and cohesiveness
(a task that confronts every teacher), his teachers get the message.
The consequence (as certainly was the case at Du Sable) is a rigidly
bureaucratic school with a vacuous sense of purpose and lack of
community.

MANAGEMENT VS. EDUCATIONAL LEADERSHIP

In its job description for principals, the Chicago Board of
Education makes it clear that principals have considerable autonomy:

> Principals of schools are responsible administrative
> heads of their respective schools and are charged with
> the organization, supervision, administration, and
> discipline thereof. They shall establish and enforce
> such regulations, not contrary to the rules of the Board
> of Education or the regulations of the General Super-
> intendent of Schools, as in their judgement may be
> necessary for the successful conduct of their schools.

Through my observations of high school principals in various settings, however, I have found that most principals choose to focus
on those aspects of their jobs that call for management skills rather
than thoughtful educational leadership.

In a study of 24 building principals in Chicago, Morris and
others (1982) also found that the main concern of principals was
management—not instructional leadership. After "shadowing" the
principals from 1977 to 1980, they concluded that the flux of
events in urban schools was not conducive to reflective, thoughtful
decision making on problems directly related to instruction. Instead, principals needed the ability to move rapidly from one
problem to another. One principal observed by Morris (p. 689),
for example, "was wrestling with a critical problem in the school's
curricular program . . . [when] the entire matter was elbowed
aside, denied a position of deserved prominence, by a cascade of
other concerns—vandalized auditorium seats, a foul-mouthed girl
intimidating her teacher, bomb threats by anonymous phone callers,
and cockroaches in the locker room."

Given the wide range of responsibilities involved in leading a
ghetto school (not the least of which is balancing the demands of
sometimes hostile teachers, students, parents, and community),
it is no wonder that principals are sidetracked by tasks not immediately related to pupils' learning. While such problems in the

day-to-day operation of the school must be handled (members of a
management team could do this), the principal should have as his
primary goal improving the quality of instruction for all students.
Tragically, such leadership among principals is rare, and, as
Enochs (1981, p. 175) suggests, "Managing may be an artful way of
preventing a job from exceeding the limits of [the principal]."

As examples of how Du Sable's principal focused on issues
unrelated to increasing pupils' learning, I offer the following bulletins culled from my files:

SPECIAL BULLETIN #17:
CHALKBOARDS

We are not to glue, paste or afix [sic] any paper or
other materials to chalkboards. Please use cork-
boards provided for this purpose. Any one [sic]
willfully disregarding these instructions may be held
pecuniarily liable for such damage.

DAILY BULLETIN #84

Classroom Doors:
All classroom doors must have an opening for view-
ing the interior of the room per the Fire Code. All
teachers should ensure that their door windows are
not totally obstructed.

DAILY BULLETIN #58

Door Safety:
The practice of putting a chair in a doorway to prop
open a door is unsafe. This practice is to cease immediately. Anyone placing a chair or some other
obstruction in a doorway will be held liable in the
event of an accident. Anyone encountering such an
unsafe act should remove the obstacle on the spot
if possible.

SPECIAL BULLETIN #21:
FIRE DRILLS

You have been requested to read Permanent Bulletin
#18 regarding fire drills. The false alarm on Thurs-
day was a disgrace. Any teacher not following procedure by NOT TAKING his/her class out of the building
will be given an E-1 [Unsatisfactory Rating].

DAILY BULLETIN #251

6" Window Openings:
Teachers are directed not to have windows open more
than 6" from the bottom. Because of many reasons,
windows are not to be open more than 6" from the
bottom. Windows may also be opened from the top.

THE PRINCIPAL AS TEACHER AND
TEACHER-EDUCATOR

Positions of educational leadership should be earned only
through demonstrated, and continued, excellence in teaching. The
head of every school should be first and foremost a master teacher
who, through his daily teaching, models for his staff an intelligent,
professional approach to education.

Central to his role as instructional leader should be the
dialogue he promotes between himself and his teachers. The thrust
of this intensive dialogue should be, of course, how to increase
student learning. In short, the principal would not only teach students in his building, he would (through inservice sessions and
daily interactions with faculty) teach his teachers what he knows
about teaching. As Rosenberg (1982, p. 630) suggests, such communication would herald new relationships between principal and
teacher:

> No longer would there be an endless series of "Do
> as I say" directives. Instead, there might well be
> a new mutual exchange: "Come and see how I do,
> and I will go see how you do. Together we will
> strive to raise the quality of our children's school-
> ing to the highest level."

Principals capable of perceiving their role in this manner would
demonstrate clearly to their faculties that promoting excellence in
teaching—not management—is their primary mission. Once again
(as he was earlier in the history of our nation's schools) the principal would be known as the "principal-teacher."

Du Sable's principal, as I believe the following "Message
from the Principal" makes clear, was not a thoughtful and alert
student of education. With fuzzy logic and the conviction that erod-
ing educational standards had resulted from "informal," "liberal,"
and "general" approaches to education, he directed his teachers to
implement a systematic, behavioristic approach to instruction:

MESSAGE FROM THE PRINCIPAL

Informal education, which has dominated the education scene over the past twenty (20) years, has proven not to be as effective as a formal education which preceded it. ACT scores, standardized test scores, and even scores of locally produced tests have served as barometers indicating a trend toward a high rate of failure.

Universities are forced to provide remedial courses in English, reading, and math because high school graduates are not competent in those areas. Universities, becoming alarmed at the lack of competencies among incoming freshmen, criticize secondary schools. However, the universities conveniently ignore the fact that the universities produced the teachers who are producing academically crippled high school graduates.

The universities led the movement away from formal education by dropping "methods" courses and diluting "skills" education. Content courses were dropped in favor of "humanities" courses and "liberal," generalized courses.

As a result of the education teachers received, teachers did not teach specific skills and concepts but rather they taught in general areas. Students, then, did not learn specific skills because they were not taught specific skills. Students did not meet standards because no standards were established.

We are now attempting to be more specific about what is to be taught and how it is to be taught. There is hope for the future if we establish standards, develop testing objectives, spell-out [sic] activities and materials, and prepare CRT's [criterion-referenced tests] and other tests.

We must assess student's [sic]; teach appropriate objectives; test objectives with CRT's; and proceed to the next appropriate objective. Continuous evaluation must take place. If we do this, then we will achieve Excellence Plus.

Two additional examples of my principal's systematic approach to instruction follow. These are indicative, too, of the meager dialogue about education that occurred between the principal and his teachers.

DAILY BULLETIN #46

Classroom Routines:
Classroom routines should be posted in all classrooms. Trouble sometimes develop [sic] simply because students do not know what is expected of them.
To avoid this in-limbo [sic] situation, it helps to
establish a routine.

DAILY BULLETIN #251

Instructional Planning:
Effective September 1977, Long Term Plans are to
be submitted with these components in detail: testing objectives, materials, activities, and criterion-
referenced tests. Materials and activities are to
be written as "Use and Do."

SUPPORT OF TEACHERS

The following letter, submitted by a group of my Du Sable colleagues to their principal, reveals not only the stress teachers experienced but also the lack of support they felt while on the job:

Dear Mr. Krimbill:

We the undersigned teachers wish to inform you that
the climate in the halls is growing progressively
worse. There are dangerous numbers of unauthor-
ized and unruly students in the halls during all
periods. This hazardous situation runs the gamut
from a few scattered violators before division,
through numerous agitators during lunch periods,
to threatening numbers of "professional" hall-
roamers who disrupt 8th, 9th, and 10th period
classes. In addition, it is often not safe in the
classroom, as many students either have keys to
the rooms or have become proficient in the art of
opening doors with their ID cards.

These citizens of the halls are generally of the law-
less and antisocial variety. They are devoting their
school years to becoming skilled at the use of pro-
fanity and the terrorizing of teachers, other students,
and personnel in the halls.
This situation has now reached the point where a
teacher is not safe standing (as directed) in the corridor between passing periods. Some students will
attempt to enter classrooms by forcing their way past
teachers who stand in doorways trying to prevent "outsiders" from entering the room and disrupting classes.
If the accosted teacher tries to stand his ground, he is
often met with repeated obscene verbal attacks, threats
to his life, or threatening pushes and shoves. When the
teacher looks around for aid he finds himself alone—
without help, without security. As we know, staff
members have already been hurt in confrontations
with students, and more will be hurt unless adequate
steps are taken to control the situation.
We are tired of being pushed, of being verbally assaulted and threatened, and of having our classrooms
disrupted. Some of us have brought our individual
complaints through all of the proper channels, and
now we bring our concerns directly to you. We demand that we be able to work in a safe school. If
you won't accept the responsibility for making this
school safe, we will be forced to make our plight
known to the Chicago Board of Education and the
concerned citizens of Chicago.

While no teacher at Du Sable expected the principal to solve
wondrously all his teaching problems, teachers did hope for support
based on an adult, objective assessment of the situation. Instead,
directives from the principal ranged from those that either denied
actual conditions or those that, in a condescending and inane tone,
implied that teachers were somehow to blame for school conditions.
While such responses to problem situations might have been the
"best" course of action for a white principal at an all-black school
to follow, they only heightened the stress experienced by teachers
and promoted an adversarial, rather than professional, relationship
between the principal and his teachers.

To illustrate further this lack of administrative support, I
offer the following memos which implied that uncommitted and lazy
teachers were the "cause" of problems within the school:

SPECIAL BULLETIN #43:
STUDENT ATTENDANCE

Unfortunately for the school and the students only
eleven teachers submttted the names of [parent volun-
teers] to reduce absenteeism. There are some teachers who would say that the teachers did not cooperate
because the idea did not originate with the teachers.
They would go on to say that any idea not originating
from the teachers was doomed to ignominious failure
because the teachers resent being told what to do. On
the other hand, there are those who might say that
some teachers were just too lazy or indifferent and
could care less about doing anything, positive or
otherwise.

DAILY BULLETIN #107

Thank You:
Thank you to those few teachers who are assisting
to clear the halls during passing time. Unfortunately they cannot handle the problem alone. It's
interesting to see who does and who doesn't.

DAILY BULLETIN #181

Teacher Responsibility:
Teachers shall be held responsible for the discipline of their classes. Recent court rulings have
held teachers responsible for discipline in and
around the school. A recent court decision held
a teacher negligent for an incident that occurred
a block away from school as the teacher went to
her car.

DAILY BULLETIN #172

Did You Know:
A new tree (price $800.00) was planted near the
southeast end of our building. The bark has been
stripped off and branches have been broken. This
is food for thought.

DAILY BULLETIN #5

Example:
Let us, as adults, set an example for our students to
emulate in dress and behavior. Let's upgrade ourselves in both areas so that students will have a
positive image to observe and follow.

SPECIAL BULLETIN #10

Some positive actions for staff to take are to be on
time to school, class, duty post, meeting, etc. and
to exert a forceful personality in enforcing school
rules. If students know we mean business they will
cooperate. Students must realize that EVERYONE
is going to enforce the rules and not every OTHER
one.

The following bulletin items, on the other hand, suggested
that the school had few major problems, and that the principal's
primary task was to convince others of Du Sable's "Number One"
status:

DAILY BULLETIN #69

Pride in Du Sable:
Staff members should guide students to develop
pride in Du Sable High School, which is one of the
best High School's [sic] in the City. Do this by
talking up the school. Discuss the positive aspects
of the school—there are many.

SPECIAL BULLETIN #13

There are some priceless and more precious as-
sets which Du Sable High School possesses. Our
students are the best in the City. . . . Our school
offers one of the finest educational programs in
the entire City.

SPECIAL BULLETIN #28

We have the expertise among adults, the talent
among students, and the will to be Number One.
Now we need the "where-with-all" [sic] to do
our thing first class.

COMMUNICATION

Authentic, two-way, face-to-face communication between principal and teachers is the cornerstone upon which efforts to improve schooling should be built. If teachers believe that their administrative leaders do not truly listen to their concerns, that policies are formulated without regard to their intimate, firsthand experience with students, then professional demoralization follows. Professional initiative is transformed into apathy or resignation; all that remains is the desire to "get through" each day until sign-out time.

Just as teachers can alienate an entire class through being glib, subtly disrespectful, and parental rather than adult, a principal with similar habits can seriously limit communication with his faculty. Yet effective communication cannot be legislated into being; it must spring out of the natural desire of two parties to enter into a meaningful dialogue.

Communication at Du Sable, as the following bulletins attest, was so highly structured that it was highly unlikely that administrators and teachers would communicate freely, openly, and with reciprocal professional regard:

DAILY BULLETIN #40

Internal Communication:
As imperfect as it is, we do have a communication
network loop at Du Sable High School. Inputs and
feedback plus the dissemination of information are
looped as follows:

TEACHERS ⟷ INSTRUCTIONAL TEAM LEADERS ⟷ PLANNING GROUP ⟷ ADMINISTRATIVE TEAM

This is in addition to the normal channels of communication such as: Faculty Dismissal Meeting,
Daily Bulletins, Special Bulletins, Permanent Bulletins, Teacher-Counselor Meeting, Meeting with
Assistant Principals, etc.

DAILY BULLETIN #147

District Superintendent:
The District Superintendent is asking that everyone
follow proper procedures and go through channels.
It is only proper and courteous that teachers

communicate with the principal first. So henceforth, no one is to make direct contact with the District Superintendent either verbally or in writing.

DAILY BULLETIN #190

Line of Communication:
District personnel are not to contact High School personnel directly. Staff members should report such incidents immediately.

Perhaps the most effective way to assess the effectiveness of any principal would be to observe the patterns of interaction between him and his teachers. The operating question is the extent to which principal and teachers express, through their dialogue, professional respect for one another and a willingness to inquire intelligently into educational problems. The unfortunate reality of this dialogue as it occurred at Du Sable was that principal and teachers conspired to bring out the worst in each other.

REFERENCES

Brookover, W., and Lezotte, L.   "Changes in School Characteristics Coincident with Changes in School Achievement." Institute for Research on Teaching, Michigan State University, May 1979.

Enochs, J.   "Up from Management." Phi Delta Kappan 63 (1981): 175-78.

Kean, M., et al.   "What Works in Reading?" Office of Research and Evaluation, Philadelphia School District, May 1979.

Morris, V., et al.   "The Urban Principal: Middle Manager in the Educational Bureaucracy." Phi Delta Kappan 63 (1982):689-92.

New York State Office of Evaluation Performance Review.   "School Traits Influencing Reading Achievement: A Case Study of Two Inner-City Schools." March 1974.

Rosenberg, M.   "School Principals Should Teach." Phi Delta Kappan 63 (1982):630.

Venezky, R., and Winfield, L. Schools That Succeed Beyond Expectations in Teaching Reading. Newark: University of Delaware Studies on Education, Technical Report #1, 1980.

Weber, G. Inner-City Children Can Be Taught to Read: Four Successful Schools. Washington, D.C.: Council for Basic Education, 1971.

13

THE WINDS OF CHANGE: INNOVATION COMES TO DU SABLE

Now I see the futility of altering
the direction which Du Sable is
taking to bring about change. The
only successful curriculum reform
will come after we, the teachers,
have thoroughly examined our
situation and have arrived at some
consensus of what the best course
of action is. I don't consider this
a radical position by any means.
I feel that the school is now committed to an unfathomable waste
of money and human effort. I hope
that time will prove me wrong.

From an English Teacher's
Letter to the Principal

MOST of the teachers felt pretty good about the week-long inservice
workshop that began that Monday morning. After all, it wasn't
every day that the Board of Education was willing to pay teachers
a full week's salary just to get ready for the new school year.

Even the school's advanced placement U.S. history teacher,
Mr. Goldman, a squat, balding white man who railed constantly

Portions of this chapter were first published under the title "Innovation in a Chicago Inner-City High School," Phi Delta Kappan 57,
no. 6 (1976).

about the ineptitude of the kids, the principal, and especially the "stooges" downtown at the board, was more hopeful than usual.

"Well, just maybe we'll get something done now," he said to me between slurps of his early morning black coffee. I nodded agreement across our table in the first floor lunchroom, the location of the workshop's opening session.

"We've gotta stop passing these kids on. I've been here seven years, and do you realize I've had only one or two kids who could read at grade level. I got kids in my advanced placement class that read on the sixth grade level. You call that advanced placement?"

"You're right," I said. "It's hard to teach an A-P course if the kids can't read." My response to Goldman was calm and even, so that his critical remarks about the school might not, as they almost always did, become louder and more emotional. I didn't want the two black teachers seated at the other end of our long table to be offended.

"Last week in the Trib they interviewed the district superintendent. She said the average incoming freshman reads at 3.5. Not even at the fourth grade level! These are the kids that end up, three or four years later, in my A-P class."

"Do you know what this meeting is about?" I asked Goldman. I decided to try to change the subject because I never knew quite how to respond to his criticisms of the school. "I hear we're going to develop a new curriculum."

"What the hell difference will a new curriculum make if the kids can't read," moaned Goldman, unwilling to leave the matter of the kids' low reading scores.

Just then Miss Franco, a young white math teacher joined us. "Did you guys get your workshop packets?" she asked as she tossed two orange folders stuffed with papers on the table. Before sitting down, she brushed away the food crumbs left on her lunchroom chair.

"It looks like the Board is really going all out with this one," she said, spreading one of the folders open on the table. "They brought in some consultants from California." She then pulled out, one-by-one, the stapled handouts inside the folder and read aloud the title printed in headline size type on each cover.

"HIGH SCHOOL: A PART OF THE TOTAL PROCESS."

"Terrific, now all we have to do is figure out what the hell that means," quipped Goldman as he rose to get us both folders from the big stack on a table nearby.

Teachers were arriving quickly now, and Mr. Krimbill was just about ready to begin. Coach Tanner and Coach Washington strolled into the room just as the 8:00 bell rang. They decided to sit at our table.

"MODULE A: CRITERION FOR INDIVIDUALIZED LEARN-
ING—GIVE THEM A BREAK!" Miss Franco read this title in a
singsong voice.

"Shit, I'll give these goddam kids a break all right. Right
over their fool empty heads," Coach Washington growled as he bent
his huge body to fit the small lunchroom chair he selected.

"Listen to this one: MODULE B: HOW TO USE OBJEC-
TIVES—LET THEM KNOW WHERE THEY'RE GOING!"

"Where they're going?" said Coach Washington, responding
again to the title Miss Franco read. "Shit, three-quarters of these
kids are going right out onto the streets, 47th and State, with their
reefer and Ripple. And half a them's gonna wind up in jail—or
dead. That's where they're going."

"MODULE C: HOW TO USE CRITERION TESTS—MEASURE
THEM ACCORDING TO THEIR OWN GROWTH, NOT EVERYONE
ELSE'S."

As Miss Franco continued to familiarize us with the workshop
materials, I thumbed through a 75-page booklet titled ADDENDUM:
SHORT AND LONG RANGE GOALS. Inside were futuristic-looking
diagrams with bold arrows and circles and architectural drawings
of modern buildings. These pages had titles like "Total Community
Career Development: Satellite Resource Development Special
Projects," "A Total System for Continuing Education," and "The
Career Oriented Interdisciplinary Curriculum."

I was intrigued. How was all of this going to fit into the program of Du Sable? I went back through the booklet, trying to make
sense of it. The pages appeared to be taken from several different
sources, and no narrative tied it all together.

Though confused, I was hopeful. The materials had a kind of
high-tech, slick advertising quality to them; maybe, then, these
professional consultants knew what they were doing. Innovation had
finally come to Du Sable, and I was ready to give it a try.

By this time Mr. Krimbill had gotten the bugs out of the
portable amplifier he would use to address us from the front of the
lunchroom, and he was ready to begin. Seated behind him were
four men and two women I had not seen before. All six were nat-
tily dressed, three-piece suits and color coordinated shirts and
ties for the men and chic business suits for the women.

Mr. Krimbill began the meeting by welcoming us to the start
of another school year. He then read the names of 11 new teachers
and had them stand up so the rest of us could see who they were.

"Welcome to the Black Hole of Calcutta," mumbled a mus-
tachioed young teacher at the table behind me.

Following the introductions, Krimbill got right down to business.

"For the information of new teachers and to update the rest of us, let's review our long-range goals. First—career education is to be our guiding theme. Preparing our students for the world of work."

"Yeah—pimp, con artist, mugger," said a doubtful Coach Washington.

"Eventually, we hope to develop Learning Activity Packages (LAPs) for our career education offerings. The components of these LAPs are: sets of measurable objectives, learning guides, criterion-referenced tests in two forms, a teacher's manual, and a resource booklet."

"He's gone around the bend," Miss Franco whispered to me and Goldman. "He's completely flipped out on this behavioral objective bull crap."

"Teachers have to become more precise in stating measurable objectives," Krimbill went on. "And they must develop criterion-referenced tests to measure those objectives. This week, then, under the direction of our six guests, whom I will introduce now, we will write criterion-referenced behavioral objectives and criterion-referenced tests for all of our course offerings at Du Sable."

Krimbill then introduced the six consultants from a California-based firm I will call California Learning Corporation (CLC—a splinter group of a nationally known educational corporation). One by one, each member of the CLC staff gave a short talk extolling the virtues of computer instructional management systems, career clusters, instructional delivery system, and the like. The objectives and test items we were to write that week, they explained, would be banked in a computer. We were also told that CLC methods had dramatically "turned around" problem schools such as Du Sable.* The key, they informed us, was simple: "give the students a break" and acquaint them with the teacher's requirements.

By the time the workshop broke for lunch, my colleagues and I felt overwhelmed by the unfamiliar rhetoric of the "systems approach" to education. In addition, some of the teachers were

---

*I was never able to verify this alleged success of CLC methods. For example, the principal of a Watts high school in Los Angeles, where a CLC-engineered system had to be abandoned because of financial and political "difficulties," failed to answer my inquiry about his school's involvement with CLC.

angry because none of us knew that outside "experts" were to be brought in. However, most of us were generally optimistic and wanted to believe what we had just heard.

The remainder of that week we spent writing behavioral objectives according to a specific format and learning about the changes CLC planned to implement at Du Sable. At the conclusion of the workshop, CLC's vice-president remained at the school to form a six-member planning team made up of that year's department chairmen. The team was later given the acronym D-COES, for Du Sable Community Occupational Education System.

DU SABLE'S INNOVATIONS

The innovation described above was actually one of three changes that began at Du Sable that year. In this section, then, I will describe, in the approximate order in which they were considered for implementation, these three innovations: (1) a year-round time schedule, (2) mini-course offerings, and (3) the educational management system. My vantage point during that period of change, 1973-77, was that of the concerned teacher involuntarily isolated from actual planning and decision making. When I became English department chairman in 1974, however, I was "allowed" to move in closer to the innovative planning process.

The Year-Round 45-15 Time Schedule

In February, 1973, Du Sable's principal was informed by an area superintendent of the opportunity for a Chicago high school to go on the 45-15 plan; (a school is divided into four "houses" and, on a staggered basis, each house attends school for 45 days and then takes a mini-vacation of 15 days before returning for another 45-day cycle). Du Sable's administrative staff decided to pursue the year-round plan as an initial step toward career education. Department chairmen thereupon met with their departments in March and presented the proposal to teachers. The teachers approved the plan by a 117 to 28 vote.

Du Sable students, eighth grade students in seven feeder schools, and parents were informed of the proposal through meetings, fact sheets, and radio and newspaper announcements. Students rejected the year-round plan by a 1,924 to 1,119 vote. The parent vote, however, was a favorable 586 to 368. The student vote notwithstanding, 45-15 received Board of Education approval, and Du Sable began year-round operation in July, 1973.

Mini-course Offerings

Prior to 45-15, Du Sable's principal, impressed with reports of mini-courses taught at innovative schools in Illinois, Michigan, and Florida, had recommended that Du Sable's curriculum be reorganized into mini-courses. With the advent of the 45-15 plan, he mandated nine-week mini-courses throughout the school.

The Educational Management System

The educational management system teachers were introduced to during that one-week workshop was difficult to see in a total configuration. Though CLC prepared a 32-page prospectus explaining D-COES, the booklet's futuristic art and slick advertising rhetoric created an image of the Du Sable-to-be that would boggle the mind of anyone familiar with the school. The booklet was filled with photos of blacks engaged in occupations such as airline pilot, city planner, chemist, model, and computer expert. Also included were high sounding, yet meaningless, passages such as the following:

> Now is a time in which industry, education, and government urgently need to direct their resources toward a <u>Continuing Educational System</u> which emphasizes the worth of the individual and his potential in an environment providing the comprehensive resources and educational guidance to relate <u>all learning</u> to "real" experience and expanding human dignity.
> As we point out in the following pages, the total community and its resources must be involved if truly individualized experiences are to be provided for each learner. <u>The school, taken alone, is a closed system, and no matter how large and comprehensive schools become, they can never equal the variety of experience to be found in the community at large.</u>

My description of Du Sable's multifaceted educational management system is based on careful study of CLC and D-COES materials and on occasional talks with CLC's president and vice-president, who gave me, rather grudgingly, their "up-to-the-minute" projections for implementation of the project's various phases.

Phase I: Instructional Management System—
Measurable Objectives

During this phase, teachers were required to write behavioral objectives for over 500 mini-courses. As mentioned earlier, these objectives and their corresponding test items were eventually to be banked in a computer.

Following are two objectives, from a total of fifteen, for a nine-week unit of junior English grammar and two objectives, from a total of nineteen, for a unit in U.S. history. In preparation for the computer-based management system, computer code numbers were assigned to objectives as they were written:

121102 Given a sentence, you will be able to select the appropriate verb form when presented with a choice between past tense and past participle.

121103 Given a sentence, you will be able to select the appropriate verb form to make the verb agree in number with the subject.

210115 Given an explanation of the Boston Tea Party and the resultant Intolerable Acts, you will be able to identify the major acts.

210116 Given a description of the Mercantile System tenets, you will be able to choose the main tenets.

Phase II: Instructional Management System—
Criterion-Referenced Tests

Phase II required that teachers write at least two multiple-choice criterion test items for each Phase I objective. Following are two objectives and their corresponding test items from a unit on Greek and Roman mythology:

131001 You will be able to define the word "myth."
  1. A myth is:
     (a) a long narrative poem in elevated style relating the deeds of a legendary or historical hero
     (b) a prose narrative dealing with a few characters and aiming at developing a single episode or creating a single mood

(c) a legendary narrative that presents parts of the beliefs of a people or explains a practice, a belief, or a natural phenomenon

(d) a narrative poem usually in stanzas of two to four lines and suitable for singing.

131002 <u>Given any of its elements, you will identify</u> the term "creation myth."

1. The elements chaos, father god, mother god would be an essential part of a (an):

(a) creation myth
(b) explanatory myth
(c) epic
(d) legend

Phase III: Instructional Management System—Implementation and Field Testing

Phase III began in October, 1974 and ended in April, 1975. During this phase, teachers were to teach selected units (120 out of 500) using the new objectives and test items.

Teachers who began field testing were given the following suggestions for using the new materials:

Explain to your students just exactly why you wrote this particular group of objectives or why a member of your department did. . . . What would you want a student to take with him from your course: What are the basic skills you wish the student to gain as a result of the course. [<u>sic</u>] These are the skills? [<u>sic</u>]

Students involved in field testing were given, on the first day of the unit, a list of behavioral objectives and a letter of explanation signed by "Everyone at Du Sable." The letter provided the following clarification of the program:

For the past year and a half, your teachers here at Du Sable have been working very hard to bring you a kind of education that would be up to date and give you what you need to build skills. . . .
It is called "individualized instructions" [<u>sic</u>] that means "breaking things down so you can work according to your own speed, interest and ability."

It makes school personal. It lets you know what is
"going on," lets you in on the act, and allows learning
to be your scene.
This kind of system or way of working in class lets
your teacher say "every student is working the way he
works best." Everyone in the class is a star—everyone in the class is a Super Star! and thats [sic] you.

Phase III: Instructional Management System— Learning Guides and Correlations

Concurrent with field testing, Phase III also included training
teachers to use individualized instruction and continuous progress
methods in the classroom. To accomplish this, the Elementary
and Secondary Education Act (ESEA), Title I funded two "human
resource laboratories" at Du Sable. Each lab was given a teacher
manager and learning modules prepared by CLC.

Phase IV: Instructional Management System— Revision of Course Units

Phase IV, which was completed during the 1975-76 school
year, called for the revision of objectives and test items based on
teacher feedback gained during field testing.

Phase V: Instructional Management System— Implementation of Remaining Units

During Phase V, which began in January, 1975, the remaining units in the curriculum were used in the classroom. CLC materials and comments by the principal implied that Phase V could
lead to some form of teacher accountability, to be based on the
number of objectives students mastered.

Career Education and Career Clusters

Du Sable was also to become, again with the help of CLC, a
career education school. Just what Du Sable's career education
was to be and how it was to be financed were not clear; however,
the D-COES prospectus set forth the following goal:

To provide by 1981 (1) career development programs,
including guidance services, for all students; (2) comprehensive occupational preparation programs within
reach of all adults; and (3) comprehensive postsecon-
dary occupational preparation programs within reach
of all youth and adults.

Du Sable's career education program was to be structured around specific "career clusters" and "applied learning laboratories." According to the D-COES prospectus, a career cluster was to increase a student's learning experiences:

> The whole concept of a career cluster is to focus available resources for a learner and personalize his or her educational experience. . . . A cluster program accommodates the learner into a system with respect for his unique abilities, aptitudes, and goals. He is given choices as his self-actualization process unfolds with reinforced bridges to the real world.

Elsewhere, the prospectus defined the applied learning laboratory:

> Applied learning laboratories provide the learner with a broad base of resources and experiences at each step in his learning process. He is exposed to the real world of business, industry, and the professions in simulated work situations and real work experiences. So that what he learns is "in sync" with what he is doing and is the now activity that motivates and generates the need to learn.

According to the D-COES planning team, the business occupations and health occupations career clusters were implemented during the 1976-77 school year. (At best, however, business and health teachers merely devoted additional class time to discussing the possible careers in business and health; in no substantive way were Du Sable students "prepared" to work in these two areas.) Industrial technology, agriculture and biological systems, and public services were to be implemented later.

OUTSIDE SUPPORT FOR THE INNOVATIONS

Within the D-COES project there was a tentativeness that was difficult for one outside the decision-making process to gauge. While CLC rhetoric promised to transform and to revitalize Du Sable, CLC's president hinted at the obvious experimental nature of the undertaking and the factors (principally, lack of money) that might thwart implementation of the "total system." In the D-COES prospectus, he stated:

Massive curricular change for an ongoing program
requires considerable planning and action on a number of fronts over an extended period of time. . . .
In some of the possible solutions, action can be taken
on the district level without consideration of additional funds. Other component funds will have to be
supplied by the Board of Education for instructional
management by objectives and technological "house-
keeping" for staff and district support. Additional
federal and state support must be sought for developing applied learning systems in which to research and
develop learning management.

FOUR CRITERIA FOR MEANINGFUL CHANGE

Virtually all critics of ghetto schools are in agreement on two
central points. First, these schools must change. Second, their
organizational climates typically inhibit change, or preclude it entirely.

For meaningful change to occur at schools such as Du Sable
(and, indeed, at any school), four conditions must be met:

1. Change must begin with a courageous, honest
   inquiry into the actual state of education within
   the school.
2. Meaningful change must be seen as a gradual
   growth process, the final form of which cannot
   be determined, or administratively mandated,
   beforehand.
3. Change should originate, and end, with the professionally autonomous teacher; worthwhile
   change involves new teacher-student relationships that enhance the educative process.
4. The likelihood of worthwhile change is greatest
   in an organizational setting characterized by an
   authentic spirit of community and open, honest
   communications.

In my evaluation of Du Sable's innovations, I will consider
first the innovations, then the process through which those innovations were to be implemented. While I treat the two elements—
innovation and process—as though separate, their relationship is
more symbiotic than exclusive. The degree to which an organization

is able to change is a function of both the innovation itself and the quality of the innovative process possible within that organizational setting. At Du Sable, deficiencies in the systems package triggered negative teacher reactions. Conversely, the poorly conceived process through which change was to be implemented caused teachers to see little merit in the proposed systems package.

ADVANTAGES OF THE CLC APPROACH

So seldom do schools attempt innovations of any sort that I am tempted to say that any change is better than none. If nothing else, then, Du Sable's systems package moved teachers to react, to think—and those were no mean achievements. Systems thinking, if used as part of a multidisciplinary approach to the problems of inner-city education, can be a useful analytical tool for the teacher. (Smith and Geoffrey's The Complexities of an Urban Classroom [1968] is an excellent example of systems thinking applied to urban education.) However, it seems unlikely that the CLC system (in the absence of demonstrated proof of its worth anywhere) could have been the solution to Du Sable's problems.

An educational management system also has the potential to provide teachers, especially those weak in developing a substantive cohesiveness in their courses, with a "ready made" structure that students could master only through self-discipline. The management system itself, with its clear organizational and immutable requirements, might prove to be the teacher's "ally" in bringing students "under control." No longer would demands be made by the capricious-seeming teacher alone; the "system" would also have its demands.

And for some students a fully functioning management system might add a degree of "scientific" objectivity (though admittedly illusory) to the learning process. It is possible that CLC technology, with its allusions to the computer and its mystique, might, through a glorified Hawthorne effect, have motivated those students who were locked into a self-destructive pattern of resistance to teachers.

LIMITATIONS OF THE CLC APPROACH

The greatest limitation of the CLC system was its failure to consider, in any way, the culture and learning styles of Du Sable students, or to examine what Churchman (1968) calls the "environment" within which a system is expected to function. In this regard, it was difficult to see how Du Sable's principal could conscionably state in the D-COES prospectus that "our professional staff and members of the community feel that education today must meet the needs of the students as opposed to students meeting the requirements of the system."

While Du Sable students seemed to function best in highly structured courses, many teachers found that the syntactical sophistication of the objectives' sentences, their vocabulary level, their dulling effect when presented in list form, and the thought processes necessary for mastery all led to frustration for the majority of Du Sable's students. As I suggested in Chapter 10, students with severe reading problems learn best from teachers who first meet students within the context of their own experiences and then proceed to a "traditional," symbol-based mode of instruction.

Systems approaches per se are not "wrong"; the risk is that the purposes of the system and the purposes of the local school can be mismatched, as they appear to have been at Du Sable. The CLC system wrongly assumed that instructional goals could be decided upon and reached in expedient, straight arrow fashion. While this design may have helped the Department of Defense and industry meet their goals, it proved to be an insufficient model for education at Du Sable.

The value of any systems model depends on whether its components form a "closed," as opposed to "open," system. In other words, to what extent can all eventualities be determined beforehand? Schools, which the CLC staff viewed as closed systems, are actually open to significant influence by the environments in which they are embedded.

Because a system of the CLC sort could "take in" only that which was quantifiable and directly observable, it had to neglect many of the unmeasurable, though important, facets of teaching and learning. The result, therefore, was meaningless trivia to be memorized (as the examples of objectives and test items presented earlier in this chapter confirm) and a simplistic, reductivist conception of education.

It is ironic (nay, even tragic) that those whom the D-COES approach was to affect the most, the students, should have experienced no significant change in their daily educational lives. After more than four years of involvement with CLC, Du Sable's only accomplishment was the creation of a bank of behavioral objectives and a series of tests of extremely low validity and reliability. Furthermore, many teachers confided to me that they simply did not use the approach; students, they found, were more turned off by lists of objectives than they were with traditional materials.

Many Du Sable teachers were disturbed by the conflict they saw between CLC values and those of educators whose job is to teach—not to make a profit. CLC materials, with their inflated, semantically ambiguous rhetoric and mediocre intellectual quality, caused me to suspect the ethics of the CLC staff (which, following the demise of Du Sable's innovations in 1978, submitted to the Board of Education a proposal to construct a criterion-referenced testing program for the Board's minimum competency high school graduation test in mathematics, science, English, and social studies—at a cost of $520,000). The values of the marketplace, as Goldberg (1972, p. 10) asserts, are not likely to be accepted by the teaching profession:

> Until the educational technology projectors and promoters face and try to answer the basic psychosocial, psycho-ethical normative challenges being directed to them, they will continue to experience hard resistance to what they want to sell; and such resistance, to my mind, is intelligent. It is prudent and large-visioned. It is to the credit of the teaching profession.

Oettinger (1969, p. 102) also warns against unscrupulous systems technologists:

> An administrator of the Air Force Office of Scientific Research is quoted as cracking: "We sold them the sizzle, not the steak."
> . . . . Although the time for similar official candor in what Tom Lehrer calls the "ed biz" is not yet here, the available evidence points to the same phenomenon at work.

While this manipulation by the military might seem inconsequential, even humorous, it becomes tragic if the ultimate victims have been unwitting youth seeking an education as a way out of the ghetto and the real beneficiaries were those promoting the system.

EVALUATION OF THE INNOVATIVE PROCESS

On an attitude survey I gave to a random sample of 32 of Du Sable's 150 teachers, only 6.3 percent felt they "were adequately represented during the planning stages of Du Sable's new programs," and only 9.3 percent felt that "teachers themselves [were] able to influence the direction [of change] at Du Sable."

I found it ironic that teachers were expected to implement, and were held accountable for, innovations that they were not allowed to help plan.

Du Sable's administration, however, felt that teachers did have input into the change process. In response to a letter from a female teacher who felt the school was "committed to an unfathomable waste of money and human effort," the principal wrote:

> The administrative staff, the planning group, and the teachers through the department chairmen were all involved to varying degrees.
> Our position is that we have an open-door policy. All teachers may involve themselves in what is happening. The teacher-department chairman-planning group is one avenue for teacher involvement. Other involvement of the teacher can be in whatever manner desired.

Teachers' opinions, however, were received in such a systematized and controlled manner as to blunt or eliminate thoughtful, open inquiry into alternate proposals. Teachers who resisted complying with the CLC approach were usually questioned by the principal through written memos which ended with a request to "please advise." Copies of these memos were also placed in the files the principal had for each teacher.

Several successful, creative, and individually "innovative" teachers were militantly against the CLC system. A few teachers even transferred amid rumors of their unwillingness to "go along" with the system. For example, one teacher, who held a Ph.D. in history, was transferred involuntarily after he had suggested there be a faculty vote on whether or not to continue the D-COES program. In a thoughtful letter to the principal, he said:

> The idea that any branch of History may be reduced to a series of facts to be remembered is simplistic and actually inimical to understanding. The idea of an entire faculty teaching the same list of facts is irreconcilable with professionalism. The advantages which should be gained from a variety of backgrounds and approaches are necessarily lost, innovation is stifled, and teaching as well as learning become rote activities.
> Certainly, and with justice, the Chicago School System has been subject of late to penetrating and unfavorable criticism. We have failed to motivate,

we have failed to socialize, we have failed to educate.
And the situation grows steadily, discouragingly
worse. Few would be so bold as to offer solutions
to problems which have festered for decades, and
which stem from such diverse causes as public
apathy, bureaucratic ineptitude, political corrup-
tion, and racial prejudice. However, the fact that
one cannot suggest a ready solution does not obli-
gate one to accept and participate in a proposed
solution which, from the outset, seems philosoph-
ically and practically wrong.
It would seem expedient, at this point, before more
money and time are expended on the present program at Du Sable, that there be a pause for evaluation. It is suggested that the next inservice training
session be devoted to an open discussion of this
program, and that there be a faculty vote on whether
or not this program is to be continued.

In actual fact, the CLC system was foredoomed because pro-
visions for ongoing evaluation and modification were not built in.
Strangely, CLC preached flexibility in the D-COES prospectus, but
was unable to achieve it:

Education can no longer be isolated (as it has been
since the Industrial Revolution) from the vital flow of
society's growth pattern and social development. It
should be at the service of all people, and it must be
flexible in order to meet their diverse needs.

Real change within the school's organization, therefore, must be
seen as a gradual growth process, one which can adapt itself as
unforeseen consequences emerge.

In retrospect, it is evident that the architects of change at
Du Sable attempted too many innovations too fast. A change such
as the 45-15 time schedule obviously would have to be schoolwide,
but an innovation such as instructional management might ultimately
have gained wider acceptance if it had been assimilated through a
single entry point—perhaps a group of volunteer teachers or an
academic department.

A MEETING WITH THE PRINCIPAL

Two days before one of Du Sable's few inservice meetings to
explain the CLC innovations to teachers, I had requested a meeting

with Mr. Krimbill. Nearly all of the school's English teachers
were strongly against management by objectives, and I thought he
ought to know about it.

At the appointed hour that Monday, I entered Krimbill's office
and took a seat just across from his big oak desk. A small plaque
attached to the front of his desk confronted me head-on. It read,
"Panic Button—In Case of Panic Push Here."

Krimbill eased into his chair, a fancy executive, swivel-
based model that, I noticed, was appreciably higher than the low
chair I sat in. "What can I do for you?" he asked, leaning forward
in his chair as though he knew beforehand the message Du Sable's
English teachers wanted me to convey to him. I sensed that he
was ready to do battle.

"I'll get right to the point," I began. "I've held several small
group discussions in the English department during the last week
and a half, and I believe that nearly everyone in the department is
opposed to writing behavioral objectives."

"Bah," he scoffed. "I can't see that."*

"Well, I think I'm assessing the department's feelings accurately," I said.

"Just what is it you teachers disagree with?" he asked.

"Basically, it's the philosophy behind behavioral objectives.
The people from CLC just don't know how teaching really is."

"Oh, come on now!" Krimbill said, his skeptical jowly face
flushed with irritation. "When I came to Du Sable five years ago,
we had no direction. We were just like every other school. We
just took it a year at a time, repeated everything each year. Now
we have a direction and a goal." Krimbill paused for a moment in
his impassioned spiel, then continued.

"Some teachers are afraid of change because they feel threatened and don't want to do any work. Others are just negative because they don't understand."

"They don't understand?" I asked, nonplused. "Don't you
think teachers might resist change efforts which they understand
only too well?"

"Teachers will have to be accountable," Krimbill went on,
ignoring my question. "Some new teachers have even been told by

---

*Later that month, 83 percent of the school's English teachers
signed another teacher's petition requesting that the English department be allowed to devise its own approach to curriculum im-
provement. The petition was never acted upon.

others, 'Oh, you're lucky to have been assigned to Du Sable, you don't have to do anything there.' We have to be accountable. We have to have goals and objectives. It's just like building a new house. Everybody has their own ideas which they think are good. Someone might want a family-room here, and somebody else might want a workshop here, and somebody else another kind of room. Why, you'd end up with something like the House of the Seven Gables."

"No one is suggesting that we teach without goals and objectives," I said. "It's just that we ought to be allowed to use our own format for writing them."

"We couldn't have everyone doing their own thing," Krimbill countered. "You know, we've never had a direction here at Du Sable. It used to be like someone trying to climb a big hill of sliding sand. The more they'd climb, the less likely they were to make it to the top. Now we've got a direction. A goal."

"Well, you're right, it is good to have a goal." I said. By then, I had given up on trying to convince Krimbill that an educational management system was not the answer to Du Sable's problems, and I thought I ought to agree with something he said.

I then moved to the edge of my chair, signaling Krimbill that it was okay to end the meeting. He made a few additional comments about goals and accountability, to which I nodded approvingly, and then we both rose and walked to the door. There we paused for a moment.

"You know," he began, "this Wednesday's inservice would have been unnecessary if department chairmen had been communicating with their departments. This meeting is going to be a big hassle."

THE INSERVICE MEETING

In preparation for Wednesday's inservice, Krimbill had requested that teachers turn in to Mr. Prokop written comments or questions about the CLC innovations.

The meeting, which was preceded by a false fire alarm and evacuation of the building, began with reports by various planning team members about several workshops they had attended recently. The stony silence of the more than 100 teachers in the auditorium was a telling comment on our interest in the reports. I saw at least two teachers who appeared to be napping.

Then a black science teacher rose to comment about a report made on a workshop at a Chicago university. "I was also at the workshop, and I got a different opinion. I didn't think it was worth much. I look around the auditorium now and I see that everyone is either reading a newspaper or a book or is sleeping. The only reason I was awake was because I was waiting to talk next."

Her remarks brought everyone to life. Loud applause and laughter indicated how accurately she had assessed her fellow teachers' feelings about the meeting.

Undaunted, Krimbill went on to read in a stilted manner from an article that said education should "meet the needs of students" and be a "total process."

Finally, with twenty minutes of the two-and-a-half hour meeting remaining, he turned to the questions we had submitted. Many were from the English department. The first asked whether CLC methods were not "dehumanizing" and "counter-educative."

"That sounds like a quote from the petition that's been circulated," he quipped, and made no further comment.

He read another comment: "'The whole thing with CLC seems overwhelming. Like 1984 or Future Shock.' Future shock—someone wrote a book by that name, didn't they?" He did not discuss the statement any further.

Another question, this one mine: "'If we are to be held accountable, will this accountability be in terms of the criterion-based objectives? And if so, won't teachers be forced to teach for the objectives which, needless to say, many think are worthless?' No," Krimbill explained. "The computer doesn't write the objectives. You write the objectives." Satisfied with the adequacy of his response to my question, Krimbill went on.

After he had gone through the remaining questions and comments, Krimbill said that some teachers were like "Ping-Pong balls." With his tongue he made sounds into the public address system microphone like a bouncing Ping-Pong ball. The ball began bouncing vigorously and then gradually slowed to a halt.

The meeting was concluded when Krimbill urged teachers to come to him, or to the planning team, with suggestions and comments. "Come to us. Come to us," he said as he beckoned teachers in his direction.

A slight pitter-patter of applause trickled throughout the auditorium as teachers rose to sign out from school.

THE PRINCIPAL AS THE KEY FACILITATOR OF CHANGE

Though painful for me, I have been purposely frank in portraying the professional relationship between Du Sable teachers and their principal, for it is impossible to consider the success or failure of an innovation apart from the personalities of the principal and his faculty. While I knew Du Sable's principal to be a well-meaning administrator, I have presented his actions as I feel they were interpreted by the majority of Du Sable's teachers. Furthermore, I should add that I was unable to determine the extent to which my principal had been "ordered" by his superiors to implement the CLC approach. The district superintendent, for example, was instrumental in securing the services of CLC and was rumored to be vigorously "behind" the system.

Nevertheless, the morale of Du Sable's teachers and their effectiveness in the classroom were related to their perceptions of the principal. The operating questions for any school contemplating change, then, are threefold: Is the principal able to foster good group processes by allowing his faculty to share meaningfully in the decision-making process? Is he able to develop a school climate characterized by a spirit of community and thoughtful inquiry into educational problems? And is his attitude toward teachers one of professionalism—not paternalism—so that the growth inhibiting polarization between teachers and administrators is lessened? If the answers to each of these questions is no (as I would have to say it was at Du Sable), then the success of any innovation is doubtful.

THE NEED FOR ORGANIZATIONAL HEALTH

In an article on change and organizational health, Miles (1965, p. 11) suggests that the school desiring to be innovative might be able to change through efforts to improve its organizational health:

> It is time for us to recognize that successful efforts at planned change must take as a primary target the improvement of organizational health—the school system's ability not only to function effectively but to develop and grow into a more fully functioning system.

The most expedient and logical way to improve the organizational health of a school, to move the institution from one that is suppressive to one that is supportive, is to see that the environment encourages, in every way possible, the human dialogue.

However, the move from a suppressive climate to one that is supportive may be impossible for schools such as Du Sable. The environment in which these schools are embedded may make change in the organizational climate impossible. Little may be done about the adverse conditions that bring out the worst in both principal and teachers—defensiveness and rigidity on the part of the principal as he tries to meet the complex demands of his job, and easily roused hostility on the part of teachers who daily experience frustration and limited success.

CONCLUSION

Carlson (1967, p. 4) states that "the full account of the life cycle of an innovation is the story of its invention, development and promotion, adoption, diffusion, and demise. . . ." After more than five years of work, Du Sable's innovations went through their full life cycle. The "causes" of the program's demise were several: (1) outside financial support was seriously limited and eventually disappeared altogether; (2) teachers found the systems approach unworkable in the classroom and therefore abandoned it in numbers unknown to the administration; (3) morale and support for the project declined seriously, as increasingly militant teachers became concerned about the gap between the system's rhetoric and classroom reality; and (4) students all along exercised their ultimate veto and rejected the system.

The administration, as one might imagine, had its own view of the effect that the change process had on the school. In a special bulletin notifying teachers that Du Sable would cease the 45-15 year-round time schedule, the principal said:

> I would like to thank each and every one who worked to make this program a success. For a success, it was!
> The school climate improved, attitudes became more positive, and everyone felt more relaxed and satisfied. These things are hard to measure but it is my opinion that the learner did benefit from this program in many ways, including academically, socially, and emotionally. The 45-15 did contribute to a more positive academic program and more success among students.
> We are extremely grateful for having had the opportunity to be a part of this activity and for being able to experience success in a learner oriented program. We pledge to continue to provide academic excellence at Du Sable High School.

It seems clear that the planners of Du Sable's innovations underestimated the complex factors involved in bringing about educational change. Yet the key to change is deceptively simple,

as Thelen (1954, p. 73) points out: "To change teaching means that
the teacher himself must, in some respects at least, change. And
only the teacher can change the teacher."

Change must begin with what the teacher does in the classroom. The real innovative "experts" in inner-city education are
to be found among the teachers. They ought to be found and they
ought to be listened to. If so, we might have more schools such as an
innovative Boston school that Schrag (1967, pp. 109-10) describes:
It has "demonstrated what, tragically, must be demonstrated again
and again, and that is that when teachers are given a little time,
are treated like professionals, and are given the freedom to function, they will respond."

REFERENCES

Carlson, R. Adoption of Educational Innovations. Eugene, Oregon:
Center for the Advanced Study of Educational Administration,
University of Oregon, 1967.

Churchman, C. W. The Systems Approach. New York: Delacorte
Press, 1968.

Goldberg, M. Cybernation, Systems, and the Teaching of English:
The Dilemma of Control. Urbana, Illinois: National Council of
Teachers of English, 1972.

Miles, M. "Planned Change and Organizational Health: Figure and
Ground." In Change Processes in the Public Schools. Eugene,
Oregon: Center for the Advanced Study of Educational Adminis-
tration, University of Oregon, 1965.

Oettinger, A. Run, Computer Run: The Mythology of Educational
Innovation. Cambridge, Mass.: Harvard University Press, 1969.

Schrag, P. Village School Downtown: Politics and Education—A
Boston Report. Boston: Beacon Press, 1967.

Smith, L., and Geoffrey, W. The Complexities of an Urban Classroom: An Analysis Toward a General Theory of Teaching. New
York: Rinehart and Winston, 1968.

Thelen, H. Dynamics of Groups at Work. Chicago: University of
Chicago Press, 1954.

14

TOWARD A PROFESSIONAL
ENVIRONMENT: MY
PRESCRIPTION FOR CHANGE

We as teachers cannot be expected
to change must less identify the
many causes that have made
[ghetto schools] a jungle. The
President, the Congress, the Su-
preme Court, the intellectuals,
and a hell of a lot of money have
all failed to ameliorate the conditions that make [these schools]
impotent institution[s]. So I cannot understand how a classroom
teacher can be expected to get at
the root causes. I think our only
alternative is to try to protect
ourselves and do the best we can
in the classroom.

Alan Jones, Students! Do Not
Push Your Teacher Down the
Stairs on Friday

THE angry teacher whom Jones (1972, p. 129) quotes above bluntly
summarizes the sense of powerlessness that ghetto teachers experience when they contemplate the possibility of improving ghetto
schools. During the eight years that I taught at Du Sable, I, too,
wondered whether anything could be done to improve the quality of
education that kids received.

While I do not wish to imply that the situation in ghetto schools is hopeless, the multiplicity of "causes" responsible for the deficiencies in these schools and the forces (seemingly beyond anyone's control) that severely limit the probability of success of most reforms are staggering indeed. It is, therefore, an oversimplification (usually made by those not in daily contact with a troubled ghetto school) to assert that ghetto schools are failing solely because "teachers are not teaching," or students are not "expected" to learn, or the biases of middle-class, mostly white, teachers "prevent" ghetto kids from learning.

It is only in the complex interaction of the family, school, community, and national cultures that one could ever find the causes of ghetto school failure. Clearly, we must examine this "larger picture" when we consider how to improve schools such as Du Sable. It is just such a view that the Urban Education Task Force of the U.S. Department of Health, Education and Welfare (1970) advocated more than a decade ago and Passow (1982, p. 522) has restated as the appropriate emphasis for improving urban education in the 1980s:

> The shape of urban education in the 1980s will be determined by the extent to which education planners and decision makers relate their activities to other facets of "the larger urban problems" and conceive their plans "within a framework of overall urban problem solving." To do otherwise will be to restrict development to goals that are achievable but fall short of what we are capable of becoming.

Nevertheless, ghetto schools will open each fall—whether or not solutions are found to "the larger urban problems." The question, then, becomes what can school personnel do—given their inability to influence the larger social problems of poverty, racism, crime, a faltering national economy, and urban decline—to improve conditions at their individual schools?

A PRESCRIPTION FOR CHANGE

If ghetto schools such as Du Sable are to change significantly, their environments must become more professional. Those who work in the schools must do all they can to promote professionalism—their own and that of their colleagues.

This prescription is more a set of attitudes or beliefs that ought to guide change efforts in ghetto schools than it is a set of specific steps for action. In an atmosphere of free inquiry and discussion, the wisdom of this stance (along with the merits of other proposals) would first be debated; later, specific plans for action would emerge.

INCREASED PROFESSIONALISM

What is needed among ghetto school personnel is a high level of serious, reflective thought about education and the ability to perceive accurately and sensitively the forces that impinge upon such schools. Needed also is the vision to create innovative approaches based on a thorough analysis and honest discussion of these perceptions. At the moment, change efforts at ghetto schools are little more than reflex reactions to conditions that few understand or, perhaps, wish to understand. Unfortunately, Getzels' (1967, p. 297) recommendation for changing urban schools a decade-and-a-half ago is as apt today as it was then: "there must be more than sporadic tinkering—there must be long-term conceptual analysis and reconstruction based on the analysis."

My approach to change at Du Sable is also contingent upon the teacher's freedom to experiment and, as Kohl (1968, p. 232) advises, the "freedom" to fail:

> What is really needed, however, is the chance for good
> people to spend their time discovering what is good.
> After sufficient time to experiment freely, they can for-
> mulate hypotheses, test, and replicate their work. But
> they must be allowed time to entertain many possibilities
> and fail many times before they can be expected to "pro-
> duce" results.

Unfortunately, the Chicago school system is unable, or unwilling, to offer teachers the autonomy needed to develop carefully researched approaches to change. Frequently, supervisors covetously guard their authority and maintain the status quo by advancing only those individuals who are not threatening to their role. Thus, the entire educational hierarchy can, if staffed with the "right" people, appear to function in a legitimate manner while its membership excludes those with deeper insight into the problems of education and the visionary wisdom and courage to suggest constructive changes.

An environment of professional autonomy can be maintained only by teachers who themselves are committed to improving professional competence and practice through sustained inquiry. In the main, this sort of staff was not present while I taught at Du Sable, nor, tragically, does it exist at many other ghetto schools.

It is no secret that teaching, perhaps more so in urban areas, attracts many whose intelligence, insight, and sense of professionalism are less than those found among other professions. Teachers' meetings at Du Sable, for example, were often characterized by a collective mindlessness and ignorance that I found troubling. Ideas for improving the school were usually limited to a search for better textbooks, a call from the law-and-order element for the enforcement of all school rules, and a final plea for all to "do their jobs" and "pull together." A valid argument, then, could be made for improving urban schools by assigning teachers on the basis of scores made on an appropriate intelligence test. While intelligence per se does not guarantee effectiveness as a teacher (though I suspect there is a high, positive correlation between the two), bright teachers would be capable of deeper insight into the dynamics of educational problems and better equipped to formulate appropriate solutions. Moreover, they would appreciate the fact that educational problems are profoundly complex and, as such, are beyond the single, simple solutions often proposed.

THE TEACHER'S PROFESSIONAL QUEST

The truly professional teacher commits himself to a continuous quest to grow in the ability to provide students with educative experiences. In doing so, he develops a rationale for integrating his objective, "scientific" knowledge of classrooms with the more subjective, intuitive, and fleeting awareness of his own and his students' inner worlds. To the extent that the teacher is able to integrate these two modes of knowing and, through his actions, able to give each its appropriate emphasis, we may say that he possesses a sound, comprehensive approach to instruction and has transformed the practice of his craft from a skill to an art.

In the following, I will pull together the strategies discussed and illustrated in the previous chapters and present five maxims that ought to be the sine qua non of the teacher as a professional. In other words, what are the priorities of the teacher who wishes to maximize the educativeness of his relationships with students? What policies guide his decision making? Next, I will present two models: one, an adaptive process model for the individual teacher to follow in implementing the five maxims; the other, a model for an entire school faculty to follow in bringing about schoolwide change.

Five Maxims for the Professional Teacher

Our first maxim is that the teacher's primary purpose is to establish relationships with students—relationships that are founded on caring, authentic, two-way communication and are characterized by an affective quality that is nurturant.

Such a teacher tries continuously to communicate with students in a way that he feels intuitively is educative, in a way that promotes—rather than hinders or blocks altogether—the student's own personal quest for meaning in life's experiences. The teacher possesses what Dewey (1904, p. 14) terms "insight into soul action"—the ability to achieve psychological insight into the mind of the student and thus determine what experiences will be most educative for the student at any given moment.

Also, the teacher stands ready to promote such teacher-student relationships outside of the classroom (in the halls, lunchroom, on the street, etc.) because he recognizes that educative moments almost always emerge spontaneously and may have little or nothing to do with the planned "lessons" in the classroom. In addition, he recognizes that interpersonal relationships are much more important in the ghetto culture because students can only count on each other and trusted teachers—not already learned modes of inquiry and accumulated knowledge of and experience in the dominant middle-class culture.

Our second maxim is that the teacher's actions are informed by (1) continuous, careful, and sensitive observation of classroom events and (2) careful, analytical reflection on the significance of these observed events. In other words, the teacher continuously theorizes about how to make his classes more educative, and he formulates hypotheses that he tests and modifies in view of his sensitive understanding of the ebb and flow of classroom events. He recognizes that there exists no one right set of specific procedures to guide his actions. In order to make spontaneous, appropriate professional decisions to best meet the stream of events encountered in the classroom, then, he must devote himself to the process of continuous professional inquiry. In short, he solves educational problems by first asking the following: What kind of data can I obtain that will enable me to understand better my situation?

Our third maxim is an extension of the second in that the teacher takes the established mental habits of observation and reflection and turns them inward. The teacher's willingness to engage in this introspection is crucial—for how can the teacher know his students if he doesn't know himself? Moreover, the teacher understands that true self-understanding ultimately leads to self-acceptance and, finally, to love of self—an optimum state which is, after all, the origin of respect and love for others.

In practical terms, what must the teacher do to facilitate his personal growth? He must first have the intellectual and emotional courage to confront himself, to ask what the experience of teaching means and what his deeper feelings are about the students he teaches.

Second, he must have the energy, the integrity, to act on the results of his self-examination. Finally, he must be willing to endure some discomfort, possibly pain, as he "works through" his present feelings in order to develop a more sensitive, humane style of teaching.

Our fourth maxim is that the teacher recognize that the aim of teaching is to provide students with experiences that are, educationally, growth promoting. Content per se, the teacher understands, does not have educational value; it is only through the experience of acquiring that content that students are (or are not) educated. In other words, education occurs only if the acquisition of any bit of knowledge contributes to the growth (now and in the future) of students. And the teacher, as Dewey (1938, p. 40) points out, is continuously alert for ways to utilize the surrounding environment to further students' growth:

> A primary responsibility of educators is that they not only
> be aware of the general principle of the shaping of actual
> experience by environing conditions, but that they also
> recognize in the concrete what surroundings are condu-
> cive to having experiences that lead to growth. Above
> all, they should know how to utilize the surroundings,
> physical and social, that exist so as to extract from
> them all that they have to contribute to building up ex-
> periences that are worth while.

Hence, the teacher not only provides students with activities that he believes will have educational value for the most students, he also tries to keep students "on task," encouraging those who are only tangentially involved to take the plunge and reinforcing those who are meaningfully involved to remain so. And when the activity seems to lose its momentum, when it becomes purposeless, the teacher intervenes and either reclarifies the task so that, once again, it is educative, or the teacher redirects students' energies to a new activity that is educative in another way. The former activity, of course, is returned to when the teacher senses that students are once again "ready."

Our final maxim is that the teacher work to understand the "groupness" of each class and realize that, as group leader, he is the member who most influences the group's purpose(s) and climate. In short, the primary responsibility of the teacher is to direct, as much as possible, the group's energy toward learning and growth and away from the temporary emotional gratification of acting out via battling the teacher or other members of the group.

The teacher realizes, too, that the climate or tension level of any group—as measured by its predominant emotional state, its cohesiveness, and the energy it wishes to devote to the task or to fighting the leader—is not constant but rather shifts from day to day, moment to moment. In light of individual needs and purposes, each member contributes to the group and is simultaneously influenced by the group. Thus the teacher must try to direct the group so as to maximize, at any given moment, the educativeness of its activities and minimize those activities that are growth inhibiting. This means that, on occasion, the group will be capable of impressive forward movement and growth for nearly all members; on other occasions, the group as a whole may be unable to move ahead and will instead "drift" aimlessly and nonproductively; and at yet other times the group may be unalterably intent on destructive acting out.

An Adaptive Process Model for a
General Theory of Instruction

Figure 5 presents an adaptive process "model" for a general theory of instruction. It is an attempt to show the sequence of steps a teacher might follow in developing a style of teaching that embodies the preceding five maxims. The model emphasizes the ongoing process of inquiry into education rather than the attainment of immediate, predetermined ends or products. The model offers not a technique or a set of specific procedures to guide instruction, but a blueprint for a way of thinking about instruction and how to create a classroom climate that is educative.

The model's nine stages (their sequence is suggested for the purpose of explication only; moreover, the stages are likely to be compacted in time so that they occur nearly simultaneously), require that the teacher continuously gather information and formulate hypotheses that he evaluates and modifies in terms of a sensitive understanding of himself, his students, and the total situation. Through insights drawn from this process of observation and reflection, the teacher grows and learns so that he is increasingly effective in providing his students with educative, growth-promoting experiences. The teacher who is able to internalize the stages of the model or, more generally, the inquiring habit of mind it seeks to nurture, will be able to make spontaneous, appropriate professional decisions in the classroom.

Organizing Principle: A Conception of Education

At the base of the model is the broad conception of education that vitalizes and directs any subsequent manifestation of the model

FIGURE 5

AN ADAPTIVE PROCESS MODEL FOR A
GENERAL THEORY OF INSTRUCTION

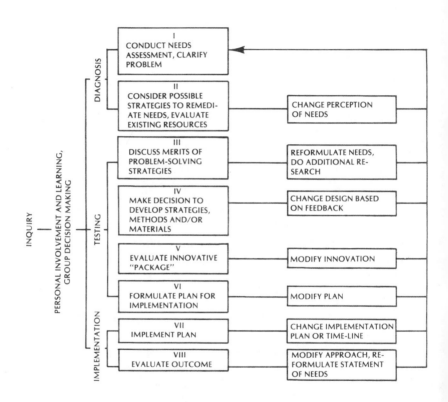

itself. Here, we view education as a humane, purposive activity designed to help human beings develop through confronting and interpreting their experiences. Throughout the stages of the model, the influence of this general conception of education should be felt as well as reevaluated and refined.

Stage I: Initial Perceptions

Instruction begins with the teacher initially perceiving or getting the "feel" of his total teaching situation. These perceptions range from experiencing the school's ethos, its culture and way of life, to experiencing the school's orientation toward education, what Dewey (1904) terms the "educational movement of the school as a whole."

The organizing theme for this stage of instruction, as well as for subsequent stages, is the need for accurate, relevant information that leads to understanding. The teacher strives continually to deepen and enrich his understanding of the school and the culture in which it is embedded. The knowledge so gained, he will find, is both intuitive and rational. And his subsequent actions will be determined by what he feels intuitively will "work" as well as by his more thoughtful, rational knowledge of the situation. Furthermore, this process of understanding is dynamic and emergent, not static; the approach requires that the processes of interpreting and reevaluating the meaning of experience be ongoing.

The observations described above are made not for the sake of acquiring specific teaching strategies or materials but for the broader purpose of orienting the teacher to his students' experiences of school and to their perceptions of its meaning for them. These early stages of observation build up the teacher's informational context (possibly suggesting incipient hypotheses for instruction), so he can respond spontaneously and effectively to the events that will later confront him. With this fund of background information to draw from, he will be more likely to cope sensitively with the total situation and less likely to find himself in conflict with or alienated from the flow of events around him.

Stage II: Understanding of Pupils

Stage II involves an extension and refinement of the faculties of observation discussed in Stage I. Here, the teacher tries to empathize with and to understand his students' reactions to instruction. Through dialogue, he strives to get undistorted feedback regarding the effect his methods have on students. In short, he "diagnoses" the situation through carefully observing his students. And he conducts these observations while simultaneously carrying out the more "technical" aspects of instruction.

Stage III: Understanding of Self

The process of information gathering characteristic of Stages I and II is now turned inward in Stage III. We may suppose that the teacher begins this stage with some level of tension or arousal. He needs first to become aware of his feelings and secondly to confirm the validity of his perceptions through an accurate appraisal of how his students perceive him. The teacher must be willing to engage in an honest, sometimes painful, internal dialectic; for his understanding of his students is a direct reflection of his own efforts at self-understanding.

Not only does the teacher reflect on the meaning of the present moment, but he scans previous experiences for possible insights to guide present action. Dewey (1904) indicates the fruitfulness of this stance:

> The greatest asset in the [teacher's] possession—the greatest, moreover, that ever will be in his possession [is] his own direct and personal experience. . . . He must accordingly have in his own experience plenty of practical material by which to illustrate and vitalize theoretical principles and laws of mental growth in the process of learning.

Stage IV: Establishing Goals

In Stage IV, the teacher attempts to formulate instructional goals in terms of the various patterns of information, or subjective "input," he has received. He also applies his knowledge of teaching skills and knowledge of subject matter and of educational theory, all in light of his internalized conception of education and his now emerging style of teaching. This stage requires not only the ability to envision how theory and practice may be integrated (by no means easily done!) but also competence in understanding the objective, consciously knowable "facts" relevant to the teaching-learning situation. Thus, we would expect the teacher to have, for example, knowledge of the structure of the disciplines and their respective modes of inquiry, knowledge of students' socioeconomic backgrounds and culture, knowledge of how to use available resources and materials, knowledge of classroom management techniques, and knowledge of students' interests.

Intuition, as I have suggested throughout this book, is an important factor in the teacher's methods. A well-developed, accessible intuitive sense functions as an internal "feedback loop" on the teacher's efficacy. Intuition draws from previously internalized knowledge and experience and gives the teacher an immediate pene-

tration into (or "hunch" about) his present situation. This awareness cannot be developed through an easily catalogued set of procedures, and, as Jackson (1968, p. 145) found out through his study
of life in elementary classrooms, the method is finally to be felt
rather than described logically:

> The unquestioning acceptance of classroom miracles is
> part of a broader tendency that reveals itself in several
> ways in the talk of teachers. This is the tendency to ap-
> proach educational affairs intuitively rather than ration-
> ally. When called on to justify their professional deci-
> sions, for example, my informants often declared that
> their classroom behavior was based more on impulse
> and feeling than on reflection and thought. In other
> words, they were more likely to defend themselves by
> pointing out that a particular course of action felt like
> the right thing to do, rather than by claiming that they
> knew it to be right.

Finally, as the teacher decides on objectives, he is influenced
by values—personal, professional, and societal. However, as I
suggested earlier, the ultimate value that energizes and directs the
teacher's activity is his understanding of education as the facilitation
of other persons' growth.

Stage V: Selection of Teaching Model

In Stage V, the teacher is ready to act on judgments made in
earlier stages and select a model, or strategy, for attaining his instructional goals. However, we now see that this decision is made
within a rich context of prior understandings—increasing the likelihood that the teacher's selections will be wise.

A model is not chosen willy-nilly but results from an informed,
purposeful scanning of strategies, each of which creates a different
learning environment. Joyce and Weil (1972) suggest that teaching
styles may be divided into four families, each representing a different orientation toward man and each resulting in different instructional and nurturant effects: information processing models, personal development models, behavior modification models, and social
interaction models. Clearly, no one "right" model exists; many
models for "good" teaching exist, depending upon the teacher's purposes.

Stage VI: The Emergence of a Personal Model

In Stage VI, the teacher's personal model emerges. The "personal" characteristics of this model may result from nothing more

than a model being executed by a teacher with a unique style and personality. Or, the emergent model may represent a synthesis of several models. What is important, however, is not the model of teaching one selects but the kind of person one is while employing the model.

Stage VII: Further Reflection and Evaluation

Stage VII involves additional feedback and reflection of the sort found in earlier stages. Through his alertness to verbal and nonverbal cues, the teacher decides whether he and his students share a common image of classroom reality and, most importantly, whether they share a common purpose. The teacher must, as Dewey (1938, p. 39) suggests, possess keen judgment regarding the actions and attitudes of others:

> It is his business to be on the alert to see what attitudes and habitual tendencies are being created. In this direction he must, if he is an educator, be able to judge what attitudes are actually conducive to continued growth and what are detrimental. He must, in addition, have that sympathetic understanding of individuals as individuals which gives him an idea of what is actually going on in the minds of those who are learning.

If the teacher finds that his purposes and those of his students are not congruent, he appropriately alters the execution of his teaching model, or he may even, depending upon their relationship, collaborate with students and "negotiate" a new model. This self-corrective capacity (characteristic of all stages of the model) enhances the probability that the teacher's personal model maximizes learning—for the students and for the teacher.

Stage VIII: Further Execution of Model

If the teacher, in the previous stage, finds that feedback confirms the appropriateness of the model—for his students and for himself—he further employs the model to create the desired environment and to attain the specified goals.

Stage IX: Attainment of Goals

In Stage IX, the teacher perceives that his immediate goals appear to have been reached. Evidence that these goals have been met is often more subjective than objective, and, in the final analysis, the teacher's decision to begin a transition from one activity to the next is based on his qualitative judgment and impressions of the total situation.

An Adaptive, Inquiry-Oriented Model for Schoolwide Change

Figure 6 presents an adaptive, inquiry-oriented model for bringing about change in ghetto school settings. The model is designed to promote the individual teacher's professionalism and autonomy. In particular, the model purposively encourages: (1) an extensive, thorough diagnosis of "the problem," (2) a careful selection from among alternative "innovations," (3) extensive staff involvement, from early planning and diagnostic stages to final implementation, (4) an approach to change that would depend more on staff creativity, initiative, and thoughtfulness than on extensive sources of outside money, (5) open, direct channels for two-way, face-to-face communications, and (6) a flexible time line for implementation.

FIGURE 6

AN ADAPTIVE, INQUIRY-ORIENTED MODEL FOR CHANGE

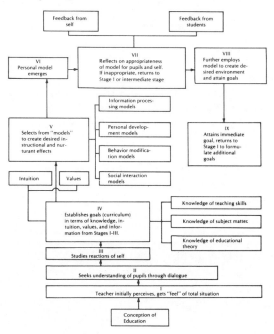

The model is termed adaptive because all stages emphasize environmental feedback, followed by modification if indicated. The advantages of an adaptive model are many. Planning is highly flexible and, of necessity, maintains contact with the reality of the situation, and implementation occurs as a logical consequence of diagnostic and testing phases.

In general, the model specifies that a particular innovative goal is shaped as a result of feedback from all involved. If modification of a certain stage is deemed necessary, all previous stages are resurveyed to insure that the total process is responding to valid, relevant input. By thus "recycling" the stages of the model as many times as necessary, the effectiveness and appropriateness of the proposed innovative solution is enhanced.

The model is furthermore termed inquiry oriented because it seeks to avoid deterministic, preformulated solutions. What is emphasized is change as an emergent process—a process of exploration designed to enable the school system to identify its, sometimes shifting, goals. It may be only at the conclusion of the process, and upon reflection, that specific, identifiable changes may be noted.

Although the goals of my model are not specifically stated (the problems of schools such as Du Sable are frustratingly complex, and few are presumptuous enough to state specifically what the goals of change should be), all participants are involved in inquiry and learning. This learning approach to change increases the likelihood that participants will cope successfully with unforeseen consequences

Diagnostic Stages

The diagnostic stages of the model begin with a clarification of "the problem," or an inquiry into the tension-producing factors that seem to warrant change. An attempt is made to view the problem from a variety of vantage points—the perceptions of administrators, teachers, pupils, parents, and unbiased outside observers are all considered. Once an approximation of the problem is achieved and it concurs with the judgments of most of the participants, the environment is further "researched" in an effort to adduce the full pattern of forces influencing the problem.

Testing Stages

In general, the testing stages are hypothetical and involve the formulation of "if — then" statements. Those involved draw from their present knowledge of and "feeling" for the situation and try to envision what might "happen" if various proposals were adopted. On the basis of these scenarios, decisions for action are made that generate the need for new, more comprehensive and detailed scenarios. As the planners move toward an innovative approach, they learn new attitudes, beliefs, and competencies that enhance the eventual sophistication and wisdom of their final solution. At the end of the testing stages, a plan for implementation (the product of group inquiry) is formulated.

Implementation Stages

As procedures are implemented, the flexibility of earlier planning stages is maintained. Testing also continues. Each action is followed by reflection and an appraisal of feedback. If necessary, the implementation plan, the time line, or the innovative approach itself are modified.

CONCLUSION

Questions of how to teach, what every teacher ought to know, or even what every teacher ought to believe about the teaching-learning process have long been debated—and will continue to be so. The preceding models for improving the quality of teacher-student relationships in ghetto schools have therefore given priority to the process of teacher inquiry rather than to the attainment of immediate, specified ends. To the extent that teachers emphasize this process they will be successful, for success is measured primarily by the doing rather than by particular plateaus of accomplishment.

While the notion of "one right way" to teach is perhaps appealing, instructional problems vary from classroom to classroom, from school to school. Effective teachers employ highly divergent methods, and then—as if to compound the problem—not even these teachers are effective with all students. In the final analysis, then, teaching methods are individual matters that teachers must explore and discover for themselves. Toward that end, each teacher must privately assess the effect of his classroom methods on students and continue his quest to develop and to implement a style of teaching that will enhance students' learning.

REFERENCES

Dewey, J. "The Relation of Theory to Practice in Education." In Third Yearbook for the National Society for the Scientific Study of Education, Part I. Bloomington, Indiana: Public School Publishing Company, 1904.

Dewey, J. Experience and Education. New York: Macmillan Company, 1938.

Getzels, J. "Education for the Inner City: A Practical Proposal by an Impractical Theorist." School Review 75 (1967):283-99.

Jackson, P. Life in Classrooms. New York: Holt, Rinehart and Winston, 1968.

Jones, A. Students! Do Not Push Your Teacher Down the Stairs on Friday. New York: Quadrangle Books, 1972.

Joyce, B., and Weil, M. Models of Teaching. Englewood Cliffs, New Jersey: Prentice-Hall, 1972.

Kohl, H. "Some Modest Proposals." In Equal Educational Opportunity, ed. Harvard Educational Review, 1968.

Passow, H. "Urban Education for the 1980s: Trends and Issues." Phi Delta Kappan 63 (1982):519-22.

Urban Education Task Force, U.S. Department of Health, Education and Welfare. Urban School Crisis: The Problem and Solutions. Washington, D.C.: National School Public Relations Association, 1970.

EPILOGUE

IT is now four years since I last taught at Du Sable. During that
time I've been an assistant professor of secondary education at a
Texas university that graduates more teachers per year than any
other university in the state. Ironically, most of my students now
are white, middle-class, attentive, and reasonably eager to learn.
Once in a while, I'll have a black student. The building I teach in is
modern and well equipped; the hallways are quiet; I don't have to
lock my door when I teach; and my colleagues and I probably experience less job stress than most other workers anywhere else.

My job now is to teach my students how to teach and how to
survive (maybe even make a difference) at places like Du Sable.
But I'm not sure I can do that—make them understand what teaching
is really all about so that they won't be numbered among the burned-
out teachers five to seven years from now. Maybe this book will
help them avoid that slow professional death. I know I could have
used that kind of help when I closed the classroom door and met my
first Du Sable class. My evolution as a teacher would have been
smoother, less painful if I had been able to recognize then that the
only person whose behavior I could control was myself. That the
only person whom I could "make" grow was myself. And that the
most sensible approach to teaching was to try to understand my particular situation as deeply as I could—and then use that understanding to guide my actions.

Around the university, I'm sort of unique because I taught for
eight years at an all-black high school on the South Side of Chicago.
Often, my students or my colleagues will ask about my experiences
at Du Sable: "Did you have discipline problems?" "Were you ever
afraid?" "Did you teach them anything?" "Were you ever threat-

ened?" "Assaulted?" I understand their concern, but their questions trouble me. I wonder why they have to be asked in the first place. Why does our educational system, our entire society, have to be divided so that one group cannot even imagine what it is like to interact with another group? Perhaps the day will come when there will be bridges of understanding, not barriers of ignorance, between people.

I also feel the difficulty of making others, including teachers at schools like Du Sable around the country, see what I saw and feel what I felt while I taught at Du Sable. I worry that they might not really hear me when I say, yes, the job was stressful, frustrating, and painful—but it was also satisfying and important work. And, if I chose to see it as such, it was an opportunity for me, along with my students, to grow.

I've returned to Du Sable a few times since I left Chicago. Four months ago, while in the city for a conference, I took a bus down State Street, past Du Sable, just to take a look. Nothing had changed. The bars, the record shops, the barbecue joints, the pawnshops were still there. The kids, huddled in tight clusters around the outside of the building, might have been the brothers and sisters of the students I used to teach. For all I knew, inside were Krimbill, Coach Washington, and Miss Wacker; and, of course, the kids were there. I'm sure I could have gotten right off that bus and gone into the building and picked up where I left off.

After rereading this book I realize just how much those eight years at Du Sable have influenced me as a teacher and as a person. I recognize, too, how much I owe the hundreds of students with whom I shared so much time. Their names have faded, but their faces and voices are as clear as ever. They opened my eyes and forced me to recognize the importance of being able to understand the richness and complexity inherent in any classroom.

They also made me see that being a "good" teacher involved much more than subject matter competence or being able to show kids "who's boss." What I needed, as all teachers anywhere need, was to grow in the skills of observing and interpreting the dynamics of interaction in the classroom.

Finally, they helped me to see that building relationships—caring, loving, educative relationships—with kids is what teaching has always been about. For their authenticity, for their energy, and for their courage, I respect—and, yes, love—my former Du Sable students. In a very real sense, they held me accountable. And they did it in a way that seemed logical to them and, I must confess, to me as well. When I bored them, they told me. When I made them angry, they told me. And when I taught them something important, and taught it well, they told me that, too.

INDEX

ABOUT THE AUTHOR

FORREST W. PARKAY is a teacher educator, educational researcher, and writer. Born in central Illinois, he grew up in Normal-Bloomington and attended the University of Illinois-Urbana where he received his B.A. and M.A. degrees in English and American literature. He received his Ph.D. in education from the University of Chicago.

He taught rhetoric for two years at the University of Illinois-Urbana. For nine years he taught high school English in Chicago—eight years at all-black Du Sable High School on the City's South Side. He was also Chairman of the English Department at Du Sable for four years. He is the editor of Teacher Inquiry: A Strategy for Improving Secondary Basic Skills Instruction and co-editor of Quest for Quality: Improving Basic Skills Instruction in the 1980s. His articles have appeared in School Review, Phi Delta Kappan, Urban Education, Journal of Humanistic Education and Development, Journal of College Student Personnel, and Texas Tech Journal of Education.

Dr. Parkay is presently Associate Professor of Education at the University of Florida. He lives in Gainesville with his wife, Arlene, and two daughters, Anna and Catherine.